THINKING THROUGH THINGS

What would an artefact-oriented anthropology look like if it were not about material culture? And what could it offer disciplines that continue to separate 'things' from the meanings that they attach to them?

Thinking Through Things makes a highly original contribution to the burgeoning literature on the role of artefacts and materiality in social theory. From cigarettes in a Papua New Guinea prison, to talismans in northern Mongolia, via property law in New Zealand and kingship in Swaziland, it seeks to ask how and to what degree might the artefacts which inspire these moments be engaged with on their own terms? It explores how material anthropology can inspire moments of ethnographic 'revelation' – in which unanticipated, previously inconceivable things become apparent – which may be taken seriously in anthropological discourse. The collection expands on the concerns about the place of objects and materiality in analytical strategies, and the obligation of ethnographers to question their assumptions and approaches.

Editors Amiria Henare, Martin Holbraad and Sari Wastell head a group of leading contributors in the field, weaving together threads drawn from the work of some of the most influential and complex theorists writing today. They articulate clearly the implications of this work for the study of artefacts and society, arguing for the futility of segregating the two. *Thinking Through Things* demonstrates the quiet revolution growing in anthropology and its related disciplines, which has shifted the philosophical foundations of the study of anthropology, and puts forward a positive programme for future research.

Contributors: Adam Reed, Amiria Henare, Sari Wastell, Andrew Moutu, Rebecca Empson, Morten Axel Pedersen, James Leach, Martin Holbraad.

Amiria Henare is a Curator at the University of Cambridge Museum of Archaeology and Anthropology. **Martin Holbraad** is a lecturer in Social Anthropology at University College London. **Sari Wastell** is a lecturer in Anthropology at Goldsmiths College, University of London.

THINKING THROUGH THINGS

Theorising artefacts ethnographically

Edited by Amiria Henare, Martin Holbraad and Sari Wastell

Routledge
Taylor & Francis Group

LONDON AND NEW YORK

First published 2007
by Routledge
2 Park Square, Milton Park, Abingdon, Oxon OX14 4RN

Simultaneously published in the USA and Canada
by Routledge
270 Madison Avenue, New York, NY 100016

Routledge is an imprint of the Taylor & Francis Group, an informa business

© 2007 Amiria Henare, Martin Holbraad and Sari Wastell for selec-
tion and editorial material; individual contributors their contributions
Typeset in Goudy by Taylor & Francis Books
Printed and bound in Great Britain by
MPG Books Ltd, Bodmin, Cornwall

British Library Cataloguing in Publication Data
A catalogue record for this book is available from the British Library

Library of Congress Cataloging in Publication Data
Thinking through things : theorising artefacts ethnographically / edited
by Amiria Henare, Martin Holbraad & Sari Wastell.
p. cm.
1. Material culture. I. Henare, Amiria J. M., 1973- II. Holbraad,
Martin. III. Wastell, Sari.
GN406.T53 2006
306--dc22
2006022250

ISBN10: 1-84472-072-1 (hbk)
ISBN10: 1-84472-071-3 (pbk)
ISBN10: 0-203-08879-4 (ebk)

ISBN13: 978-1-84472-072-9 (hbk)
ISBN13: 978-1-84472-071-2 (pbk)
ISBN13: 978-0-203-08879-1 (ebk)

CONTENTS

CONTENTS

NOTES ON CONTRIBUTORS

Rebecca Empson is a British Academy Postdoctoral Fellow at the Department of Social Anthropology, University of Cambridge. She is currently working on a monograph, based on fieldwork among Buryats from the north Mongolian-Russian border, concerned with the mobility of kin relations from the perspective of children and daughters-in-law.

Amiria Henare is a curator at the University of Cambridge Museum of Archaeology and Anthropology, where she lectures for the Department of Social Anthropology. She is the author of *Museums, Anthropology and Imperial Exchange* (Cambridge University Press, 2005).

Martin Holbraad teaches anthropology at University College London. His monograph, provisionally titled *Cuban Divination and Anthropological Truth*, is in preparation.

James Leach is Research Fellow in Anthropology at King's College, Cambridge, and the author of *Creative Land: Place and Procreation on the Rai Coast of Papua New Guinea* (Berghahn Books, 2003).

Andrew Moutu is a British Academy Postdoctoral Fellow in the Department of Social Anthropology at the University of Cambridge, and Curator of Anthropology at the Papua New Guinea National Museum. His doctoral fieldwork was among the Iatmul in Papua New Guinea.

Morten Axel Pedersen is Assistant Professor at the Department of Anthropology at the University of Copenhagen. He is the author of several articles about religious and political forms in post-socialist Mongolia, and is currently completing a monograph on Darhad Mongolian shamanism.

Adam Reed teaches in the Social Anthropology Department at the University of St Andrews. He has conducted research in Papua New Guinea and Britain. His interests lie in colonial and postcolonial governmentality, the politics of vision, money, popular narratives of nationhood and the city, cultures of fiction reading and literary subjectivities.

Sari Wastell holds a lectureship in anthropology at Goldsmiths College, University of London, where she teaches social theory and the anthropology of rights. She has worked in Swaziland since 1997, studying divine kingship and the legal forms, political subjectivities and social improvisations divine kingship fosters.

ACKNOWLEDGEMENTS

This book arose from a series of discussions that began among a group of doctoral students in the University of Cambridge's Department of Social Anthropology in the late 1990s. The inspirational influence of our teachers in the department, under the successive headships of Marilyn Strathern, Stephen Hugh-Jones and Caroline Humphrey, is evident in the chapters that follow. While freedom from the restrictions of a 'Cambridge school' was a blessing of our intellectual formation, we are also aware that the underlying motivation of the present volume, namely a desire to re-formulate the relationship between ethnographic method and anthropological theory, was very much in the air in Cambridge at the time. As it became evident after Amiria Henare's suggestion to give this conversation form in an edited volume, so was a concern for the role of artefacts in the re-vamped methodology towards which we were reaching. So the title *Thinking Through Things*, as well as making an anthropological point about what our informants do and how we might deploy versions of their approaches to things for our own analytical purposes, captures the tenor of the graduate conversations that precipitated this volume.

Ideas for several of the papers were workshopped in the interdisciplinary graduate seminar 'Artefacts in Theory', run by Amiria Henare at the University of Cambridge Museum of Archaeology and Anthropology. We thank the participants of this group, and particularly Ludek Broz, Liana Chua, Fernando Dominguez-Rubio and Tao Sule for their engagements with the book's various themes. Many thanks also to the Ethnographic Museum of the University of Oslo, who invited Amiria to give a paper outlining our developing ideas for the book and for the helpful comments which she was able to bring back to us from their interventions.

The conference in which the majority of contributors to the book were first able to publicly air their analyses in concert, generating valuable observations and feedback, provided the first testing ground for our project as a whole. We are extremely grateful to Ludmilla Jordanova, Catherine Hurley and the team in the University of Cambridge Centre for Research in the

Arts, Humanities and Social Sciences (CRASSH) for their generosity in both funding and hosting the conference. For their roles as chairs and discussants, and for substantial comments on subsequent drafts, we thank Keith Hart, Ludmilla Jordanova, Tim Lewens, Daniel Miller, Marilyn Strathern, and Chris Wright.

We are very grateful to Giovanni Da Col, Fernando Dominguez-Rubio, Stephan Feuchtwang, Maryon Macdonald, Daniel Miller, Morten Pedersen, Nancy Ries, Anne Salmond and David Turnbull for their comments on drafts of the Introduction. Two anonymous publisher's readers provided very valuable feedback on the manuscript as a whole. Finally, we would like to express our deep gratitude to Eduardo Viveiros de Castro for his detailed commentary on drafts of most of the chapters, and for his unwavering stimulation and support throughout the writing of the volume.

1

INTRODUCTION
Thinking through things

Amiria Henare, Martin Holbraad and Sari Wastell

What would an artefact-oriented anthropology look like if it were not about material culture? And could such a project develop, not as a new sub-genre within the discipline, but as a means of reconfiguring anthropology's analytic methods more generally? These are questions that preoccupy the contributors to this volume, all of whom share common concerns about the place of objects and materiality in their analytical strategies. Living in places where powder is power, where costumes allow access to other planes of existence, and where legal documents may not primarily concern reason or argument, ethnographers are obliged to question the assumptions underpinning their own surprise at such things. Rather than dismiss informants' accounts as imaginative 'interpretations' – elaborate metaphorical accounts of a 'reality' that is already given – anthropologists might instead seize on these engagements as opportunities from which novel theoretical understandings can emerge. The goal of this volume is to gather a range of approaches that show how such moments of ethnographic 'revelation' – in which unanticipated, previously inconceivable things become apparent – may be taken seriously in anthropological discourse. In particular, how and to what degree might the artefacts that so often occasion these moments be engaged with on their own terms? Too often, perhaps, the anthropologist's immediate reaction is to explain away their own surprise with recourse to more familiar conceptions – not least the presupposition that these artefacts are analytically separable from the significance informants seem to 'attach' to them. What would happen, we ask, if this wonderment were held in a state of suspension so as to resist the urge to explain it away? The idea is to develop a language for writing and speaking about ethnographic experience that unsettles distinctions central to the very origins of the discipline, the tools which underpin the work of anthropological explanation.

At least since W. H. R. Rivers declared in 1914 that 'the whole movement of interest' in anthropology is 'away from the physical and material towards the psychological and social', anthropologists, even while working to undermine such distinctions, have tended ultimately to reiterate them. Oppositions

1

between the concrete and the abstract, the physical and the mental, the material and the social have thus endured, becoming hegemonic in the strict sense, in that efforts to overcome them have often contributed to their repro-duction (cf. Argyrou 2002: 2–6). Even scholars dedicated to re-integrating materiality and culture in response to the Riversian (and earlier Cartesian) segregation continue to struggle with theoretical languages that presume an *a priori* distinction between persons and things, matter and meaning, repre-sentation and reality. Like the modish notion of 'hybridity', the impetus toward reconnection turns on the presumption of an initial separation.

Such presumptions are, of course, what many working in the field of material culture studies have attempted to overcome by employing theoret-ical strategies as diverse as phenomenology, cognitive psychology and Marxist analyses of fetishism (see e.g. Ingold 2000; Küchler 2005; Spyer 1998). By positing the relationship between human subjects and the objects they create as mutually constitutive, for example, scholars like Daniel Miller have sought to retrain anthropology's analytic gaze away from an exclusive focus on the social, toward the materiality of social life (Miller 1987; 2005a). The focus of this book, by contrast, cuts a rather different tranche through the philosophical territory approached by such analyses. Being concerned less with the ways in which subjects and objects emerge, or with questions of materiality, it turns attention rather to the relationship between concepts and things in a way that questions whether these ought necessarily be considered as distinct in the first place. The distinction between concepts and things (which broadly compasses other familiar dichotomies such as sense versus reference, signified versus signifier, etc.) may be unhelpful, obscuring theo-retical possibilities that might arise were the pre-emption of such contrasts by the artefacts we study taken seriously. By confirming the authority of formulations peculiar to Euro-American philosophical traditions, recourse to familiar analytical concepts can inhibit effective engagement between researchers and the phenomena they study.

The purpose of this introduction is to elucidate what the editors see as implicit in the contributions to this volume. While the contributors were not asked to write to a specific remit, we see in their papers a variety of attempts to sidestep habitual analytic distinctions. Instead of advancing yet more complex and ostensibly sophisticated theoretical models (piling up the assumptions as it were), each explores the peculiar mileage afforded by the ethnographic method itself. What they offer collectively is the promise of a new way of approaching the often-segregated tasks of fieldwork and anal-ysis, in short, the germ of a new methodology. With purposeful naïveté, the aim of this method is to take 'things' encountered in the field as they present themselves, rather than immediately assuming that they signify, represent, or stand for something else. Adopting an approach that might be called 'radi-cally essentialist' (see below), the papers that have been assembled here can be seen as exploring a more open, heuristic approach to analysis that allows

2

'things', as and when they arise, to offer theoretical possibilities (and it will presently be explained why the term 'things' is considered apposite in this context).

Things as meanings

It remains a commonplace within anthropology and related disciplines that meanings can only be thought of as abstractions – ideas that somehow circulate in the ether, over a material substrate primordially devoid of significance. 'Understood as a realm of discourse, meaning and value', Tim Ingold has observed, 'culture is conceived to hover over the material world but not to permeate it' (2000: 340). On this model, meanings attach to things, impose themselves on things, may even be inscribed or embodied in certain things, but are always presumed to be – in the first instance – distinct from the things themselves. Marilyn Strathern (1990) has attributed this view to the epistemological preoccupations of a modernist anthropology that takes as its task the elucidation of social and cultural 'contexts' – systems or frameworks used to make sense of social life (see also Pinney and Thomas 2001). In this scheme, she notes, the primary task of anthropologists is to slot things into the social and historical systems (such as 'society' or 'culture') wherein their significance is produced. One effect of this procedure is that the system itself becomes the object of study, its artefacts reduced to mere illustration:

> For if one sets up social context as the frame of reference in relation to which meanings are to be elucidated, [. . .] then explicating that frame of reference obviates or renders the illustrations superfluous: they are become exemplars or reflections of meanings which are produced elsewhere. It was in this sense that social anthropology could proceed independently of the study of material culture.
>
> (Strathern 1990: 38)[1]

This volume is designed to test the limits of such enduring analytical assumptions. Rather than accepting that meanings are fundamentally separate from their material manifestations (signifier v. signified, word v. referent, etc.), the aim is to explore the consequences of an apparently counter-intuitive possibility: that *things might be treated as* sui generis *meanings*. Such a formulation will appear paradoxical only to those who see the anthropologist's task as one of putting things into context (which of course turns precisely on the distinctions we seek to overcome). So the starting-point instead is to treat meaning and thing as an identity – and if the Aristotelian notion of essence was meant to allow things to carry their definitive properties on their sleeve, then the essentialism entertained here is indeed radical. For in the image put forward, meanings are not 'carried' by things but just

3

are identical to them. Such a starting-point neutralises the question of 'knowledge' at the outset, because meanings – be they native (relativism) or supra-cultural (universalism) – no longer need to be excavated, illuminated, decoded and interpreted. What is proposed, in effect, is an anthropology that holds issues of interpretation at bay. The point is not that anthropologists might be wrong (or indeed unique) in their predilection for structuring the world according to proverbial 'binary oppositions', but simply that such notions are not universally shared (even within 'the West'), and therefore may not be particularly useful as a lens through which to view other peoples' lives and ideas. Indeed, the strategy of refusing to apportion meanings and things separately – of taking them as one – provides a way out of such familiar anthropological dilemmas. For it focuses attention away from the business of adjudicating between competing 'theories' that may be more or less appropriate to ethnographic material, toward that of articulating a method by which the material may itself enunciate meanings.

What things?

The project, then, is primarily *methodological*. It encourages anthropologists to attend to 'things' as they emerge in diverse ethnographic settings, and to begin such investigations with what, for the ethnographer, may appear as a logical reversal: rather than providing data to which theory is applied, revealing the strengths and flaws of an existing theoretical model, the things encountered in fieldwork are allowed to dictate the terms of their own analysis – including new premises altogether for theory. In this sense, of course, the project is not new. The promise of methodologies that 'think through things' has long been implicit in the ethnographic method itself, with its imperative to go out and 'see for oneself' and to participate in, as well as observe, other peoples' lives. Ethnographic fieldwork compels its practitioners to engage with people and their things in a variety of ways, not simply by talking to them or reading about them in their own or others' texts. Anthropologists prepare and share food with their informants, help to build houses and participate in producing all manner of artefacts, from blowpipes to photographic records to legal claims. So the injunction to let these interactions speak for themselves is not an innovation. What the approach advanced here attempts to add to these routine activities is a collapse of the experience/analysis divide, such that the experience of things in the field is already an encounter, *simpliciter*, with meanings.

But first, why 'things' at all, and why an 'artefact-oriented' anthropology? At first glance it might appear that this terminology upholds the very oppositions we are calling into question (sociality v. materiality, culture v. nature, meanings v. things). The prescription to think through things would appear to require a clarification as to what may count as a thing in the first place. Such a clarification, however, is one which we are not just reluctant, but patently committed, to denying the reader. Things, it is suggested, ought not to be delineated in advance of the ethnographic encounters from which they emerge. To pre-empt an ethnographically defined understanding of what constitutes a thing would be to simply offer an alternative *theory* of things.

'Thing-as-heuristic' v. 'thing-as-analytic'

The advantage of 'things' as a term is that, unlike 'objects', 'artefacts' and 'materiality', they carry minimal theoretical baggage. The term is, as Lévi-Strauss' point about *truc* and *machin* as 'floating signifiers' would suggest, distinguished by its peculiar vacuity (Lévi-Strauss 1987: 55, and see Holbraad, this volume) – though we would of course retort that even calling the term 'thing' a 'signifier', floating or otherwise, freights it with particular theoretical weight. The denuded usage of 'things' put forward in this volume is thus intended to signal a shift in the term's status – described here as a transformation of 'thing-as-analytic' to 'thing-as-heuristic'. Rather than going into the field armed with a set of pre-determined theoretical criteria against which to measure the 'things' one already anticipates might be encountered, it is proposed that the 'things' that present themselves be allowed to serve as a heuristic with which a particular field of phenomena can be identified, which *only then* engender theory. So, the difference between an analytic and a heuristic use of the term 'things' is that while the former implies a classificatory repertoire intended for refinement and expansion, the latter serves to carve out things (as an appropriately empty synonym for 'objects' or 'artefacts') as the field from which such repertoires might emerge. Analytics parse, heuristics merely locate.[2]

Take Holbraad's contribution as an example. The thing through which he sets out to think is *aché*, a particular kind of powder Cuban diviners use during their séances. This powder, the diviners say, constitutes their divinatory power. Now, if one were to take this powder as a 'thing' in the *analytic* sense, the ethnographer would have to devise a connection between two distinct entities (powder and power), only one of which appears as 'obviously' thing-like, according to their pre-conceived notion of 'things'. The task then becomes one of interpretation – explaining to those who have not encountered such a 'thing' before how it can be considered powerful (given that the 'things' we know do not exercise power in and of themselves) and how power itself may be considered a (powdery) thing – a strategy which not only presumes the reader's familiarity with the concepts being deployed, but insists upon their authority as an accurate account of reality. 'They' *believe* the powder is power, 'we' *know* that this belief derives from a peculiar cultural logic in which powerful powder makes sense. What remains undeveloped (or even precluded) in this scheme are the theoretical possibilities afforded by powerful powder itself.

Where one recognises the 'thing-ness' of powder in *heuristic* terms, on the other hand, the connection with power is already immanent in the powder (the thing is both powder and power and is accepted as such). The task for the ethnographer, then, is not to explain how certain people might counter-intuitively connect powder with power, contrary to his own presumption that only one of them (powder) can properly be considered a thing. After all, his informants attest that this powder does not just happen to be powerful, but *is* power. This begs the question of how an adequate account of this 'thing' can be achieved. Instead of seeing this as a problem of interpretation, that is, of expanding familiar categories to illuminate unfamiliar instances, we suggest that it might rather be treated as one of assembling a satisfactory description – if it seems odd that powder should be power, the problem is 'ours' and not 'theirs'. But crucially, such a task involves a further move. Having accepted powder as power, and allowed others to approach its unfamiliar contours through skilful description, the ethnographer is then obliged to deal with the theoretical implications of this heuristic engagement. One possibility, under-taken here, is to use the ethnographic analysis of powder as an occasion to advance a theory that refuses the dichotomy between materiality and power in the first place. The scheme of classification appropriate to the analysis of powder is thus no longer a pre-condition of the analytical strategy, but its product.

So in summary, behind the hope that an ethnography of things may lead to a revision of our analytical assumptions about what counts as a 'thing' lies the possibility that those assumptions may be inappropriate, and that other people's understandings on this score (including not just their ideas about things but also their assumptions) might be different from what we take to be our own when writing anthropologically. The heuristic approach advocated here seeks to animate these possibilities.

A heuristic use of the term 'thing' has also been adopted by Bruno Latour, who, after Heidegger, has worked to transform the semantic emphasis of 'things' from 'matters of fact' to what he describes as 'matters of concern' (2004a). Drawing on older etymologies in which 'thing' denoted a gathering place, a space for discussion and negotiation, Latour has rehabilitated this sense of the term as a way out of the twin culs-de-sac of constructivism and objectivity. His argument that we have never been modern turns on his exca-vation of a dual separation, whereby modernism is only able to purify (i.e. separate) objects from subjects, non-humans from humans, by denying the proliferation of what he calls 'hybrids' or 'quasi-objects' – things that are simul-taneously natural and cultural, subject and object, ideal and material. The point is that one cannot 'purify' – or separate non-human from human – without simultaneously creating more hybrids. These hybrids are constituted in the living fabric of a world that is not just mentally constituted or physically given, but both of those things and more. Their resistance to being teased out into ontologically 'acceptable' categories actually provides the very conditions of possibility for the attempts to segregate persons and things which characterise modernism (why would purification be necessary if there was no contamination in the first place?). So Latour has exposed the lie of our modernist leanings, and in so doing has offered a new ontology, which he would claim universally, irrespective of time or place. Our presumed ontological bearings have proved inadequate in his terms, but he has given us new ones to think through.

Where the approach of this volume differs from Latour's work is in the status accorded to the new and more 'democratic' world that emerges from his heuristic usage of 'things'. While our goals may appear comparatively modest in contrast with his re-writing of the Euro-American ontological 'constitution' based on what he has called a 'parliament of things' (2004b), our methodological bent holds out a very different promise. For at the end of the day, Latour offers a new meta-theory whereby the inclusion of non-human/human hybrids portrays everything as a network of entities that breache the object/subject divide. We want to propose a methodology where the 'things' themselves may dictate a *plurality* of ontologies. Where he presents us with a unifying, revisionist theory of things, we advocate a methodology that might generate a multiplicity of theories. It may be the case that not everything works like a network of hybrids.

So the distinction between 'things-as-analytics' versus 'things-as-heuristics' points toward the absolute productivity of non-definition – towards a new impulse within anthropology to move beyond the development of ever more nuanced filters through which to pass phenomena, through to engagements with things as conduits for concept production. Neither definition nor negative definition will suffice. To speak of absolute productivity in this sense is to suggest an openness of method that treating things as meanings dictates, contrasted here with the strategic foreclosures of elevating this principle to the level of a theoretical dictum.

A quiet revolution: from epistemological angst to the ontological turn

Some of the potential of 'thinking through things' has of course already been realised in the work of a number of authors responsible for what could be seen as something of a quiet revolution in anthropology. This shift has been relatively unselfconscious until recently, performed in the shadows of far more flamboyant theoretical gyrations which took place in the 1980s and 1990s under the banner of 'reflexivity'. Discrete enough to remain nameless, promulgated too loosely across otherwise divergent works to deserve the name of a movement, the tenets of the anthropology we have in mind can nevertheless be gleaned from the works of a number of influential anthropologists, including not only Bruno Latour, but also Alfred Gell, Marilyn Strathern, Eduardo Viveiros de Castro and Roy Wagner. We say 'gleaned' because, despite the impact that each of these authors is having individually, their collective message about a new way of thinking anthropologically is yet to be woven into a positive programme for future research (though for an explicit manifesto see Viveiros de Castro 2003, and for a more enigmatic one see Wagner 2001). Our project draws immediate inspiration from the ways in which this body of work has quietly, almost surreptitiously, radicalised the very aims of anthropological endeavour.

What these authors have in common is that their work points in varying degree toward the analytic advantages of shifting focus from questions of knowledge and epistemology toward those of ontology. What is exciting about such an approach is that, instead of just adapting or elaborating theoretical perspectives – often pillaged from other disciplines – to reconfigure the parameters of 'our' knowledge to suit informants' representations of reality, it opens the way for genuinely novel concepts to be produced out of the ethnographic encounter.[3] The question then becomes not just how human phenomena may be illuminated (through structuralism!, no, semiotics!, no, phenomenology!, no, Marx showed the way!, etc.) but rather how the phenomena in question may themselves offer illumination. How, in other words, the ways in which people go about their lives may *unsettle* familiar assumptions, not least those that underlie anthropologists' particular repertories of theory.

It is precisely the difference between these two strategic alternatives that is captured by the distinction between epistemological and ontological orientations in anthropological analysis. Since these terms – 'epistemology' and 'ontology' – are much used and abused in present day discourse, however, it is important to be quite explicit about what work we want them to do for our argument on 'things'. Perhaps the clearest statement of the distinction was given by Eduardo Viveiros de Castro in the last of four lectures delivered to the Department of Social Anthropology at Cambridge in 1998, when contributors to this volume were students (Viveiros de Castro 1998a). In closing the argument of the lectures, which concerned the radical alterity of Amerindian cosmology, Viveiros de Castro offered a diagnosis as to why, despite their professional investment in the task, anthropologists find such cases of alterity difficult to handle:

> [A]nthropology seems to believe that its paramount task is to explain how it comes to know (to represent) its object – an object also defined as knowledge (or representation). Is it possible to know it? Is it decent to know it? Do we really know it, or do we only see ourselves in a mirror?

> (Viveiros de Castro 1998a: 92)

Anthropologists' epistemological angst, for Viveiros de Castro, is a symptom of a deeper tendency in the history of modernist thought:

8

The Cartesian rupture with medieval scholastics produced a radical simplification of our ontology, by positing only two principles or substances: unextended thought and extended matter. Such simplification is still with us. Modernity started with it: with the massive conversion of ontological into epistemological questions – that is, questions of representation –, a conversion prompted by the fact that every mode of being not assimilable to obdurate 'matter' had to be swallowed by 'thought'. The simplification of ontology accordingly led to an enormous complication of epistemology. After objects or things were pacified, retreating to an exterior, silent and uniform world of 'Nature', subjects began to proliferate and to chatter endlessly: transcendental Egos, legislative Understandings, philosophies of language, theories of mind, social representations, logic of the signifier, webs of signification, discursive practices, politics of knowledge – you name it

(*Ibid.*)

The assumption, then, has always been that anthropology is an *episteme* – indeed, the *episteme* of others' *epistemes*, which we call cultures (cf. Wagner 1981; Strathern 1990). The inveteracy of this assumption, argued Viveiros de Castro, is owed to the fact that it is a direct corollary of 'our' ontology – the ontology of modern Euro-Americans, that is. It is because, in our Cartesian-Kantian bind, we assume that the manifold of the universe cannot but consist at most of mind or matter (representation or reality, culture or nature, meaning or thing) that we also cannot but assume that both anthropology and its object are epistemic in character. If we are all living in the same world – one best described and apprehended by science – then the task left to *social* scientists is to elucidate the various systemic formulations of knowledge (epistemologies) that offer different accounts of that *one* world. This just follows from the way the dualism of mind and matter apportions questions of difference and similarity. Matter is deemed 'indifferent' (our term)[4] in the most literal sense: it qualifies as matter just to the extent that it instantiates universal laws. Things of the world may appear different, but the point is that they are different in similar – universal – ways; nature in this sense is 'one'. Culture, on the other hand, is 'many'. After all, while matter (nature) just is what it is indifferently, mind (culture) can represent it in different ways. So, to the extent that anthropology takes difference as its object, leaving the study of the indifferences of nature to natural scientists, it cannot but be a study of the different ways the world (the one world of Nature) is represented by different people – and particularly by different *groups* of people (Durkheim 1982: 40).

The circularity of this position is part of its remarkable power. For, like a Popperian 'closed system' (Popper 1995), it assimilates all dissent as confirmation – as grist to its mill. Were one merely to contemplate the possibility of a different ontology, one would be forced to capitulate immediately by recognising that such a possibility, by its very virtue of being 'different', cannot but be an alternative *representation*. Such is the power of the dualist ontology of difference: it exposes all possible adversaries – all putatively alternative ontologies – as merely different *epistemological* positions (artefacts of knowledge). Thus it compasses them within its own terms, much like old-styled Marxists used to do in debate with the bourgeoisie ('your critique of Marx's idea of false consciousness is just an example of it!'). In keeping with its monotheistic origins (Viveiros de Castro 1998a: 91), ours is an ontology of *one* ontology. If 'ontology' simply means the study of the nature of *reality*, then to speak of multiple ontologies seems an oxymoron at best, or a sign of social pathology and schizophrenia at worst. In any event, the proponents of 'multiple ontologies' can be dismissed as simply promoting a fractured and deliberately incoherent rendering of the 'real world' that (we all know, so the argument goes) is 'out there' – a utopian and polyvocal epistemology emitting from a confused mind which mistakes multiple representations of the world for multiple worlds. What an impasse.

Indeed, the risk of seeking to conceptualise anthropological concerns in ontological terms is precisely that of falling prey to the monomania of 'one ontology'. One of the reasons for which appeals to ontology are often treated with suspicion is surely the ease with which this term can descend into synonymy with 'culture'.[5] Rhetorical gestures towards a vague idea that culture has something to do with 'being' are a dualist bugbear. They simply confirm the supposition that differences – as to 'being' or otherwise – are a matter of cultural perspective – perspective, that is, on (definite article) 'the world'.[6]

'Worldviews' v. 'worlds'

The way out of anthropology's epistemological bind turns on a denial of the key axiom of dualist ontology, namely that difference has to be to similarity what representation is to the world. For if one refuses to attribute difference to culture and similarity to nature, the circular coercion of dualism is rendered limp. In the scheme advanced here, therefore, the presumption of natural unity and cultural difference – epitomised in the *anthropos* – is no longer tenable (cf. Argyrou 2002). If we are to take others seriously, instead of reducing their articulations to mere 'cultural perspectives' or 'beliefs' (i.e. 'worldviews'), we can conceive them as enunciations of different 'worlds' or 'natures', without having to concede that this is just shorthand for 'worldviews'.

Now, this shift in orientation may have an air of scholastic preciousness about it. Aren't the two options, of rendering difference as a property of representation or of the world, just symmetrical? And isn't the choice between epistemology and ontology merely a matter of vocabulary – a matter of whether one prefers to speak of 'worldviews' or 'worlds'? Ultimately, do these differences about difference really make any difference? They do, because the apparent symmetry is only grammatical. This becomes clear as soon as one adds a third pair of terms to the equations in question, the traditional corollary of representation versus world, namely the contrast between appearance and reality. In its traditional rendition (representation = appearance, world = reality), it is just this extra implication that makes the power of dualism so pernicious to anthropological thinking. For if cultures render different appearances of reality, it follows that one of them is special and better than all the others, namely the one that best *reflects* reality. And since science – the search for representations that reflect reality as transparently and faithfully as possible – happens to be a modern Western project, that special culture is, well, ours (cf. Latour 2002).

This implication, of course, lies at the heart of the resilient positivist agenda of a 'social *science*'. Differences between people's representations can be explained (or even, more evangelically, settled) by appeal to our most privileged representations, whose chief difference from others is that they are true – true, that is, 'to the world'. But a very similar notion underlies the habitual anthropological retort to positivism, namely cultural relativism (cf. Sperber 1985: 38–41; cf. Latour 1993: 103–14). True, relativists will deny that certain representations have a superior claim to reality. If the world can only be apprehended through representations, they will argue, then 'reality' or 'truth' are just properties with which *we*, representationally, invest it. Nature is a mirror, goes the argument, and our sense of its reality is constructed in our own image, just like others construct it in theirs.

Nevertheless, relativists are paradoxically just as inclined as positivists to accord special status to their own representations. Having barred themselves from appealing to 'truth', they appeal instead to what philosophers of social science called 'adequacy' (e.g. Taylor 1971: 4–5). According to this view, since all we have is alternative world*views*, the fantasy of explanation must be replaced by the necessity of interpretation – rendering others' representations in the idiom of our own. While such an image of anthropological work is clearly more pluralistic than positivism (inasmuch as interpretation is a game everyone can play – even scientists), upon close inspection it turns out to be no less universalistic. This is because, as positivists like to tease (e.g. Sperber 1985: 41–9), for the notion of interpretation to get off the ground at all (i.e. for it to avoid the logical pitfall of the cultural agnosticism we call 'ethnocentrism'), relativists must assume that their representations, though partial, are nevertheless adequate *in principle* to the task of translating the nuances of others'. How, logically speaking, can relativists assert without contradiction that our representations are *both* partial with respect to others' *and* rich enough to translate them? The answer, anathema to them no doubt, is logically unavoidable. Cross-cultural translation must be mediated by some point of *comparison* – an element that can be posited, if not as supracultural, then at least as a point of cultural convergence. Enter 'the world', as itchy as a phantom limb following metaphysical amputation. 'They see things differently than we do', relativists say, thereby carting the 'things' of 'the world' back into the picture, against their own better judgement, to guarantee the possibility of adequate cross-cultural translations. It is just for this reason that that perfect Cartesian capsule of a word – 'world-view' – does not strike our otherwise avid anti-Cartesians as oxymoronic. And it is for this reason also that they can be as presumptuous about the merits of their own analytics – their interpretative 'tools' – as positivists are about their 'truths'. Though each of us may talk partially, we all talk about the world, and therefore we can talk about others' versions too.

An ontological turn in anthropological analysis refutes these presumptions wholesale. The mysterious-sounding notion of 'many worlds' is so dissimilar to the familiar idea of a plurality of worldviews precisely because it turns on the humble – though on this view logically obvious – admission that our concepts (*not* our 'representations') must, by definition, be inadequate to translate *different* ones. This, it is suggested, is the only way to take difference – *alterity* – seriously as the starting point for anthropological analysis. One must accept that when someone tells us, say, that powder is power, the anthropological problem cannot be that of accounting for why he might think that about powder (explaining, interpreting, placing his statement into context), but rather that if that really is the case, then we just do not know what powder he is talking about. This is an ontological problem through and through. For its answer is patently not to be found by searching 'in the world' – maybe in Cuba? – for some special powerful powder. The world in which powder is power is not an uncharted (and preposterous!) region of our own (cf. Viveiros de Castro 2005; Ardener 1989). It is a different world, in which what we take to be powder is actually power, or, more to the point, a third element which will remain ineffably paradoxical for as long as we insist on glossing it with our own default concepts – neither 'powder' nor 'power' but, somehow, both, or better still, the same thing.

Two steps to ontological breakthrough

So since these 'different worlds' are not to be found in some forgotten corner of our own, then where *are* they? The answer to this question, which goes to the heart of the method of 'thinking through things', involves two parts – two steps to ontological breakthrough, as it were. In order to understand the first step, consider what the epistemologically informed reaction to the question would look like. Since different worlds are not parts of *the* world, then they must somehow be a function of our representations – what else? Now, obviously such a reply is no more than a throwback to epistemological orthodoxy (one world, many worldviews). But what it serves to illustrate in its seeming inevitability, is that the logical consequences of the notion of 'different worlds' go deeper than just inverting the familiar formula of 'difference is to similarity what representation is to the world'. For as long as our ordinary intuitions as to what 'the world' *is* remain untutored, the notion of 'different worlds' will remain contradictory (surely such worlds can only be imagined – i.e. represented – because part of the very definition of the world is that it is single). Thus, for the notion of 'different worlds' to make any sense at all it must be understood without recourse to its putative opposite, that is, different representations. Indeed, the difficulty of this notion – as well as its logical coherence – lies precisely in the fact that it denies the opposition of representation v. world altogether, rather than merely inverting its implications.[7]

It is for this reason, for example, that the claim that when Cuban diviners say that powder is power they are speaking of a *different powder* (and a different power also) is not a 'constructivist' claim (cf. Latour 1999: 21–3). To put it in Foucauldian terms, the point is not that discursive claims (e.g. 'powder is power') order reality in different ways – according to different 'regimes of truth' – but rather that they create new objects (e.g. powerful powder) in the very act of enunciating new concepts (e.g. powerful powder). Though Foucault would say that discourse creates its objects, he still works from the presumption that there is some real-world fodder out there. For example, while a body may not be male or female until a discourse of gender invokes this as an operative distinction, there is still a body to which the discourse refers.[8] By contrast, what is advanced here is, if you like, an entirely different kind of constructivism – a *radical* constructivism not dissimilar to that envisaged by Deleuze (Deleuze and Guattari 1994: 7, 35–6).[9] Discourse can have effects not because it 'over-determines reality', but because no ontological distinction between 'discourse' and 'reality' pertains in the first place. In other words, concepts can bring about things because concepts and things just are one and the same (one and the same 'thing', we could say – using the term heuristically).

So, in summary, the syllogism is this. We start with the ordinary (representationist/epistemological) assumption that concepts are the site of difference. Then we argue that in order for difference to be taken seriously (as 'alterity'), the assumption that concepts are ontologically distinct from the things to which they are ordinarily said to 'refer' must be discarded. From this it follows that alterity can quite properly be thought of as a property of things – things, that is, which *are concepts* as much as they appear to us as 'material' or 'physical' entities. Hence the first answer to the incredulous question of *where* 'different worlds' might be, is *here*, in front of us, in the things themselves (things like powder or – as we'll see in the contributions to this book – photographs, legal documents, shamanic costumes, cigarettes, and so on). So this is a method of 'back to the things themselves', as the phenomenologists had it, but only with the caveat that this is *not* because the 'life-world' of our 'experience' of things has priority over a 'theoretical attitude' (Husserl 1970), but precisely because our experience of things, if you will, *can be conceptual* (see also Holbraad, this volume).

But this immediately provokes another – and surely equally incredulous – question, which precipitates the second step towards locating these seemingly elusive 'different worlds'. If things really are different, as we argue, then why do they seem *the same*? If 'different worlds' reside in things, so to speak, then how could we have missed them for so long? Why, when we look at Cuban diviners' powders, do we see just that – powder? And what would we have to do to see it as 'powerful powder'? – whatever *that* might be . . . Still, if incredulity finds its credentials in 'common sense', it should be obvious that these questions make no sense for precisely that reason. True, common sense would insist on casting the question of 'different worlds' in terms of the ways in which they may or may not 'appear' to a knowing – or 'seeing' – subject. Such a visualist key, however, may not always be appropriate, depending on how far one takes 'seeing' as a metaphor (cf. Empson and Pedersen, this volume). The very notion of perception simply reiterates the distinction that 'different worlds' collapses. The point about different worlds is that they cannot be 'seen' in a visualist sense. They are, as it were, *a-visible*. In other words, collapsing the distinction between concepts and things (appearance and reality) forces us to conceive of a different mode of disclosure altogether. The question then arises of how the things encountered in the course of ethnographic work become apparent.

This is where the first term in the title of our project, namely *thinking*, is important. If, as we argue, the notion of 'different worlds' stands or falls by the identification of things with concepts, then it follows that on such an image things disclose themselves not as perceptions but as *conceptions*. Consider the Cuban diviners once more. Their assertion that 'powder is power', we have argued, is not to be taken as some kind of bizarre empirical claim – an 'apparently irrational belief' about powder, demanding anthropological 'explanation' or 'interpretation' (cf. Sperber 1985). This is not a statement about what we know as powder at all. It is the *enunciation of a concept* of powder with which we are quite unfamiliar; or, better put, it is the enunciation of an unfamiliar 'powder-concept', where the hyphen serves to emphasise that the possibility for such an enunciation depends on collapsing the distinction between the concept of powder and powder 'itself'.

But if in saying that powder is power Cuban diviners are expressing a powder-concept that is new to us, then how can we possibly hope to understand it? How can we conceive of a world in which powder *is* power, without falling prey to the accusation of social pathology or schizophrenia mentioned earlier? How do we maintain our footing on ontological rather than epistemological ground? And if such an act of conception is emphatically *not* a matter of merely imagining – i.e. representing – a world in which powder is power as a possibility (for this would be just to imagine powder differently, whereas what is at stake here is a *different powder*), then what does it involve? The answer is embedded in the questions. To conceive of a different powder (a 'different world') is to *conceive it* – to think it into being,

because thought here just *is* being. Conception is a mode of disclosure (of –
metaphorical – 'vision') that creates its own objects, just because it is one
and the same with them, so to 'see' these objects is to create them. Think of
it. You, the reader, 'see' the point we are striving to 'make' here by making it
for yourself, perhaps lifting your eyes from the text occasionally, to 'think
the point through' (much as we have had to do while writing it). So too
anthropologists may 'see different worlds' by creating them. Creating thing-
concepts like 'powerful powder', not so much in our mind's eye, as in our
eye's mind.

So, if the first step to 'ontological breakthrough' is to realise that
'different worlds' are to be found in 'things', the second one is to accept that
seeing them requires acts of conceptual creation – acts which cannot of
course be reduced to *mental* operations (to do so would be merely to revert
to the dualism of mental representation versus material reality). On this
view, anthropological analysis has little to do with trying to determine how
other people think about the world. It has to do with how *we* must think in
order to conceive a world the way they do. In this sense the method of
'thinking through things', geared towards creating new analytical concepts,
is a recursive one. As each of the contributions to this volume illustrates, it is
because our informants (e.g. diviners, lawyers, prisoners, shamans, nomads,
etc.) think through things (e.g. powder, legal texts, cigarettes, costumes,
photographs) that we might think of doing the same.

This point about recursivity will be taken up later, in examining the debt
this method owes to Roy Wagner's holographic notion of 'invention'. But it
should be noted here that there is an important asymmetry between informants' conceptual creations and the second-order creativity advocated for
anthropological purposes. This has to do with the way the 'game' of anthropology, as Viveiros de Castro has called it, is set up (2002). For while the
outcome of our analytical acts of conception is, in the proposed method,
required to be the same as our informants' (e.g. to conceive a powder that is
power), their point of departure is by definition quite distinct. We may or
may not know what assumptions precipitate our informants' conceptual
creativity (e.g. what concepts of powder and power they seek to elaborate
upon when they are motivated to 'make the point' that the two are the
same). This is a matter of ethnographic remit. But even if we do know, we
cannot take it for granted that these 'obviated' concepts – to use Wagner's
terminology (e.g. 1981: 44; 1986: 50–1) – do not enunciate worlds that are
just as perplexingly 'different' as the ones upon which our informants
proceed to elaborate. So whatever end of this infinitely regressive stick we try
to grasp will not be so much wrong, as a-visible in principle. On the other
hand, what we *can* grasp is our own assumptions. We *have* concepts of
powder and power, and we 'know' that they are *not* the same, contrary to
Cuban diviners' (apparent) claims. This, we would argue, is an enabling
(perhaps the *only* enabling) starting point for conceptual creation. How far

and in what direction must we change our *own* concepts before we too can assent to our informants' initially bizarre claims? How far do we need to change our assumptions about what counts as 'powder' and 'power' before we too can say consistently that they are one and the same?

It should further be noted that 'our' ability to conceive both powder *and* powder-power does not suddenly give us the ontological upper hand over our informants. It is not that the old assumption of an anthropological 'episteme of all epistemes' has merely been replaced by an ontology of all ontologies. Rather, handicapped by a dualist ontology (and the scientific rationalism to which it gives rise) anthropologists need a method to recuperate a facility their informants may already have. We need to seize on a methodology that allows for concept production that makes worlds. And this is a 'humbling' method, inasmuch as it depends on our admission that our own concepts are inadequate, and therefore need to be transformed by appeal to those of our informants.

As will be shown in the next section, contributors to this volume explore the potential of this kind of concept creation in a variety of ways, not least because the things they think through are so variedly 'different'. For the sake of clarity, however, it may be useful to illustrate the preceding discussion about the ontological turn in anthropology by returning to what is perhaps the most seminal anthropological attempt to think through a thing, namely Marcel Mauss' famous account of the relationship between persons and things in Mäori 'gifts' (Mauss 1990). Mauss' argument can be interpreted in a way that illustrates the rudiments of the ontological remit of 'thinking through things'. However, some of his most influential followers have cast his argument about persons and things in 'epistemological' terms (as defined above), exemplifying the ease with which ontological questions can retreat back to the safer ground of epistemology.

Precedents in Maussian anthropology

Mauss' seminal contribution, in terms of the issues explored here, was to take seriously the 'primitive' identification of aspects of personhood with the things that he collectively described as 'gifts'. Instead of dismissing ancestor-artefacts and objects imbued with the personality of former owners as evidence of primitive animism or superstition, he embraced these unfamiliar entities, marshalling them in a critique of assumptions that prevailed within his own society. Henare's chapter in this volume revisits the classic passage on which Mauss based his discussion of Mäori gift exchange, from a letter written by the Mäori elder Tamati Ranapiri to ethnologist Elsdon Best. As every anthropology student must learn, Ranapiri's identification of *taonga* (valued articles) with *hau* (the 'spirit of the gift') led Mauss to develop his theory of social obligation that impels reciprocity.[10] Just as we propose using 'things' that arise in the course of ethnography as heuristic devices, then, so Mauss engaged with Mäori *taonga*, among other things, to explore their theoretical potential.

Yet there are two significantly different ways of understanding Mauss' argument about the alterity of 'gifts' and the ways in which they collapse persons and things into one another, each of which has been played out in the anthropological literature. The first, which we would characterise as epistemological, starts by treating the categories of 'person' and 'thing' as analytically separate, then seeks to explain why these seemingly separate entities are – for Mäori – the same. Chris Gregory's Marxist gloss of gifts as 'inalienable objects' (1982) is a particularly influential example of this approach. Along with other criteria, the question of alienability is supposed to show the difference between 'objects', when viewed as gifts (inalienable) or as commodities (alienable). The difference is made, in the former case, by adding persons to things and, in the latter, by keeping them separate. Thus the gift registers as an analytic oxymoron: a thing that is unlike things, for it is inalienable from persons. The aggregative logic of this mode of analysis (thing + person) can be characterised as epistemological because the job of anthropological analysis in this scheme is to determine how a set of analytical concepts (e.g. 'things' and 'persons') may relate to different ethnographic settings (gift economies involve things + persons, commodity economies involve things). The anthropologist, in other words, determines how (analytical) concepts apply to their informants' representations, an essentially interpretive exercise.

A similar argument might be advanced with respect to Alfred Gell's influential attempt in *Art and Agency* to elaborate what he, like Gregory, explicitly calls a Maussian theory of artefacts (1998: 9; cf. Pinney and Thomas 2001). Proposing to 'consider art objects as persons' (*ibid.*), Gell sets out a sophisticated conceptual framework with which to show how objects come to possess social agency, much like people. Perhaps the most inspiring aspect of his argument is the attempt to conceive a form of agency that emerges as 'a global characteristic of the world of people and things in which we live, rather than as an attribute of the human psyche, exclusively' (*ibid.*: 20). Yet ultimately, as Leach argues in this volume, Gell casts objects as 'only secondary agents' whose capacity to act is rendered metaphorical by its dependence on the context of social relationships (*ibid.*: 17). Insofar as their agency originates in the minds of their creators (at least as much as in 'the material world'), his art objects stop short of *revising* our commonsense notions of 'person' or 'thing'. For agency, here, remains irreducibly human in origin, and its investment into things necessarily derivative; things gain social agency insofar as they are embedded in social relationships between persons. Though Gell's avowed intention is 'to take seriously notions about agency which even [. . .] philosophers would probably not want to defend' (*ibid.*: 17), in retaining the analytical distinction between 'person' and 'thing' he stays closer to received philosophical wisdom. Whilst his work hints at the possibility of a plurality of worlds, rather than simply worldviews, his appeal to Mauss, like that of Gregory seems to entail only an unfamiliar aggregation of familiar concepts.

Now, the alternative approach, described here as ontological, regards the identification of 'person' and 'thing' in Mauss' 'gift' as an act of concept production rather than one of mere aggregation. Gell's work could also be read this way, as Pedersen's contribution to this volume maintains. In this scheme, 'person' and 'thing' are no more than heuristic tags used to account for *something else*, namely what Gell invokes with the term 'agent', and what Ranapiri was trying to convey when he said that the *taonga* 'is' the *hau* of the gift. The reason why Ranapiri's statement is difficult to understand, and why it has led to a century's worth of anthropological debate, is not that it necessarily challenges familiar assumptions about 'persons' and 'things' – requiring scholars to expand their concepts to accommodate, for example, animate pieces of wood – but because it offers an alternative definition altogether of what elements constitute gift relations – *hau* and *taonga*, rather than persons and things. In this reading, Ranapiri was not assuming that Best shared his understanding of what persons and things are, only to proceed to explain how in certain contexts a thing (a special Mäori one, called a *taonga*) may count as a person. Instead he was showing that, when it comes to gifts of *taonga*, these concepts are altogether insufficient. For what is at stake here for the anthropologist is a third concept: one that results when our notions of 'thing' and 'person' are mutually transformed through an encounter with Ranapiri's assertion that 'the *taonga* is the *hau*'. This illustrates the difference between epistemology and ontology as we understand it. While the former seeks to find ways to apply concepts that are already known to unfamiliar instances, the latter treats the unfamiliarity of those instances as an occasion to transform concepts, so as to give rise to new ones. It is not that 'persons' and 'things' have different referents for Mäori – an epistemological question. It is that 'persons' and 'things' *are* different from that which animates Mäori gift exchange – an ontological claim.

While it is beyond the scope of this introduction to offer a comprehensive review of the literature in which the shift from epistemological to ontological orientations has so far been manifest, it may help to draw out aspects of the work we consider has precipitated this move. Despite the fact that Marilyn Strathern has not couched her own efforts in terms of an ontologising anthropology, we believe that such a perspective can be read back into much of her material. Indeed, while the Maussian character of Strathern's analysis of Melanesian gift-giving is well established (e.g. Graeber 2001: 37), perhaps the principal affinity of her strategy to Mauss's lies in her willingness to use Melanesian gifts as an occasion to transform analytical assumptions. In other words, if Strathern is Maussian, she is so in the ontological sense outlined above.

When asking questions about the nature of 'persons' in Highland Papua New Guinea, Strathern rejects an approach that would seek merely to broaden the Anglophone concepts of 'person' and 'thing' to accommodate Melanesian data. Rather, faced with a situation in which gifts contain the gendered relations which they instantiate, she is willing to pursue the conceptual effect that such an occasion implies – to tackle the theoretical implications of the gift-as-heuristic, in other words. It is not that Melanesian gifts are also 'persons' in terms familiar to the anthropologist – they are not 'individuals' in terms of the 'possessive individualism' that animates Euro-American conceptualisations of what constitutes a 'person'. Rather, Strathern treats the insufficiency of 'persons' and 'things' as concepts through which to apprehend Melanesian gift-giving as an opportunity to transform those very concepts. Where a gift *instantiates* a social relation rather than merely being a symbolic *representation* of that relation, it follows that Melanesian 'persons' can no longer be conceived as existing prior to relationships in which they subsequently become implicated through exchange. Instead, Melanesian persons have to be construed as relations *per se* (hence Strathern's famous evocation of the 'dividual' as a 'distributed person' (1988: 13, 15; 1991: 53). This forces us to re-think our concept of the person, and particularly its relevance to social situations less familiar than our own. Against possessive individualism, which turns on the assumption that people are discrete entities that can enter into relations, Strathern has effectively created a new concept of the 'person' that follows Melanesians themselves in locating personhood in the relations that exchange entails.[11]

However, the differences between Strathern and Mauss are as significant as the similarities. While Mauss is incited by the seeming inadequacy of 'person' and 'thing' with respect to *hau* to subvert those categories, he stops short of formulating alternative categories. Consider the excerpt from *The Gift* below:

> However, we can go even farther than we have gone up to now. One can dissolve, jumble up together, colour and define differently the principal notions that we have used. The terms that we have used – present and gift – are not themselves entirely exact. We shall, however, find no others. These concepts of law and economics that it pleases us to contrast: liberty and obligation; liberality, generosity, and luxury, as against savings, interest, and utility – it would be good to put them in the melting pot once more. We can only give the merest indications on this subject. Let us choose, for example, the Trobriand Islands. There they still have a complex notion that inspires all the economic acts we have described. Yet this notion is neither that of the free, purely gratuitous rendering of total services, nor that of production and exchange purely interested in what is useful. It is a sort of hybrid that flourished.
>
> (Mauss 1990: 72–3, references omitted)

Effectively, Mauss here posits the 'hybridity' of the Trobriand concept, as the endpoint of his analysis. This made sense in terms of his political project, which sought to utilise the analytical subversion of the concepts of 'person' and 'thing' to perform a political subversion. The present programme takes its cue more from Strathern's endeavours to move beyond the negative gesture of hybridity – where a third concept emerges that is still somehow predicated on the familiar concepts fused in the putative hybrid – toward the positive analytical end of genuine concept creation. It is not that the hybrid is not new. It is simply that it is not new enough insofar as it still refers recursively back to those concepts it seeks to replace. Where Mauss throw up his hands and cannot see beyond giving the 'merest indications' that a third concept is at stake – one that is more unique than a mere colouring of our given concepts would imply – Strathern's use of the concept of the 'dividual'[12] can be seen as taking up exactly that challenge.

In fact the contrast between Mauss' strategy and that developed here can perhaps be taken even further. While Mauss recognises that the concepts at his disposal are too 'thick' or freighted to enable his ontological revision, he settles for a 'colouring' or 'combining' (the melting pot metaphor) in order to keep working through them. This, we would suggest, signals a use of concepts as analytics rather than heuristics. Strathern, on the other hand, might be said to use the concept of 'person' heuristically in just the sense we have sought to outline. Her use is heuristic in that it under-determines what a 'person' might be, such that it allows (in her case) for attention to be focused on 'relations' rather than entities. So, arguably it is only because her initial conception of the 'person' is so peculiarly empty that her analysis is able to arrive at the concept of the 'dividual', as much more than simply a re-colouring of the Western concept of the 'individual.'

Strathern's strategy with regard to Melanesian gifts thus exemplifies the approach proposed here. The difference, of course, is that whereas in this part of her work, it is 'persons' that Strathern treats as the enabling heuristic (cf. Strathern 1988: 18), the contributors to this volume chart a similar course with respect to 'things'. We propose to think through things because our informants do. While persons may be just as salient a category for reflection, we suggest that the application of this analytical strategy to 'things' yields new and different kinds of insights. What draws together all of the contributions to this volume is a shared concern for things – not solely on the part of the ethnographer/analyst, but by the informants themselves in these varied contexts.

This loop – the recursive relationship between informants' concerns and the methodological stances of ethnographers – owes much to Roy Wagner's concept of cultural 'invention'. For one of the major strands of Wagner's *Invention of Culture* (1981) is a systematic account of the roles anthropologists play in 'inventing' the cultures they purport to study (see also Wagner 2001).[13] The twist – so central to the argument made here – is that Wagner's notion of invention is neither counterposed to 'reality' nor construed as an exclusive property of human genius.[14] Rather, it is presented as the mode by which reality (or 'worlds', as we would say) is constituted – an ontological exercise *par excellence*. For Wagner, invention is just the process by which concepts are transformed in the very act of being 'applied' in new contexts, so that, strictly speaking, concepts come to carry their contexts within themselves (Wagner 1986; cf. Strathern 1990: 33).[15] So, like Strathern after him, Wagner sees the encounter between anthropologists' own concepts and those of their informants as a productive one because of their divergences. As the two are brought into contact, their sense is transformed through what Wagner calls 'metaphorical extension' (1981: 38–9).

But what is pertinent about Wagner's strategy here is not only the analytic purchase of this theory of metaphor, but also the recursive tactic by which he arrives at it. The very novelty of his proposition to Euro-American ears is perhaps owed to its peculiarly Papua New Guinean provenance. As he remarks, the meta-anthropological proposal of *The Invention of Culture* originates from his earlier ethnography of invention as the central modality of Melanesian social life, as explored in *Habu*, his treatise on the role of 'the innovation of meaning in Daribi religion', as the book's subtitle puts it (Wagner 1972; cf. 1981: xiv–xvi). Such a recursive relationship, between what informants do and the techniques anthropologists bring to bear in their study of them, is also central to the strategy of this collection. In this light, the meta-anthropological argument about the value of 'thinking through things' is merely a holographic capitulation – to use the Melanesianist idiom – to the collective impact of the ethnographic studies collected in this volume.

While our contributors may not necessarily subscribe without qualification to the more didactic aspects of the editors' argument about 'thinking through things' as a method, the ways in which people think through things is the *ethnographic* theme that brought these essays together in the first place. Writing from widely varying ethnographic settings, the contributors are all motivated by their informants' evident concern with 'things' and their conceptual effects. So, for example, a central claim in Reed's account of smoking in a Port Moresby prison is that inmates' preoccupation with cigarettes, far from being an extra-curricular activity born of boredom or despair, stems rather from the fact that smoking is constitutive of the very concept of prison sociality (much as for Holbraad powder is constitutive of Cuban diviners' notion of power). Similarly, the two Mongolianist contributions (by Empson and Pedersen) show how ceremonial objects – altars and shamanic costumes respectively – act as conduits through which their informants are able to 'see' – conceptually create, that is – salient aspects of Mongolian kinship and religion. Wastell and Henare both turn their interest to the law – often seen as the discursive, abstract form *par excellence*. Wastell's focus is on the way in which Swazis engage with the received law as a civic totem – a reified thing – which presences a non-Swazi form of power and efficacy. Henare, meanwhile, addresses the role of Māori *taonga* (treasured items including things from traditional lore to scientific knowledge) in a much-debated legal claim in New Zealand. Finally Leach, looking at creative collaborations between artists and scientists in Britain, shows what happens when informants' attempts to think through things falter. While the 'sci-art collaborations' he studies were set up with the explicit aim of producing new forms of creativity through artists' and scientists' joint production of artefacts, collaborators' preoccupations with personal authorship foreclosed the more experimental aspirations of this project.

So 'thinking through things' is recursive as an anthropological method, in that it draws mileage (the potential for producing novel analytical concepts) from informants' own ontological projects. Indeed, the idea of 'native ontology', as it were, is problematised most explicitly by Moutu, who in his contribution sets out to show that the activity of collecting can be seen as 'a way of being', as he puts it, that has 'ontological effects'. Bringing together an eclectic variety of 'ethnographic vignettes' – his own 'collection', as he points out – Moutu seeks to dispel the assumption that collections are merely a practical implementation of a collector's pre-established classificatory scheme – a view he brands as 'epistemological', in a manner confluent with the argument laid out above. Drawing on his own fieldwork among the Iatmul of Papua New Guinea, as well as that conducted by Gregory Bateson, Moutu argues that in *juxtaposing* (rather than merely classifying) objects, the activity of collecting has an ontological effect in that it alters the objects it gathers together, reconstituting them by placing them in a set of relations that are internal and peculiar to the collection itself.

One of Moutu's most evocative vignettes concerns an exhibition that residents of small villages located along the north coast of Papua New Guinea helped to produce following a devastating tsunami attack in 1998. Whereas one might approach such an exhibition as an illustration or narration of the story of the tsunami and its aftermath, Moutu argues that the assembling of artefacts, film footage, photographs and even the survivors at the exhibition's opening, helped to produce a story that could not have been anticipated prior to the gathering. That is to say, what was at stake in the exhibition was not the faithful *representation* of the event of the tsunami, but rather the expectation that by bringing artefacts related to this event together, the tsunami could be understood in wholly new terms vis-à-vis the relations created in the juxtaposition of the various artefacts. Moutu analyses this in terms of a Papua New Guinean proclivity to look for the 'root causes' of such tragedies – 'human and spiritual agencies [. . .] [that] are considered integral to the explanations of devastating misfortunes'. Moving backwards in time, to excavate artefacts from the loss caused by the catastrophe, the tsunami survivors brought these objects back into the present. This very act, argues Moutu, had an ontological effect inasmuch as the juxtapositions of objects in the exhibition re-constituted the event in a unique way. From the

22

move backwards into loss, there followed an acceleration forward in time, which ultimately allowed the tsunami survivors to re-constitute themselves through a revelation of what the tsunami was (in terms of its root causes). The tsunami was not remembered, it was conceived.

When people think through things . . .

The point of this collection of essays is that 'native ontology' must always be cast in the plural. The conceptual effects of collecting may be presumed to be different from those of divining, legal claim making, and so forth. And this is precisely why thinking through things can only be understood as a methodological project as opposed to a theory in its own right, because these disparate activities may well generate equally disparate ontologies. No one theory can encompass this diversity because to theorise is of a type with these tasks and so in turn can only generate *its* ontology – in the singular. It follows that the promise of thinking through things cannot be to offer another consummate theory, but rather a method for generating a plurality of concepts or theories. The contributions to this volume are intended as examples of the ways in which these possibilities may be implemented anthropologically, and the plethora of new concepts which may emerge from such an approach.

Reed's discussion of cigarettes in Bomana gaol, Papua New Guinea, fore-grounds the agency of tobacco or *smuk* in everyday prison life. Taking seriously prisoners' claims that cigarettes 'kill memory' and 'shorten time', Reed describes a world in which '*smuk* is king', not simply in the metaphor-ical sense (as an item people will go to great lengths to acquire) but because, for the inmates of Bomana gaol, *smuk* 'is the dominant actor in prison'. More than something to do while passing time, tobacco smoking is held to alter one's state of mind in ways which Reed finds are not reducible to its chemical effects. In allowing prisoners to forget their debts and obligations outside prison, *smuk* at once creates the possibility for new relations, and provides the substance of those alliances and friendships, instantiated in the sharing of cigarettes. The shifting constellation of prison sociality is thus 'shaped by the way these objects flow', and Reed draws a parallel here between the workings of *smuk* in Bomana and the ways in which money has been analysed by economic anthropologists as central to social reproduc-tion. Like other forms of currency, *smuk*'s generative potential derives not simply from its abstract value in a system of exchange but also from its distinctive properties as a 'thing'. As with Holbraad's *aché* powder, its part-ibility is crucial to the kinds of effects it is able to produce, just as the scale of the units into which it is broken for distribution (packets, cigarettes) is dictated by the peculiar way in which it must be consumed. As the *sine qua non* of prison life, *smuk* itself provides the constitutive logic of social rela-tions inside gaol; it is the substance in which they are manifest and the thing through which they are thought. *Smuk* is thus an irreducible component not only of sociality but of knowledge, and Reed's chapter, like Pedersen's (see below), deploys the dissonance between familiar assumptions and things encountered in the field to reassess representationist theories of knowledge.

Now if *smuk* proves a generative concept for Reed, Henare's exploration of Mäori invocations of *taonga* offers a similar example. Thinking through 'Wai 262', a claim to New Zealand's Waitangi Tribunal, the body appointed by government to investigate breaches of the 1840 Treaty of Waitangi, she argues that the claim may be regarded as a concerted attempt on the part of the claimants to transform received conceptions of property. This is achieved by forcing the law to recognise (and incorporate into itself) the notion that the 'persons' and 'things' it habitually separates may be considered one and the same, as they are in the concept of *taonga*. In doing so, Mäori bring *taonga* and commodities 'into a single generative sphere' rather than simply fusing two seemingly incommensurable concepts. Just as Western property law continually expands to accommodate ever more things into the constellation of what can be owned, so too do Mäori registers of value exhibit a similar facility in the text of the Wai 262 claim. However, whereas Western law appears to expand its purview through the production of hybrid concepts (e.g. one can own an idea because an idea, although immaterial, is like a thing because both are products of human labour), *taonga* operates by generating a new conceptual dimension within the realm of property law. In exploring this intervention, Henare plays close attention to the text of the claim, proposing that the claim itself may be understood in Mäori terms as a certain kind of *taonga* – an instantiation of ancestral effect. Passages in the text, written predominantly in English, are left untranslated from Mäori, thereby 'asserting the *mana* or authority of Mäori concepts and terminology'. *Taonga* are thus deployed heuristically in two ways: first by Mäori people in their claim-making, and second by Henare herself, as a device to transform the available terms of analysis into something more appropriate to the situation at hand. Just as Moutu argues that collecting brings things into a new set of relations rather than merely illustrating a pre-existent classificatory scheme, the claimant's invocation of *taonga* refuses a pre-figured opposition between *taonga* and commodities, instead generating a uniquely Mäori modality in which 'property rights are subsumed in *taonga* relations'.

Now, if Mäori are engaging with law in such a way that two apparently incommensurable registers of value are encompassed in the invocation of *taonga*, the Swazis in Wastell's account appear to be doing quite the reverse. In her discussion of Swazi engagements with the received ('Western') law, Wastell argues that Swazis use the law to create separations and social diversity. In a world where all are one in the body and person of a divine king, it is difference and social pluralism which must be produced. Offering an analogy to the ways in which Swazi praise-names (*tinanentelo*) produce stratified clan hierarchies which allows for claims to be made, Wastell demonstrates how the Swazi reification of a 'legal thing' generates a similar sort of social distance and differentiation. Following Dumont's arguments on hierarchy (1970) she suggests that the received law serves two distinct functions for Swazis. On one level, it cuts across the (normally undifferentiated) social body that is 'the Swazi', in much the same way as praise-names do. At another level, received law instantiates the totemic authority of a non-Swazi 'other', presencing a magical authority which is of a type with, but ultimately also in contest with, the kingship. Thus, received law instantiates two disparate formulations of social diversity at once.

The concept production at work here derives from the fact that social diversity in this instance does not map onto a more familiar 'Western' notion of social pluralism as a description of a existing state of affairs. Rather, social pluralism emerges as a product of legal claims, courtroom activities and Swazis' fascination for legal paraphernalia – again echoing Moutu's argument about the ontological effects of collections. Just as collecting is not merely an 'acting out' of an already existing typology, Swazi engagements with law – far from levelling social diversity through an appeal to legal equality, as the rule of law would have it – manufacture peculiarly Swazi concepts of inequality and difference.

The key concept at work in Empson's contribution is *xishig*, a Mongolian term she translates as 'fortune' (not dissimilar to Holbraad's discussion of Cuban *aché* as power). Mongols consistently work to maintain good fortune by keeping back parts of people, animals and things from which they have been separated (for example through migration, marriage or sale). In *xishig*, Empson notes, 'something has to be given away in order for it to be kept back to support and increase the whole', a principle she also finds evident in Mongolian kinship, which 'relies on the separation and transformation of people in order for sameness, or consanguinity, to continue'. In thinking through the items kept inside and displayed on top of household chests, (arrangements which model familial networks of kin and association) Empson deploys the encounter between *xishig* and more familiar notions of fortune and relatedness to arrive at new insights into ways of reckoning Mongolian kinship.

In particular, Empson's argument turns on a second conceptual transformation, this time regarding the workings of vision and visibility (or invisibility) in the ways in which Buryat-Mongol relations are conceived. While certain (mainly agnatic and inherited) connexions are made continually visible in the photographic montages displayed on top of chests (which replaced the genealogical charts banned under socialism) other kinds of relationships are kept hidden from view inside the chest, namely those that are 'the products of the separation and movement of people between groups'. Their (a-visible) presence inside the chest instantiates the conditions of flux and movement against which the stability of the agnatic ties prominently visible on the chest's surface must be maintained, and thus throws this relative stability (expressed in photomontage form) sharply into relief. Empson analyses these two components of the chest, the visible and the invisible, as interdependent kinship perspectives that produce different kinds of relations. It is only in viewing the family chest, she argues, with all its visible and invisible components, that it is possible to see simultaneously the different perspectives through which kinship is reckoned. The chest thus becomes, in Empson's analysis, an essential component of Mongolian relationality. It is the only site in which it is possible to piece together, through the mechanism of reciprocal vision, a total sense of self. In this analysis our concept of vision is transformed. Far from being a mere physiological reaction to external stimuli, vision becomes 'the tool by which relations are created'.

Pedersen's analysis of Darhad shamanic regalia similarly draws attention to how certain kinds of artefacts enable Mongolian social relations to be reckoned – and brought into being – in ways that would not be possible in their absence. In an article weaving insights from cognitive science together with those of Melanesian and Amazonian ethnography, he describes how shamanic robes and spirit vessels serve as essential 'socio-cognitive scaffolding' that allow Darhad Mongols – and shamans in particular – to 'see' themselves and their relationships from perspectives that would otherwise be literally inconceivable. Following Gell and Susanne Küchler's analysis of the *malanggan* sculptures of New Ireland, the objects of Pedersen's analysis are more than representations of specific kinds of social knowledge produced elsewhere; they are the vehicles whose very form and substance make that knowledge possible. Yet, like Viveiros de Castro, his argument goes one step further, entailing a radical reassessment of our assumptions about the nature of knowledge.

Taking seriously the idea that shamanic costumes allow the wearer to access planes of existence normally closed to human beings, Pedersen borrows insights from Amerindian 'perspectivism' (Viveiros de Castro 1998b) to entertain the possibility of non-representational ways of knowing which, his ethnography suggests, may also be regarded as states of being. Here the semantic symmetry between 'seeing' and 'knowing' in both European and Mongolian usage is exploited to draw a contrast between two different forms of knowledge. On the one hand 'seeing' is conceived as the construction of mental representations of a (single) world 'out there' (like knowledge in the epistemological sense). On the other, 'seeing', in the perspectivist (and shamanic) sense, is 'an ontological state', defined by inhabiting a particular kind of body (world), in which different kinds of things appear. The shaman's costume enables the shaman to attain otherwise unattainable points of view understood as different (spiritual) identities rather than perspectives in the sense of 'worldviews'.

Whereas Pedersen finds inspiration in Gell's insights, reading his work as an injunction to attend to the ontological potential of fieldwork, Leach tests the limits of Gell's theory, ultimately finding it wanting in its conceptualisation of creative agency. Working through Gell's writings in relation to his own ethnographic experience of 'sci-art' collaborations (partnerships orchestrated between artists and scientists), Leach argues that Gell, like his own informants, is unable to imagine a way in which the agency of objects does not ultimately depend on individual (human) creativity.[16] Just as the 'collaborations' between artists and scientists generated tensions and disagreements over just whose skills and knowledge were instantiated in the products of the partnership and subsequently recognised within different arenas of display, so Gell's theorisation consistently refers back to an individual intellect as the source of (artistic and social) agency. While the 'sci-art collaborations' about which Leach writes were set up with the explicit aim of engendering new forms of creativity through artists' and scientists' joint production of artefacts, the collaborators' preoccupation with questions of personal authorship merely reiterated familiar assumptions about the role of individual agents in creative processes, thus foreclosing the more experimental aspirations of these enterprises.

Together, all these papers serve as concrete illustrations of the potential of the method of *Thinking Through Things*. The volume picks up the challenge laid down by anthropology's 'quiet revolution', making explicit the productivity of a methodological focus in reconfiguring anthropology's customary analytical strategies. Indeed, if the volume offers one qualification to the body of work that has inspired it, it is on the grounds that too much priority has been given in this work to theory over the methods that might engender it. After all, unifying, consummate theories can only replace one another. It is perhaps for this reason that an articulated sense of a shared movement is absent within the 'quiet revolution'. An emphasis on methodology seeks to remedy this state of affairs, joining disparate theoretical agendas made exigent through a variety of ethnographic encounters into a coherent experiment unified by a shared method. The positive programme of thinking through things promotes a plurality of theories. For as observed earlier in the discussion, there may be as many ontologies (and therefore novel analytical frames) as there are things to think through – provided we start by heeding the injunction that meanings and artefacts are of an essence.

Notes

1 Ingold similarly notes how the idea of an artefact as the product of the action of culture upon nature 'lies at the back of the minds of anthropologists and archaeologists when they speak of artefacts as items of so-called "material culture"' (Ingold 2000: 340).

2 This point about heuristics is not dissimilar to Needham's famous argument that terms like 'kinship' and 'marriage' should be recognised as anthropological 'odd-job words' (Needham 1974: 42, citing Wittgenstein 1958: 43–4).

3 For a programmatic statement of this goal, inspired by the philosophy of Gilles Deleuze, see Viveiros de Castro 2002; cf. Deleuze and Guattari 1994; Holbraad 2003.

4 But see B. Latour, 'Discussion: for David Bloor and beyond', 1999: 117 for an elaboration of this point, in which he asks what it is 'for an object to play a role if it makes no difference'.

5 We thank Morten Pedersen for clarifying this point.

6 Indeed, this is the fundamental difference between the position adopted here and a more Heideggerean approach. Although Heidegger could be said to countenance the possibility of disparate 'realities', those realities are merely permutations of how 'the world' discloses itself differentially dependent on the combination of one's corporeality and concerns in that world (the concept of 'the finitude of the knowing agent' or 'engaged agency' in Charles Taylor's (1993) terms). Indeed, Ingold's evocation of the 'affordances' of artefacts encapsulates this dilemma (1986). While any artefact may reveal itself to disparate entities differently, there is a limited variety of characteristics to be revealed because the artefact is – simply – one thing in the world – both very much in the singular (see also Viveiros de Castro 1998a: 33–5).

7 Perhaps the analogical inversion in question is best characterised as being metonymic in character, as opposed to metaphoric. A metaphoric inversion of the formula 'difference: similarity: representation: world' can only appear as a contradiction in terms: 'difference: similarity: world: representation'. A metonymic inversion is quite a different procedure, since it involves fusing parts of one side of the analogy with parts of the other. Such a logical operation can be rendered as follows: 'difference: similarity: representation: world' = 'difference: world'.

8 Note that this is a common denominator between Foucauldian ideas of discourse and phenomenology (see note 6 above).

9 Our appeal to a Deleuzian notion of radical constructivism may appear contradictory, considering we have already characterised the method of thinking through things as radically 'essentialist' (see above). But the point is that our essentialism and Deleuze's constructivism are radical in just the same way. For Deleuze, the 'virtual effects' of conceptual creation are equivalent to what constructivists dismissively call 'reality', because the virtual is defined as the plane in which concepts are real (Deleuze 1994: 208; 1990: 4–11). Conversely, we see things as worth thinking through because they are identical to the concepts essentialists would append to them as 'properties' (though see Aristotle 1956: 178–80). So radical constructivism is radical essentialism expressed backwards: if concepts are real then reality is conceptual (see also Deleuze 1993: 41–2).

10 This analysis of course doubled as a socialist polemic against the 'brutish pursuit of individual ends' in France after the Great War, which Mauss attributed to the separation of person from thing in the logic of money and contracts (Parry 1986; Godelier 1996; Graeber 2001: 155–63).

11 Strathern is, however, careful to note that her own novel concepts do not purport to map onto those of her informants, but are rather produced in the ethnographic encounter. Gell famously noted as much when he observed that *The Gender of the Gift* was an ethnography of 'system M', 'which you can take to stand for Melanesia or Marilyn, as you wish' (1998: 34).

12 Strathern borrows the terminology from McKim Marriott, who writes that in South Asia, persons or single actors are not thought to be 'individual', that is, indivisible, bounded units, as they are in much of the Western social and psychological theory as well as in common sense. Instead, it appears that persons are generally thought by South Asians to be 'dividual' or divisible (1976: 111).

13 In this more recent work, *The Anthropology of the Subject*, Wagner consummates the point about the analyst's responsibility for conceptual invention in a pandemonium of 'thinking through things' – New Guinean men's houses, Indra's net, chessmen, Australian flying foxes, the music of Johann Christian Bach, and Eve, all reinvented along with the wheel. Self-consciously written as a joke that readers won't get, the volume plays out the consequences of this responsibility – its strictly irresponsible limits – in authorial performance. If things are concepts then the tautology of stating such an identity occasions a game: take concepts and turn them into things. The 'metaphoric' analysis of things inverted as a 'literal' reification of concepts. But this Castanedian game goes some steps further than we can here. Straight-laced or dimmer, that is, we insist on getting the joke.

14 The irony here is that in many post-colonial situations, such acts of 'invention' are deemed inauthentic when performed by the 'natives' – a sign of their incorporation into Western modernity (e.g. Kuper 2003 – see Henare, this volume). Whereas Wagner insists he is following his informants' practice in extending concepts to embrace unforeseen contexts, many commentators presume this capacity to be the purview of Euro-Americans and read all similar efforts by others as signs of acculturation, or as Henare terms it, 'conceptual miscegenation'. The dilemma stems from a fundamental misreading of what Wagner has in mind, as he is not suggesting that invention here is simply a matter of elasticising old concepts for new contexts – a Euro-American epistemological impulse – but rather something more radical, namely that every time concepts are 'extended' in this way they are *ipso facto* transformed into new meanings – an ontological activity (e.g. Wagner 1981: 39).

15 In 'Artefacts of history', Strathern describes how in Melanesia 'An artefact or performance grasped for itself is grasped as an image. An image definitively exists out of context; or, conversely, it contains its own prior context' (1990: 33).

16 A similar argument is made about 'the tyranny of the subject' in Gell's work, as well as in British social anthropology in general, in Miller (2005a).

References

Ardener, Edwin (1989) *The Voice of Prophecy and Other Essays*, Oxford: Blackwell.

Argyrou, Vassos (2002) *Anthropology and the Will to Meaning: a Postcolonial Critique*, London: Pluto Press.

Aristotle (1956) *Metaphysics* (trans. John Warrington) London: J. M. Dent & Sons.

Deleuze, Gilles (1994) *Difference and Repetition* (trans. Paul Patton) London: Athlone Press.

——(1993) *The Fold: Leibniz and the Baroque* (trans. Tom Conley) London: Athlone Press.

——(1990) *The Logic of Sense* (trans. Mark Lester) London: Athlone Press.

Deleuze, Gilles and Felix Guattari (1994) *What is Philosophy?* (trans. H. Tomlinson and G. Burchell) New York: Columbia University Press.

Dumont, Louis (1970) *Homo Hierarchicus: the Caste System and its Implications*, Chicago: University of Chicago Press.

Durkheim, Emile (1982) *The Rules of Sociological Method and Selected Texts on Sociology and its Method* (ed. S. Lukes, trans. W. D Halls) London: Macmillan.

Foucault, Michel (1994) *The Order of Things: an Archaeology of the Human Sciences*, New York: Vintage Books.

Gell, Alfred (1998) *Art and Agency: an Anthropological Theory*, Oxford: Oxford University Press.

Godelier, Maurice (1996) *L'enigme du don*, Paris: Fayard.

Graeber, David (2001) *Toward an Anthropological Theory of Value: the False Coin of Our Own Dreams*, New York: Palgrave.

Gregory, Chris (1982) *Gifts and Commodities*, London: Academic Press.

Holbraad, Martin (2003) 'Estimando a necessidade: os oráculos de ifá e a verdade em Havana', *Mana*, 9(2): 39–77.

Husserl, Edmund (1970) *The Crisis of European Sciences and Transcendental Philosophy* (trans. D. Carr) Evanston IL: Northwestern University Press.

Ingold, Tim (2000) *The Perception of the Environment: Essays in Livelihood, Dwelling and Skill*, London: Routledge.

——(1986) *The Appropriation of Nature*, Manchester: Manchester University Press.

Küchler, Susanne (2005) 'Materiality and cognition: the changing face of things', in Daniel Miller (ed.) *Materiality*, Durham NC and London: Duke University Press, 206–30.

Kuper, Adam (2003) 'The return of the native', *Current Anthropology*, 44(3): 389–402.

Latour, Bruno (2004a) 'Why has critique run out of steam?: from matters of fact to matters of concern', *Critical Enquiry*, 30(2): 25–48.

——(2004b) *Politics of Nature: How to Bring the Sciences into Democracy*, Cambridge MA: Harvard University Press.

——(2002) *War of the Worlds: What about Peace?*, Chicago: Prickly Paradigm Press.

——(1999) 'Discussion: for David Bloor . . . and beyond: a reply to David Bloor's anti-Latour', *Studies in the History and Philosophy of Science*, 30(1): 113–29.

——(1993) *We Have Never Been Modern*, London: Prentice Hall.

Lévi-Strauss, Claude (1987) *Introduction to the Work of Marcel Mauss* (trans. F. Barker) London: Routledge and Kegan Paul.

Marriott, McKum (1976) 'Hindu Transactions: Diversity without Dualism', in B. Kapferer (ed.) *Transaction and Meaning*, Philadelphia: ISHI Publications (ASA Essays in Anthropology 1).

Mauss, Marcel (1990) [1950] *The Gift: Forms and Functions of Exchange in Archaic Societies* (trans. W. D. Halls) London: Routledge.

Miller, Daniel (2005a) 'Materiality' (introduction to edited volume) in Daniel Miller (ed.) *Materiality*, Durham NC and London: Duke University Press.

——(1987) *Material Culture and Mass Consumption*, Oxford: Blackwell.

Miller, Daniel (ed.) (2005) *Materiality*, Durham and London: Duke University Press.

Needham, Rodney (1974) 'Remarks on the analysis of kinship and marriage', in R. Needham, *Remarks and Inventions: Skeptical Essays about Kinship*, London: Tavistock Publications.

Parry, Jonathan (1986) 'The gift, the Indian gift and "the Indian gift"', *Man*, 21: 453–73.

Pinney, Christopher and Nicholas Thomas (eds) (2001) *Beyond Aesthetics: Art and the Technologies of Enchantment*, Oxford: Berg.

Popper, Karl (1995) *The Open Society and Its Enemies*, London: Routledge.

Rivers, William H. R. (1917) 'The government of subject peoples', in A. C. Seward (ed.) *Science and the Nation: Essays by Cambridge Graduates*, Cambridge: Cambridge University Press, 306–7.

Sperber, Dan (1985) *On Anthropological Knowledge*, Cambridge: Cambridge University Press.

Spyer, Patricia (ed.) (1998) *Border Fetishisms: Material Objects in Unstable Spaces*, London: Routledge.

Strathern, Marilyn (1991) *Partial Connections*, ASAO Special Publication no. 3, Lanham MD: Rowman and Littlefield.

——(1990) 'Artefacts of history: events and the interpretation of images', in J. Siikala (ed.) *Culture and History in the Pacific*, Transactions no. 27, Helsinki: Finnish Anthropological Society.

——(1988) *The Gender of the Gift*, Berkeley: University of California Press.

Taylor, Charles (1993) 'Engaged agency and background in Heidegger', in Charles Guignon (ed.) *The Cambridge Companion to Heidegger*, Cambridge: Cambridge University Press.

——(1971) 'Interpretation and the sciences of man', *Review of Metaphysics*, 25: 3–51.

Viveiros de Castro, Eduardo (2005) 'The gift and the given: three nano-essays on kinship and magic', in Sandra Bamford and James Leach (eds) *Genealogy Beyond Kinship: Sequence, Transmission, and Essence in Ethnography and Social Theory*, Oxford: Berghahn.

——(2003) *And*, Manchester Papers in Social Anthropology, 7, Manchester: Manchester University Press.

——(2002) 'O nativo relativo', *Mana*, 8(1): 113–48.

——(1998a) 'Cosmological perspectivism in Amazonia and elsewhere', four lectures delivered 17 February–10 March at the Department of Social Anthropology, University of Cambridge.

——(1998b) 'Cosmological deixis and Amerindian perspectivism', *Journal of the Royal Anthropological Institute*, 4(3): 469–88.

Wagner, Roy (2001) *The Anthropology of the Subject: Holographic Worldview in New Guinea and Its Meaning and Significance for the World of Anthropology*, Berkeley: University of California Press.

——(1986) *Symbols that Stand for Themselves*, Chicago: University of Chicago Press.

——(1981) *The Invention of Culture* (revised and expanded edition) Chicago: University of Chicago Press.

——(1972) *Habu: the Innovation of Meaning in Daribi Religion*, Chicago and London: University of Chicago Press.

Wittgenstein, Ludwig (1958) *The Blue and Brown Books*, Oxford: Blackwell.

2

'*SMUK* IS KING'

The action of cigarettes in a Papua New Guinea prison

Adam Reed

Fieldwork taught me to smoke, or at least how to enjoy the kind of pleasures cigarettes can provide. Prior to my time in Papua New Guinea, I only smoked as they say 'socially', to overcome nerves at parties and give my hands some occupation. But living on the outskirts of Port Moresby, without a car and in a city where public transport shut down at dusk, smoking became something to do. I would spend my evenings sitting out on the balcony of the house I shared, sweating in the night heat and slowly taking drags from one of the filter cigarettes in the packets I regularly purchased from the local trade store. These evenings, punctuated by little acts of smoking, were dominated by thoughts of the fieldwork day passed and the day to come, but also by a combination of boredom and fear. Victim to my own vivid imagination, I became convinced that my position was unsafe, that it was only a question of time before something nasty happened to me. Rather melodramatically, I would speculate on my chances of lasting the year. Too unsettled to read novels (anthropologists' solution for wishing themselves elsewhere since Malinowski [1967]), smoking became my main source of consolation. It was for me an inextricable part of conducting fieldwork.

Down in Bomana gaol (my fieldwork site), a fifteen-minute walk away, I discovered that cigarettes could have a still greater significance. For the inmates of this maximum-security installation, holding on average 700 male convicts and remand prisoners, these things, both through their circulation and consumption, were a quintessential feature of prison life. Although tobacco products were illegal in Bomana, whenever they could, men sat down together, rolled a cigarette (*smuk*), lit it and passed it round. Indeed, like any new inmate, one of the first things I learned was that in gaol '*smuk* is king'. This was the case not just because smoking provided inmates with a crucial kind of experience, but also because cigarettes were highly valued objects in the informal prison economy. Of course the significance of cigarettes as artefacts of incarceration is widely reported (cf. Morris and Morris 1963; Radford 1968; Heffernan 1972; Carroll 1974; Schifter 1999). Something about the ordeal of this modern form of punishment – 'detention plus discipline' (Foucault 1977: 248) – seems to invite inmates, from a range of societies, to smoke and to treat that material with a special kind of reverence. But at Bomana I came to appreciate that smoking was not just a coping mechanism; when men spoke of *smuk* as king, they were also referring to the fact that this activity provides a constitutive logic for gaol life and the form of inmate society.

According to Klein (1995: xi), cigarettes are a crucial integer of modernity, among the most interesting and significant objects of our time. He notes that tobacco's introduction into Europe in the sixteenth century coincided with the invention and spread of printed books, the development of scientific method and a questioning of previously assured theological positions (in this Age of Anxiety, the drug became a commonly prescribed remedy) (1995: 27). Cigarettes went on to accompany workers into the mechanised factories of the Age of Industry (eventually to spread across colonial and postcolonial empires) and to be the companion of the soldier in modern war. As well as the quality of experience that smoking provides, Klein highlights its continuing symbolic and aesthetic properties, as displayed in popular media such as literature, photography and film. He points out the uses of cigarettes as instruments of communication (smoking provides a whole language of gestures and acts) and as objects of gift and trade (see Machen 1926). And finally, he connects them with histories of moral evaluation; once an act of defiance or 'cool', smoking is now frequently an occasion for guilt (1995: 17). Particularly in Europe and North America, cigarettes are assigned a negative value, the object of public disapproval and government-backed economic sanction.

Despite such claims (and the secret history of the cigarette as a tool of fieldwork), I believe anthropologists have failed to attend to the actions of what Klein terms this archetypal modern object. The absence is more glaring when one contrasts it with the attention showered on other things. Take the example of money, which is commonly held to be another integer of modernity. The widely made claim that money is a thing that expresses the period's dominant forms of logic, consciousness and principles of social organisation (see Simmel 1978), and also informs modern debates about aesthetics and symbolisation – most notably, the relation between sign and signified (see Shell 1995), has engaged anthropology since its inception. Notions of monetisation – an increasing spread in the number of objects brought into a state of equivalence by modern currency – have provided a context in which anthropologists can explain change and/or the persistence of alternative regimes of value (cf. Dalton 1965; Bohannan 1976; Parry and Bloch 1989; Akin and Robbins 1999). Money is held up as the subject of moral evaluations, a vital measure for the state people think they are in. Indeed, however it is judged, the object is held to lie at the centre of social reproduction (see Hart 1986; 2000). In the spirit of the artefact-based anthropology this volume proposes, I want to treat cigarettes as things with an equivalent generative status. This means taking the claims of inmates at Bomana seriously. If *smuk* is king, what kind of reign does it constitute? Can one speak of a cigarette sociality? What are the analytics of smoking? By thinking through cigarettes with the same enthusiasm anthropologists have previously invested in thinking through money, I hope to illustrate one way in which the very substance of things may be construed as irreducible components of thought (see Henare *et al.*, Chapter 1 in this volume). As well as considering the meaning of cigarettes as artefacts of incarceration, this chapter explores the possibility that incarceration may also be an artefact of smoking and the action of cigarettes.

Thinking through cigarettes

One of the points that Klein (1995: 7) makes is that smoking a cigarette is not usually regarded as an act in its own right. Instead it is taken to accompany other more purposeful activities (dining, talking, travelling, reflecting, working). Indeed, smoking is often derided as doing nothing. Yet, as Klein illustrates, the time it takes to smoke a cigarette may be full of significance. Inhaling or exhaling on tobacco smoke can be act of defiance (the factory or office worker and the schoolchild thumbing a nose at the productivity requirements of work [1995: 60]). It can also be a source of consolation. Thus those who must wait, hope or fear (his favourite example is the soldier in wartime) often pull on cigarettes in order to gain composure (1995: 137). He states that smoking can provide such individuals with a 'moment of meditation' (1995: 138), periods free of anxiety. It can even allow them to open a gap in the time of ordinary experience, to achieve what Klein terms an 'ecstatic standing outside of oneself' (1995: 16). What sometimes appears a strange kind of non-activity therefore has all kinds of potentiality.

Like Klein's wartime soldiers, prisoners at Bomana are defined by a state of waiting. Most obviously convicts must wait for their date of release and remand inmates for their trial or sentence (indeed the latter are distinguished by that condition, known as *wetkot* or 'wait court'). The hopes and fears that accompany this experience of detention or confinement occupy the minds of inmates. Indeed, they distinguish their situation on the basis of their enforced separation from people they know, in particular from kin, women and friends.[1] Despite the fact that the prison complex lies just outside Port Moresby, the largest urban centre in Papua New Guinea, prisoners complain that they feel isolated, as if lost in a deep forest. Restricted to the dry dusty plateau encompassed by the high perimeter fence, they are unable to view familiar faces or landscapes (prisoners at Bomana come from provinces across the country, though they are usually arrested in Port Moresby). As a technology, incarceration is therefore held not only to make men wait but to have them dwell on what they are missing and the consequences of their absence for people outside the gaol (see Reed 1999; 2003). Thus inmates complain that they suffer from 'worry' (*wari*), a state of continual anxiety about the welfare of those to whom they owe support. For example, men express concerns about the health of ageing parents (a commonly held fear is that a father or mother will die before the inmate is released), the attitude of partners or wives (inmates fret that women will be unfaithful or desert them), and the education of children (as fathers, inmates worry about how school fees will get paid). The existence of these worries also generates further worries; inmates believe that anxious thoughts can travel, impact on the objects of worry (kin, spouse, children), thus damaging the minds of loved ones outside the gaol and making them ill. In this sense, the distress caused to inmates (some men are said to be driven crazy [*longlong*] by anxiety) is but one of the outcomes if worry is left unchecked.

In this situation, smoking is held to be crucial, acknowledged as an activity vital and sufficient on its own terms. While inmates draw satisfaction from the fact that the act is subversive, against prison rules (and also the health warnings issued by national government), they are far more impressed by what they identify as its relieving capacities. The ceremony of huddling together, either in a corner of the cell or up tight against the yard fence, pinching the tobacco along a strip of old newspaper and rolling it into a cigarette, which is set alight and passed from one cupped hand to another, provides them with a much-needed form of occupation. In fact inmates talk of smoking 'shortening time' (*sotim taim*) or making the prison day pass more quickly.[2] This is especially the case because the majority of prisoners at Bomana have nothing to do (only a small number of convicts are assigned to work parties); men spend their days inside their barrack room style cell blocks or outside in the cell yards, bored and with few diversions to occupy their attention. However, the true significance of the activity is held to lie in the effects it has on the mind of the smoker. For the whole period of sharing a *smuk* is animated by the promise of escaping the pains of confinement. Dragging on a cigarette, men claim that the smoke they inhale enters the body and makes their head spin. This action is held to impact upon inmates' capacity to remember, to briefly numb or 'kill' what they term their 'memory sense' (*kilim dispeal memori sens blong yu*). More particularly, the smoke is said to prevent them from thinking and worrying about the persons and places they left behind when they entered Bomana (*yu smuk na yu no tingting long autsait*). This ability to make men 'lose thoughts' (*lus tingting*) or forget is what makes the activity such a valued experience. As smokers, inmates learn to love cigarettes because they kill their memory and therefore change their state of mind.[3]

Central to the value ascribed to smoking is the recognition by inmates of where agency in this activity lies. While smoking can be read as a form of resistance, it is not necessarily taken to demonstrate the agency of prisoners. In fact the activity is usually figured as an event in which something happens *to* them. Men in Bomana claim to be vitally acted upon by cigarettes, subject to the actions of tobacco when set alight and smoked. Indeed, '*smuk* is king' precisely because in inmates' minds it is the dominant actor in prison. This is perhaps best highlighted by what happens to prisoners when they are forced to try and live without cigarettes. During such periods men claim to 'suffer' greatly (*ol man suffa tru long smuk*). Instead of walking around the yards, inmates sleep all day in their cells and complain of feeling sick and lethargic. Worries overcome them, so that they stop talking to one another and become quick to temper (as inmates say, 'if there are no cigarettes there are no stories' [*no gat smuk no gat stori*]). In contrast, when cigarettes reappear again the mood changes dramatically. As inmates told me, the first drag opens their eyes. Once the *smuk* is finished, they get up, wash themselves and leave the cell. Men start to smile, crack jokes and exchange stories. Although this experience might be discounted as the symptoms of tobacco addiction, prisoners who smoked outside the gaol insist that they have never felt like that before. In Bomana they claim to be constantly 'hungry for cigarettes' (*hanger long smuk*); men live for the next smoke, thinking and dreaming on how to get it. This desire, which is only exacerbated when a cigarette is found and consumed, is often said to completely dominate their thoughts. Inmates like to point to the example of the 'cigarette man' (*cigiman*), a prisoner who is so desperate to smoke that he is prepared to sell his food rations and uniform, and to offer his body for sexual services. In this case, cigarettes appear to consume the man, to make him act with them in mind. While the cigarette man is a tragic-comic figure in Bomana, other inmates acknowledge that cigarettes are also the cause of their actions.

The most immediate outcome or artefact of smoking is prison sociality. By killing memory or allowing inmates to forget the debt they owe to people outside the gaol, the activity creates the possibility of identifying alternative sets of relations (smoking enables them to stand outside that part of themselves composed before incarceration). In particular, it allows prisoners to recognise bodies of men that are present and active in gaol. As well as the outcome of the negative act of forgetting, these forms are positively elicited by practices of smoking. When new inmates arrive at Bomana they are processed at reception and then led down to the guardhouse next to the cell yards. There, warders count and search them, before opening the gates and ushering them in. Usually too scared to venture inside a cell, these prisoners stand about in the yards waiting to see what happens. Gradually other inmates crowd round them, inspecting their appearance and making inquiries about their background. One by one individuals are invited to enter a cell, sit down in a corner and share a cigarette. By this act the new prisoner is acknowledged as either a gang mate or *wantok* ('one language' mate, an elastic term for anyone from the same language group, province or region). Indeed, from the first rolled cigarette an inmate smokes, his relationship to the important bodies of men in gaol is laid out. By definition, a gang mate or *wantok* is a smoking partner, someone who occupies the same cell corner (inmates divide the space of cells by hanging blankets to create screened rooms; this is where bodies of men sleep and smoke) and who shares cigarettes.

Not only the consumption but also the exchange of cigarettes draws inmates together (Klein 1995: 137 suggests that 'cigarettes give the gift of giving').[4] The composition of a gang, for instance, is shaped by the way these objects flow. Senior members or 'big boys' (*bikboi*) are simply those gang mates who have found a means of smuggling tobacco into gaol (usually by successfully identifying a warder who will take a bribe and smuggle on their behalf). They are responsible for distributing cigarettes and keeping gang mates supplied. If their source of tobacco dries up, they immediately lose that status. One of the first things that a new prisoner learns from his gang mates is not to ask for or accept cigarettes from inmates he doesn't know (*no kan askim mangi long smuk em lo blong haus kalabus*). Gangs in Bomana are differentiated from one another on the basis of men not sharing cigarettes. Indeed, competition between them is largely measured by their relative success in smuggling and distributing tobacco; to accept a cigarette from a man in a different gang would therefore risk ruining one's own gang name (*bagarapim nem blong gang long mipela*). Outside their gang mates, men only offer cigarettes aggressively, to taunt their enemies or persuade them to switch sides (it is also possible to smoke aggressively; cell fights often start because gang mates deliberately smoke in front of others). Like its 'big boys', the status of gangs is precarious, measured by the amount of cigarettes that at any one time are consumed and circulated in its name.

Whether gang mates or *wantok*, cigarettes are the things that allow men to demonstrate who they know and how. Without *smuk*, inmates say that they would have no way of making friends (*sapos smuk no gat pren i no gutpela tumas, sapos gat smuk gat plenty pren*). Smoking is therefore the constitutive form of sociability (to smoke alone is regarded as a pure act of negation). This is the case whether the relation evinced places persons in like positions or complementary opposition. Inmates sometimes give cigarettes, for example, in order to open a debt that they know the recipient cannot return. Here, the acceptance of a cigarette can leave a man vulnerable to future demands (prisoners talk of the donor claiming 'tax' back); confronted with such a request (*mi givim yu smuk na yu givim mi wanem*), he may be forced to perform menial tasks such as washing clothes, sweeping a cell corner, collecting meals or even submitting to sexual assault. For men at Bomana, then, smoking and the action of cigarettes provide an orienting aesthetic, the constraining form by which persons and sets of relations are ordered.

But the agency of cigarettes and the claim that '*smuk* is king' is most dramatically illustrated for inmates by a different attribute. Upon entering Bomana, new prisoners are amazed to discover that cigarettes have taken on the role and function of currency.[5] Any informal transactions in the gaol are conducted with 'cigarette money' (*smukmoni*). Thus, a single cigarette or 'roll' may be used to purchase a can of tinned meat, a tube of toothpaste, a plate of cooked rice, a face towel or a bar of soap. Two rolls may buy an inmate a pair of sunglasses and four rolls may buy him half a bag of sugar. As well as hand-rolled cigarettes, men treat 'packets' of tobacco as a unit of this currency. With one packet they may purchase a pair of trousers or shoes and with two packets a watch or radio. In this way units of rolled and unrolled tobacco are seen to draw all objects into a common scale; a state demonstrated by the fact that those few inmates who do not smoke in Bomana still seek out ways of gaining cigarettes in order to make transactions.

In this economy what strikes new inmates most of all is the reversal of value between cigarettes and national currency (in Papua New Guinea notes are known as *kina* and coins as *toea*).[6] They find it astonishing that an object so inexpensive and ordinary outside the gaol, one they had previously given little thought to, can displace the authority of notes and coins (although the possession of *kina* and *toea* is prohibited by prison rules, this money is widely available; in fact notes and coins are far easier to smuggle into gaol than bulky pouches of tobacco). As inmates like to point out, a pouch of rolling tobacco, costing 95 *toea* in the trade store outside the gaol, may be purchased in Bomana for 6 *kina* (during my fieldwork in 1995 the exchange rate was roughly 1 *kina* to the US dollar). From that pouch an inmate may divide the tobacco into three packets, each one of which he can sell for 2 *kina*. To them, national currency is suddenly made cheap; not only is it unsuitable as a medium of exchange in the general prison economy, it is without value in the market for tobacco until the holder finds a warder willing to smuggle or an inmate willing to sell. In fact prisoners claim that for the first time in their lives they have too much cash, that they hold *kina* and *toea* at the moment they lose the power to spend it. Outside the gaol, in particular in Port Moresby, men claim to devote their energies to acquiring national currency. Everything, from the food one eats to the clothes one wears, the house one rents or buys, the bus one travels on and the beer one drinks, must be purchased using notes and coins. Indeed, inmates assert that in the city 'money talks' (*moni tok*), the need for it directs their actions. Many of them actually claim they are in gaol because of national currency; the presence of *kina* and *toea* is said to make young men in the city steal, become 'fools' for crime.[7] Entering Bomana, a place where this currency exists but men say that 'cigarettes talk' (*smuk tok*), is therefore a considerable shock. The experience means that inmates tend to draw out the actions and properties of cigarettes by comparing and contrasting them to the actions and properties of national currency.

According to Strathern (1999: 97) one of the ways in which people in Papua New Guinea think through national currency is by taking on board its attribute of divisibility. In particular, what impresses them is the ability of the inscriptions or drawings on the surface of notes and coins to represent abstract units of value, an account unconnected to the enumerable form of the thing itself (any *kina* note includes four reproductions of its value in

number form ['2'] and one in letter form ['Two Kina']).[8] This divisible
quality is held to have specific effects on the constitution of money users.
Indeed, the people from the Western Highlands that Strathern worked with
complained of *kina* and *toea* dividing their minds. Unlike traditional wealth
items such as pearl shells or pigs, notes and coins are never transacted whole
with a single purpose (1999: 96). Some amount of national currency is
always held back in the imagination of the money holder. Thus, while the
pearl shell is a single, non-divisible thing whose exchange elicits a specific
relationship, the capacity of *kina* and *toea* to display the objective attribute
of a number encourages people to envisage all their relationships at once.
Not surprisingly, this creates some anxiety, a sense that debts must be
returned more quickly and exchange accelerated.

Cigarettes, however, are not subject to the same mathematics as *kina* and
toea (or traditional wealth items); they provide quite different material
conditions for counting. As a currency, *smuk* lacks any form of inscription.
There is no opportunity for individual rolls or packets of tobacco to stand
for multiples or abstract units of account. A single cigarette is always 'one';
this is the case whether it is rolled long and thin or short and fat. Although
the size of the roll does not alter its numerical value, this lack of equivalence
does mean that it is impossible for inmates to predict how many cigarettes
there are in one packet of tobacco (the amount can vary from five to ten
rolls).[9] Like cigarettes, the size of a packet can vary too (it can be half or
one fifth of a trade store pouch). While these packets divide, albeit vicari-
ously, into rolls, rolls cannot be accumulated and converted back into
packets (however many cigarettes an inmate possesses the number never
becomes a packet). As an alternative to *kina* and *toea*, this currency therefore acts without the calculative property of divisibility, a fact that inmates
regard as a real advantage.

Indeed, it is precisely the non-divisible aspect of cigarettes that makes
them such an appealing prison currency. For unlike *kina* and *toea*, *smuk* acts
as a poor instrument of memory;[10] it does not keep track of the same
exchanges or register the same genealogies.[11] Part of the problem with
national currency in Bomana is that it risks activating inmates' memories of
transactions outside the gaol and of debts they have yet to return (holding
notes and coins reminds them of the money owed for children's school fees,
of the rent payment due to their wives, the money they promised their father
for prescription glasses, etc.). By contrast, cigarettes help inmates to forget
those thoughts. Not only can the act of smoking alleviate men's worries, the
fact that the money form is specific to Bomana and that it lacks divisible
qualities means it carries no record of these relationships (those that stretch
back prior to incarceration). As a token, cigarettes only register exchanges
between inmates; those debts that they know can be returned.

But the most obvious way in which cigarettes differ from *kina* and *toea* is
in the basis for their valuation. First and foremost they are held as objects to

consume rather than exchange; indeed, it is the desire to smoke them that provides the authority for this money form. In this way cigarettes contradict what are usually held to be the conventional rules of currency. According to Robbins and Akin (1999: 4), for example, modern money and indigenous currencies share two distinct qualities (first identified by Simmel 1978). First of all, as objects they cannot be consumed; users must pass currency on, convert it into something else, before they enjoy it. Second, because these objects are unable to come to rest in consumption, they must circulate continuously and gain their value as a means of exchange (1999: 4–5).[12] In fact Robbins and Akin assert that the significance of all currencies in Melanesia (and by implication elsewhere) extends from this ability of the objects to flow between persons and to evoke permanence and continuity (1999: 18–19). While this explanation makes sense of the actions inmates ascribe to *kina* and *toea* (objects that resist consumption and therefore accrue value exclusively from circulation), it does little to elucidate the actions of cigarettes. In Bomana the exchange and flow of *smuk* is certainly important (responsible for shaping the composition of bodies of men); however, the value of these things cannot be reasonably separated from the moment of their eventual consumption.

In a straightforward sense the pull to take cigarettes out of circulation and smoke them, literally to burn the currency, leads to bouts of deflation and periods of money shortage. When the tobacco stock entering Bomana falls (after breakouts or prison fights, for instance, inmates are locked up all day inside their cells and their weekend visits are suspended, making it almost impossible for tobacco to be smuggled), cigarettes almost completely stop circulating;[13] most men will smoke whatever they have rather than use them to purchase any available items for sale. The desire to consume *smuk* and the difficulties associated with smuggling mean that the informal prison economy appears to suffer regular crises of currency – too often, it has goods without the means of exchange. Despite this fact, cigarettes remain inmates' currency of choice. For them, smoking and the act of consumption do not threaten the money form, but they do draw out its unique materiality.

According to Foster (1999: 215–16), Papua New Guineans do not generally distinguish between *kina* and *toea* on the basis of the material differences between paper and metal. Nor do they worry about the increasing gap between the money form's inscription (its role as signifier of value) and its relative value as an object of substance (a division now exaggerated by the increasing electronification of national currency).[14] Indeed, he claims that people are less concerned with the specific medium of exchange and more with the ways in which the money form circulates to establish the distinctions crucial to social reproduction (hence paper, metal and electric digits can symbolise the same relationship and all stand for an abstract unit of value) (1999: 217). At Bomana it is certainly true that the attention inmates give to the materiality of cigarettes does not result in them suddenly differentiating between the substantive matter of *kina* and *toea*. But it does lead them to distinguish cigarettes as a currency whose substance vitally matters. For in gaol the reproduction of social relations depends precisely on the money form possessing the right material properties (no substitute will do). These must fit the requirements of exchange, but more importantly those of consumption (it is only by smoking tobacco that men can kill memory and thus survive the pains of confinement). Another reason, then, that inmates view notes and coins as such a poor money form in Bomana is that they never come to rest in the same way as cigarettes.

While, as Keane (2001: 69) points out, the irreducible materiality of notes and coins can always make national currencies vulnerable to slippage (undermine the authorising stamp of the state on its face),[15] this is not the same as saying that a money form is founded upon an appreciation of the object's material properties. From the beginning, the matter of cigarettes defines its status as prison currency. This attention on what appears the untranscended materiality of *smuk* makes appear a fetish object; like gold, tobacco provides the basis for a highly sensuous currency. According to Pels (1998: 99), the fetish 'maintains an aesthetic value that radically distinguishes it as a material object from the subject it confronts' (cf. Pietz 1985). For him, this kind of object status provides a useful position against the treatment of materiality in present-day cultural and social theory; in particular what he regards as the hegemony of constructivism (1998: 112). Instead of things being treated as human product, he wants to consider those times when they appear to act and emit their own messages (1998: 94). The fetish object is not animated by something foreign to it – human intention or social meaning – but by a spirit that seems its own. That spirit is not held to reside in matter, but rather it appears as the spirit of matter (1998: 101). From this perspective, material seems to mould persons, to constitute them as subjects who desire and suffer; the object is too powerful a presence to be just the sign of something else (1998: 113). At Bomana inmates identify what might be taken as the spirit in cigarettes – its role as medium of exchange and token (the same spirit they identify in *kina* and *toea*), but they also highlight what might be taken as the spirit of cigarettes – their role as consumable matter. They can identify no equivalent spirit in the substance of national currency or indeed in other indigenous currencies (prisoners resist analogies to traditional wealth items). For them, cigarettes are without complement, they are distinguished by their transcendence of what they previously expected money to do.

Indeed, cigarettes in gaol have quite different qualities from solid-specie or gold-based monies. Whereas the sensuousness of gold is linked to its durability, the material properties of cigarettes disappear at the point of consummation. For their authority is based upon a sacrifice of matter, or at least its conversion into a different material form. As inmates share a *smuk*, the solid thing (tobacco and rolling paper) is gradually turned into fragile matter (ash) and nonsolid matter (smoke), which then enters the body, circulates and exits, to dissipate in the air. If prisoners at Bomana regard the material of cigarettes as exerting its own agency, then, as subjects or actors (*smuk* is king), these things also consume themselves. As well as frustrating attempts to own or appropriate them (Klein 1995: 31),[16] the self-consuming quality of cigarettes makes them a unique kind of fetish object. *Smuk* moulds men by having them transform its material state (it is the smoke of the cigarette, not its solid matter, that acts upon the mind of inmates). From this simple action, life in Bomana unfurls; as far as prisoners are concerned, it is the point from which everything starts and to which everything returns.

Conclusion

I hope that in this chapter I have begun to suggest some of the ways in which the material properties of things can become involved in the production of meaning. The ways in which inmates at Bomana think through cigarettes surely demonstrates the kind of artefact-based anthropology this volume proposes. It would, for example, be hard to insist that in this case meanings are fundamentally separated from their material manifestations (see Henare *et al.*, Chapter 1 in this volume). In inmates' eyes, the organisation of prison life is premised on the action of smoking; when cigarettes are taken away those social forms break down and men withdraw from contact with each other. Rather than imagining that they infuse cigarettes with meaning, prisoners insist that cigarettes give their lives significance. '*Smuk* is king' because it makes men act with these things in mind. However, it is worth pointing out that as far as prisoners are concerned this state distinguishes cigarettes from other kinds of objects; in Bomana only one artefact is an irreducible component of thought. Indeed, the reign of *smuk* necessitates the devaluation of other things. Most notably, in gaol inmates stop thinking through *kina* and *toea*; they no longer act with national currency in mind. An artefact-based anthropology then would also have to acknowledge the consequences for other things of one material substance emitting its own meanings.

Further, the action of cigarettes is historically contingent. Just as I lost interest in smoking when I returned from the field, so inmates know that once they are released from Bomana the activity will cease to organise their lives. Outside the gaol cigarettes revert to the status of one among many trade store commodities; once again it is money or national currency that talks. In fact the value of cigarettes in gaol and the autonomy of the informal prison economy ultimately depend on *kina* and *toea* remaining desirable to someone. It is only by bribing certain warders with cash that a significant amount of tobacco can be successively smuggled. And while the vast majority of inmates switch their attention from national currency to cigarettes, a few men remain focused on gathering *kina* and *toea*. These prisoners, known as 'dealer men', have privileged access to smuggled tobacco. As well as distributing cigarettes among gang mates or language mates, they hold some back and secretly sell to other inmates. By continuing to think through *kina* and *toea*, they are able to accumulate vast sums of money (I was told that the most successful of them leave Bomana with bundles of notes worth up to 6,000 kina). From their perspective, it is the meanings emitted by national currency that makes sense of smoking and the action of cigarettes.

Acknowledgements

I would like to thank the prisoners and warders of Bomana maximum-security gaol. I am also grateful to the editors of this volume for inviting me to contribute, in particular Martin Holbraad. For their support and comments, I am indebted to Keith Hart, Marilyn Strathern, Tony Crook, Annelise Riles, Iris Jean-Klein, Hiro Miyazaki and Bill Maurer. Funding for my fieldwork in Papua New Guinea was made possible by a grant from the Cambridge Commonwealth Trust. Subsequent writing-up occurred during a studentship at Trinity College, Cambridge and a fellowship at Clare College.

Notes

1 Foucault (1977: 257) is suspicious of any claim that relegates the modern penal experience to the moment of confinement, to what he terms the legalistic definition of punishment as 'mere deprivation of liberty'. For him the penitentiary is crucially detention *plus* discipline; it is this extra judicial aspect of imprisonment that he believes defines (and constructs) the prison subject. However, for inmates at Bomana the kind of subject they become in jail is held to be first and foremost an outcome of the constraint of detention – being cut off and forcibly isolated from people one knows. This is the experience that counts.

2 The role of smoking in helping inmates to pass time is well observed in other prison environments. Schifter (1999: 82), for instance, who worked in Costa Rican prisons, notes that consuming cigarettes is one of the few forms of consolation available to inmates. For them, smoking serves as a method of 'time control' in a situation where they lack power over the most basic exercises – when to eat, sleep or wash.

3 According to Mosko (1999), men among the Mekeo people of Papua New Guinea drink beer in order to change their state of mind and do things they might otherwise not. Indeed, he compares the state of alcoholic intoxication to sorcery – a condition in which one's state of being is affected by the negative actions of another. However, Mosko says that beer consumption serves as a kind of 'autosorcery', a belief that through intoxicants one can bring an altered state upon oneself.

4 Klein (1995: 137) emphasises the role of cigarettes in the gift-giving economy of soldiers; in wartime, he points out, cigarettes not only help soldiers to deal with their fear, the objects allow them to exercise generosity and demonstrate kinship as comrades.

5 As Klein (1995: 136) points out, prison is not the only place and time where cigarettes take on the attributes of money. During the Allied reoccupation of Europe in the Second World War, for instance, American soldiers could buy

anything they wanted from the local population using their cigarette rations. More recently, during the Romanian revolution at the end of the Cold War, the American cigarette brand 'Kent' for a brief period replaced the national currency as the medium of exchange in Bucharest.

6 Prior to Papua New Guinea's independence in 1975, the state currency was dollars and cents. The new names for monetary units (kina is an indigenous term for pearl shell and toea for arm shell) were intended to signify the new nation and suggest continuities with traditional forms of wealth (Foster 1998: 71).

7 Bergendorff (1996) reports that the Mekeo people, who live near Port Moresby and are regular visitors to the city, recognise the power that money has over them. They claim that money can detrimentally affect the mind and cause mental illness. He quotes one Mekeo villager as saying:'Money problems. Some of them think, they do not have enough (money); some of them think they want to get more. Or, some of them think, they want to do something, but let's say, they do not have money to do that thing. But they think of money and then they get that (mental sickness)' (145).

8 Shell (1995: 131) argues that the act of numerical inscription is also crucial to the development of Western art; some artists, for instance, regard the first coin impressed with the numeral '2' as the earliest example of conceptual art.

9 As Klein (1995: 30) points out, the material conditions of counting may be very different if cigarettes are mechanically manufactured instead of being hand-rolled. Here, each cigarette is identical to another and interchangeable. Klein suggests that in this situation cigarettes lose their uniqueness and come to stand for an abstract generality, to only have a collective status as like units and thus to have number belong to their identity (30–1).

10 Hart (2000: 234) talks of money as a 'memory bank', a means of ensuring that information about the transactions between people is recorded and kept in circulation.

11 Foster (1999: 230) argues that *kina* and *toea* can be seen as the 'skin of the state', a site where government and the nation and people's relation to those bodies is made visible. Indeed, as he points out, at Independence (in 1975) government education programmes encouraged its citizens to understand the nation as a community of money users. Much was made of the fact that as a medium of exchange these notes and coins were valid translocally, co-extensive with the newly sovereign country's borders (Foster 1998: 70).

12 Criticisms of national currency in Papua New Guinea sometimes centre on the idea that *kina* and *toea* are less effective means of keeping track of exchanges. Thus Errington and Gewertz (1995: 54) discuss the distinctions drawn by Duke of York Islanders between shell money or *diwara* and national currency. They point out that while notes and coins are denigrated as 'light' or inconsequential objects, unable to sustain enduring ties, shell money is presented as 'heavy', capable of embodying genealogies and generating future sets of relations (1995: 58).

13 In his study of the economic organisation of a Second World War POW camp, Radford (1968: 403) is struck by the fact that the camp market, in which cigarettes act as currency, comes into existence without labour or production. With all goods supplied by the Red Cross and family food parcels, the emphasis of economic practice lies in the exchange and the media of exchange. At Bomana most goods (including rations of food) are supplied by the prison service, but unlike the POW camp, where cigarettes arrive free and approved, tobacco is prohibited. Inmates must work to smuggle it into jail.

14 Foster (1998: 66) states that colonial and postcolonial governments in Papua New Guinea actively encouraged the idea that the matter of national currency

was of no consequence. In contrast to traditional wealth items (taro, pigs), a colonial government information booklet stressed that notes and coins do not decay or corrupt; if soiled or dirty, individual pieces of money can be exchanged at the bank for clean, new ones. Foster claims that this message was motivated by a government fear that people might embrace notes and coins the wrong way – as material whose intrinsic properties explain its efficacy (66). However, there was some contradiction in this strategy of colonial education. In order to encourage saving, the government emphasised the fragility of individual notes and coins and the importance of depositing them in the bank for safekeeping; here they acknowledged the significance of money's materiality (67).

15 Nihill (1989) provides an example of *kina* and *toea* being revalued on the basis of their material properties. Among the Anganen people of the Southern Highlands, *kina* notes have entered into ceremonial modes of transaction and appear to have taken on the value previously assigned to wealth items. The Anganen associate coins and small denominations of notes with the female sphere of household consumption. Larger notes, in particular the 20 *kina* note, are associated with the males sphere of public exchange. Anganen men emphasise the newness or crispness of 20 *kina* notes, and their red colouration, treating them as directly interchangeable with pearl shells.

16 Referencing the critique by Sartre of conceptions of property under capitalism, Klein (1995: 31) points out that the smoker of cigarettes cannot easily claim that 'I am what I have'. Unlike the pipe smoker, for instance, whose pipe still remains a palpable object after smoking, the cigarette smoker loses the thing he claims in the act of appropriation.

References

Akin, D. and Robbins, J. (eds) (1999) *Money and Modernity: State and Local Currency in Melanesia*, Pittsburgh PA: University of Pittsburgh Press.

Bergendorff, S. (1996) *Faingu City: a Modern Mekeo Clan in Papua New Guinea*, Lund: Lund University Press.

Bohannan, P. (1976) 'The impact of money on an African subsistence economy', in Dalton, G. (ed.) *Tribal and Peasant Economies: Readings in Economic Anthropology*, Austin: University of Texas Press.

Carroll, L. (1974) *Hacks, Blacks and Cons: Race Relations in a Maximum-security Prison*, Lexington MA: D. C. Heath.

Dalton, G. (1965) 'Primitive money', *American Anthropologist*, 67: 44–65.

Errington, F. and Gewertz, D. (1995) *Articulating Change in the 'Last Unknown'*, Boulder CO: Westview Press.

Foster, R. (1999) 'In God we trust? The legitimacy of Melanesian currencies', in Akin, D. and Robbins, J. (eds) *Money and Modernity: State and Local Currencies in Melanesia*, Pittsburgh PA: University of Pittsburgh Press.

——(1998) 'Your money, our money, the government's money: finance and fetishism in Melanesia', in Spyer, P. (ed.) *Border Fetishisms: Material Objects in Unstable Spaces*, London: Routledge.

Foucault, M. (1977) *Discipline and Punish: the Birth of the Prison*, Harmondsworth: Penguin.

Hart, K. (2000) *Money in an Unequal World: Keith Hart and his Memory Bank*, London: Texere.

——(1986) 'Heads or tails? Two sides of the coin', *Man*, 21: 637–56.

Heffernan, E. (1972) *Making it in Prison: the Square, the Cool and the Life*, New York: John Wiley & Sons.

Keane, W. (2001) 'Money is no object: materiality, desire, and modernity in an Indonesian society', in Myers, F. R. (ed.) *The Empire of Things: Regimes of Value and Material Culture*, Sante Fe NM: School of American Research Press.

Klein, R. (1995) *Cigarettes are Sublime*, London: Picador.

Machen, A. (1926) *The Anatomy of Tobacco*, London: Alfred. A. Knopf.

Malinowski, B. (1967) *A Diary in the Strict Sense of the Term*, London: Routledge and Kegan Paul.

Mead, M. (1986) 'Field work in the Pacific Islands 1925–67', in Golde, P. (ed.) *Women in the Field: Anthropological Experiences*, Berkeley: University of California Press.

Morris, T. and Morris, P. (1963) *Pentonville: a Sociology Study of an English Prison*, London: Routledge and Kegan Paul.

Mosko, M. (1999) 'Magical money: commoditization and the linkage of *maketsi* ("market") and *kangakanga* ("custom") in Contemporary North Mekeo', in Akin, D. and Robbins, J. (eds) *Money and Modernity: State and Local Currency in Melanesia*, Pittsburgh PA: University of Pittsburgh Press.

Nihill, M. (1989) 'The new pearlshells: aspects of money and meaning in Anganen exchange', *Canberra Anthropology*, 12: 144–59.

Parry, J. and Bloch, M. (eds) (1989) *Money and the Morality of Exchange*, Cambridge: Cambridge University Press.

Pels, P. (1998) 'The spirit of matter: on fetish, rarity, fact and fancy', in Spyer, P. (ed.) *Border Fetishisms: Material Objects in Unstable Spaces*, London: Routledge.

Pietz, W. (1985) 'The problem of the fetish', *Res*, 9: 5–17.

Powdermaker, H. (1966) *Stranger and Friend: the Way of an Anthropologist*, New York: Norton.

Radford, R. A. (1968) 'The economic organisation of a P.O.W. camp', in Le Clair, E. and Schneider, H. K. (eds) *Economic Anthropology: Readings in Theory and Analysis*, New York: Holt, Rinehart & Winston.

Reed, A. (2003) *Papua New Guinea's Last Place: Experiences of Constraint in a Post-colonial Prison*, Oxford: Berghahn.

——(1999) 'Anticipating individuals: modes of vision and their social consequence in a Papua New Guinea prison', *Journal of the Royal Anthropological Institute*, 5: 43–56.

Robbins, J. and Akin, D. (1999) 'An introduction to Melanesian currencies: agency, identity and social reproduction', in Akin, D. and Robbins, J. (eds) *Money and Modernity: State and Local Currencies in Melanesia*, Pittsburgh PA: University of Pittsburgh Press.

Schifter, J. (1999) *Macho Love: Sex Behind Bars in Central America*, New York: The Haworth Hispanic/Latino Press.

Shell, M. (1995) *Art and Money*, Chicago: University of Chicago Press.

Simmel, G. (1978) *The Philosophy of Money*, London: Routledge and Kegan Paul.

Strathern, M. (1999) *Property, Substance and Effect: Anthropological Essays on Persons and Things*, London: Athlone Press.

Wayne, Helena (1995) *The Story of a Marriage: the Letters of Bronislaw Malinowski and Elsie Masson, vol. 1, 1916–20*, London: Routledge.

3

TAONGA MÄORI

Encompassing rights and property in New Zealand

Amiria Henare

> Ownership gathers things momentarily to a point by locating them in the owner, halting endless dissemination, effecting an identity.
>
> (Strathern 1999: 177)

> There is no specific term in Mäori for the word value. [. . .] [T]he Mäori idea of value is incorporated into the [. . .] term 'taonga' – a treasure, something precious; hence an object of good or value. The object or end valued may be tangible or intangible; material or spiritual.
>
> (Mäori Marsden in Royal 2003: 38)

This paper examines a particular intervention in conceptions of ownership on the part of Mäori people in New Zealand. It concerns a claim that asserts Mäori interests in a range of specific things singled out as objects of legal attention, among them the products of new technologies that the law has only recently, or not yet even, decided may be owned. These interests are asserted on the basis that the things concerned are *taonga*, a Mäori term which may be glossed as 'a treasure, something precious; hence an object of good or value'. A *taonga* might equally be a historic whalebone weapon, the Mäori language, a native plant or a body of knowledge; distinctions between the material and the ephemeral are not relevant here. Nor are ideas about animate versus inanimate entities; women and children may be exchanged as *taonga*, and *taonga* such as woven cloaks are often held as ancestors or instantiations of ancestral effect.

Marcel Mauss first brought the concept of *taonga* to international attention in his seminal 'Essai sur le don' (1925), published in translation as *The Gift* in 1954. Referring to a letter written in the 1890s by the Mäori elder Tamati Ranapiri, later translated by museum ethnologist Elsdon Best,[1] Mauss argued that when a *taonga* or treasured possession is exchanged, it carries with it *hau*, 'the spirit of the gift', an animate force binding those involved in the transaction – persons and things – into a cycle of reciprocity, impelling the receiver to

47

make a return. But whereas for Mauss, *taonga* appeared as mere 'vehicles' for the *hau* and *mana* of the gifting party and his kin-group, Ranapiri himself expressed things rather differently:

> The *taonga* that I received for these *taonga* (which came from you) must be returned to you. It would not be fair (*tika*) on my part to keep these *taonga* for myself, whether they were desirable (*rawe*) or undesirable (*kino*). I must give them to you because *they are a hau of the taonga that you gave me*. If I kept this other *taonga* for myself, serious harm might befall me, even death. This is the nature of the *hau*, the *hau* of personal property, the *hau* of the *taonga*.
>
> (in Mauss 1990: 11, emphasis added)

According to Ranapiri, one *taonga* exchanged for another does not simply *carry* the *hau* of the gift, it *is* its *hau*, translated elsewhere by Best as 'the vital essence or life principle' (1900: 189). There is a precise identity, in other words, between thing and spirit, aspects which Mauss separated out in his analysis. I make this point to emphasise that the concept of *taonga* is not in fact translatable into European terms, legal or otherwise. My purpose is to examine the implications of this untranslatability, in particular the strategies Māori people are developing to insist on the enduring relevance and integrity of their own concepts today within a predominantly anglophone society.

Māori rights in their *taonga* are specifically protected in the terms of the Treaty of Waitangi, the document by which New Zealand was made a British colony in the mid-nineteenth century, but which has never been fully recognised in law. The Māori version of the Treaty, first signed in the Bay of Islands in 1840, was constituted as an exchange of promises between Māori chiefs and the British Crown. In Article 1 of the Treaty, the chiefs agreed that Queen Victoria could establish a governor in New Zealand. In Article 2, the Queen's representatives promised that she would uphold the *tino rangatiratanga* or absolute authority of the chiefs over their lands, living places, *me o ratou taonga katoa*, a phrase often translated as 'and all their valuables'. At the same time the chiefs 'gifted' to the Queen the right to control *te hokonga* (usually translated as the buying and selling) of land. In Article 3, the Queen promised to protect Māori people and give them the same rights as her own people in England.[2]

All the articles of the Treaty have been contentious, not least that which guarantees Māori *tino rangatiratanga* over their *taonga* and land. Much legal, historical, and anthropological debate has focused upon this commitment in recent years, and the claim I will be thinking through is positioned in the thick of this scholarly action. At one level, dispute centres on the validity of Māori claims to ownership of *taonga* in a variety of spheres. Yet more is at stake here than property rights alone. Some who question Māori interests do so on the grounds that over two centuries of cultural engagement and intermarriage with Europeans have removed from Māori their privileged status as an indigenous people, rendering even their claims to a distinctive identity suspect. It is increasingly held that globalisation and life in a twenty-first century, first-world society have adulterated authentic Māori identity, leaving a hybrid, postcolonial relic in its place. In the course of this paper I will explore how anthropologists are providing support for this view by analysing cultural change through the lens of biological kinship. The logic of *whakapapa* ('genealogy') – a key organising principle in Māori – as we shall see, offers a rather different view.

In asserting the ongoing vitality of concepts such as *taonga*, their ability to generate and encompass new forms, therefore, Māori are insisting on the persistence and creativity of a distinctively Māori register of value. More than just a pre-emptive strike against the commoditisation of specific objects, the particular claim I will be looking at insists on the enduring vitality of Māoriness, and may be seen as an attempt to continue weaving into the *kaupapa* or body of law in New Zealand a distinctively Māori way of conceiving the nature of persons and things. As I hope to articulate in the course of this chapter, the claim's anticipated effect derives in part from distinctive assumptions about the workings of language, particularly written or printed text. In fact, as I will argue, the claim itself may be understood as a certain kind of *taonga*, one whose contours are thrown into relief by the very contrast between divergent conceptions of reality.

Wai 262: a 'cultural property' claim

Over the past century, a great deal of Māori energy has been devoted to seeking reparations for land and resources expropriated in the course of colonisation. Although the Treaty of Waitangi was declared a legal nullity by a New Zealand court not long after its signing, Māori people have consistently called for its terms to be upheld, for successive governments' failures in protecting Māori interests to be addressed, and for adequate reparations to be made for land, *taonga* and resources lost in the colonial process. In 1975 the Waitangi Tribunal was established to assess such claims, which, under its remit, must demonstrate a specific breach (or breaches) of the Treaty of Waitangi, the document signed by Māori leaders and representatives of the British Crown in 1840.

The particular claim through which I will be thinking is known as Wai 262, being the 262nd claim submitted to the Tribunal since its foundation. Wai 262 was lodged by a group of Māori representing six *iwi* or tribes, and asserts Māori interests in *taonga* including indigenous flora and fauna, genetics and genetics derivatives, silica sands and cultural motifs, as well as items identified (by the claimants and others) as 'traditional' objects of value. This latter category includes the Māori language, Māori knowledge or *matauranga* in general and the knowledge, skilled practice and artefacts of processes including carving and weaving. Interests in these objects of value are asserted with reference to Article 2 of the Treaty, in particular the section guaranteeing to Māori *te tino rangatiratanga* over their lands, living places, *me o ratou taonga katoa*. The text of the claim, and evidence submitted in its support, incorporates conceptual threads drawn both from British and New Zealand jurisprudence and from Māori principles and thinking. These are woven together into a *kaupapa* or fabric in the form of a legal document, the Statement of Claim, in which diverse conceptions are laid alongside one another and held in tension. While the term 'ownership' is not used, the claim specifically names 'intellectual property and property rights' among the 'indigenous, cultural and customary heritage rights' for which it seeks recognition.

Seen in historical perspective, Wai 262 follows a series of unexpected commodifications of things that were not originally conceived as abstractable from an all-encompassing fabric of relations. First, in the colonial period, land was appropriated and sold in transactions that (at least at first) confounded Māori notions of economic and social propriety. More recently, government plans to sell resources including fishing quotas, petroleum rights and the radio spectrum used in telecommunications, took Māori (and others) by surprise. Each of these moves resulted in claims to the Waitangi Tribunal for a Māori share of the pie. In the Fisheries Claim (Wai 307), for example, a number of tribes were successful in gaining a substantial share of commercial ocean fisheries, whereas claims for a stake in the radio spectrum and petroleum rights (Wai 776 and 796 respectively), though upheld by the Tribunal, were rejected by government. In the case of Wai 262, it seems that Māori are pre-empting the process, getting in ahead of the intellectual property lawyers and legislators who would define how things should be objectified. It is in this sense that the claim appears as an assertion of distinctively Māori values, and of a mode of objectification in which different kinds of things appear. Yet while, as with the Fisheries Claim, people seem prepared to accept that Māori value rights in resources defined by the authorities (and by the claimants themselves) as 'traditional', they are less willing to extend to Māori the capacity to encompass newness, the artefacts of technological innovation, within their relational scheme. To some commentators indeed, the claim appears little short of ludicrous in the scope of its demands (e.g. Milne 2005).

The matter is complicated by the fact that Māori clearly participate in more than one register of value – that which produces commodities as well as that which is peopled by *taonga*. As a report on the claim makes explicit:

> The concepts of te ao Māori [. . .] cannot be assimilated to categories of real, personal and intellectual property rights of ownership and/or possession in respect of tangible or intangible items with economic exchange value. The tension of living with these incompatibilities is a daily fact of life for Māori.
>
> (Williams 2001: 14)

I am interested in the relationship between these apparently incommensurable positions. According to many commentators in New Zealand, the two are inherently opposed – the more one values commodities, the less Māori one becomes, as to claim an attachment to the artefacts of global capitalism is seen as reneging upon a commitment to the world of *taonga*. Yet in Wai 262, one perspective is encompassed by the other, as property rights are subsumed in *taonga* relations. Let me give a brief example of this encompassment in action. The following paragraph is drawn from the amended Wai 262 Statement of Claim, submitted to the Waitangi Tribunal in October 2001 by counsel for claimants on behalf of the Ngati Kuri, Te Rarawa and Ngati Wai *iwi* or tribes. Although the claim is written mostly in English, many readers will not understand parts of it as they are given in Māori, often without translation. I will return to this point shortly:

> The [Wai 262] claim relates to te tino rangatiratanga of Ngati Kuri, Te Rarawa and Ngati Wai in respect of indigenous flora and fauna *me o ratou taonga katoa* (and all their treasures) within their respective tribal rohe, including but not limited to te reo, matauranga, knowledge systems, laws, customs and values, whakairo, waahi tapu, biodiversity, natural resources, genetics and genetics derivatives, Māori symbols, images, designs, and their use and development and associated indigenous, cultural and customary heritage rights (including intellectual property and property rights) in relation to such taonga. 'Taonga' in this claim refers to all elements of the claimants' estates, both material and non-material, tangible and intangible.
>
> (Wai 262 Second Amended Statement of Claim on behalf of Ngati Kuri, Te Rarawa and Ngati Wai, 20 October 2001)

The claim itself thus brings a range of objects, including intellectual property and property rights in general, into the sphere of *taonga*, encompassing them under the heading *me o ratou taonga katoa* (glossed here as 'and all their treasures'). This is achieved both explicitly, through articulating this assertion in a combination of English and Māori terms, and performatively, in asserting the *mana* or authority of Māori concepts and terminology by leaving them largely untranslated in the mainly English text. From this position, at least, incommensurability no longer appears as a problem, as *taonga* and commodities are brought into a single generative sphere. Later in this paper I will explore this encompassment and its significance for analyses of cultural dynamism and change.

The Treaty of Waitangi as a *taonga*

In Māori terms, the kaupapa (underlying principle) of all the claims made to the Waitangi Tribunal is the Treaty itself. Māori people have come to regard the Treaty as a *taonga*, as a solemn token of convenant, as 'he kawenata tapu' (a sacred convenant) and as a bringing together of Mäori custom and English law.

(Waitangi Tribunal 1992: 2.13)

The foundation of the Waitangi Tribunal, and the various claims which it has so far assessed, have occasioned heated public and scholarly debate about the terms of the Treaty, the circumstances surrounding its signing and the intentions of those who signed it. As already mentioned, much of this discussion has centred on the clause in the Treaty that guarantees to Mäori *te tino rangatiratanga* over their *taonga*, and which is the focus of the Wai 262 claim. Counsel and expert witnesses for the Crown in a number of claims have taken a conservative approach to its interpretation, attempting to restrict the definition of *taonga* to include only the kinds of things likely to have been valued by Mäori in the mid-nineteenth century. Mäori on the other hand assert that the Treaty upholds their authority over their *taonga*, period – not just those considered valuable in 1840. A conflict has thus emerged between those who consider the Tribunal's primary task to be the reconstruction of nineteenth-century understandings through the deployment of historical and ethnographic evidence, and those for whom the Treaty is a living document, protecting the salience and ongoing development of Mäori principles and values in perpetuity. Those who hold the latter view have often described the Treaty itself as a *taonga*, a sacred covenant between Mäori chiefs and the British people. As the Ngapuhi chief and scholar Sir James Henare wrote in the 1980s:

Ko öku whakaaro ake mö te Tiriti o Waitangi, he taonga tapu, he mea tä ki te moko no o rätou kiri. He tapu ra o tätou tupuna, mätauranga, he tohunga, he Ariki hoki.

Here are my thoughts about the Treaty of Waitangi. It is a sacred *taonga*, incised with tattoos from the skins of our ancestors. It is their *tapu* (sacred power), the *tapu* of their knowledge, of their priests and high chiefs.

(in Blank *et al.* 1985: 113; trans. Anne Salmond)

Henare refers here to the way in which many chiefs who 'signed' the Treaty at Waitangi and other parts of the country in 1840 did so by inscribing designs from their *moko* or facial tattoos onto the parchment of the document. In Mäori, the head is the most *tapu* part of the body, and the heads of *rangatira* or high-born people, intricately tattooed in a manner that brought the person's *whakapapa* or genealogy out onto the surface of their skin, were among the most spiritually potent objects one might encounter. In drawing their *moko* marks onto the Treaty, the chiefs extended their own *mana* to the document, rendering it an instantiation of their personhood as the 'living face' of their line. Such practice was already commonplace in transactions involving land, and there are extant deeds on which the entire *moko* pattern covering the face of the signatory is inscribed.

Māori and the power of writing

Even by 1840, though, there were Māori who had become familiar with the practice of writing, largely through the work of missionaries whose teachings focused upon the Bible, the sacred power of the word of God. Many copies of the Bible and other religious texts were translated into Māori then printed and circulated, and Māori who were taught to read and write in the mission schools sought to pass these skills onto others. A number of the chiefs who signed the Treaty thus wrote out their own names, committing these personal marks of another kind to this new and highly *tapu taonga*. This movement, from the drawing out of *whakapapa* onto the surface of the skin with *uhi* or tattooing chisels, then onto paper with pen and ink, into writing in the form of signatures, meant that for Māori (who had no indigenous script of their own), written language possessed powers with which they were familiar, as well as those with which they were not.

The same could be said for printed material. Books held a fascination right from the start, not simply as a result of missionary emphasis on the *Paipera Tapu* (Holy Bible). On Captain Cook's second voyage to the Pacific, for example, William Wales recorded that a copy of *Tom Jones* was filched by a Māori man from the ship's binnacle cupboard while they were moored at Totaranui (Queen Charlotte Sound) (Wales in Beaglehole 1969: 788–9). Later writers recorded how Māori were 'struck with wonder at hearing, as they described it, "a book speak",[3] and went to any lengths to get hold of one, regardless of whether they could read. At a church service, as one early settler recorded,

> Many of [the Māori] thought it highly proper that they should be armed with books. It might be an old ship's almanac, or a cast-away novel, or even a few stitched leaves of old newspapers.
>
> (Clarke 1903: 31)

Others wore leaves from mission books rolled up and thrust through piercings in their ears, just like valued *taonga* such as the skins and beaks of huia birds, pieces of *pounamu* greenstone that had descended through several generations, or the rare white cloth made from *aute* (paper mulberry bark) and albatross down.

Yet, according to D.F. McKenzie,

> For [Māori], the really miraculous point about writing was its portability; by annihilating distance, a letter allowed the person who

wrote it to be in two places at once, his body in one, his thoughts in another.

(1985: 19)

McKenzie's analysis presumes, though, that early Māori shared assumptions about the natural separation of mind and body with Europeans. People who regarded *taonga* as possessing many qualities in common with people, however (to the extent that a person could be a *taonga* and vice-versa), would have conceived of such things rather differently. Yes, letters and books annihilated distance, but not necessarily by enabling one's thoughts to go one way and one's body another. Given that the written and printed word alike were often treated as *taonga*, and that *taonga* were instantiations of personal (including ancestral) effect, perhaps the 'miracle' of text was that, as a special kind of *taonga*, it enabled a form of distributed personhood involving the *mana*, *tapu* and *hau* of the person – their ancestral efficacy and power, in other words – as well as their 'thoughts'. It is against this background that the notion of the Treaty of Waitangi as a *taonga*, a living document, should be understood.

Text as the instantiation of ancestral effect

When the Treaty was signed in 1840, several different versions with significantly different meanings were circulated around New Zealand; some forty-five chiefs signed the Māori version presented at Waitangi, which then travelled around the country, gathering over 500 signatures in all on various editions of the document. Thirty-nine chiefs appended their marks to an English version at Waikato Heads and Manukau, while a further version was printed by the Church Missionary Society at Paihia, one copy of which was also used to obtain signatures. In addition, five different versions in English were sent abroad, either to Sydney or London (McKenzie 1985: 33). Yet, as McKenzie warns, the fact that chiefs 'signed' the document in its various guises should not necessarily be taken as an indication of their agreement to its terms. Noting that few Māori at the time spoke English, McKenzie points out that the missionaries only taught reading and writing in Māori, so as to restrict their access to morally dangerous non-Scriptural material. (As one missionary remarked in 1842, 'having no other books to read but Scripture and productions from Scripture, [Māori] pursuits must all be of a sacred nature'.)[4] McKenzie also argues that the 'presumed wide-spread, high-level literacy of the Māori in the 1830s is a chimera' (1985: 35). Pointing to the laborious way in which the seventy-nine chiefs who appear to have actually written their own names on the Treaty did so, along with other evidence, he concludes that it is unlikely any of them would have been able to read its contents well enough to satisfy grounds for written consent. Nor, as members of a culture accustomed to

54

the flexibilities of oral contractual negotiation, he argues, would they have appreciated the binding nature of the document in accordance with British intent.

If most of the chiefs were not able to read the Treaty, however, why did they extend their *mana* to this parchment or paper by inscribing it with the marks of their authority? That the document wielded considerable *mana* was clear; the pomp and ceremony surrounding its presentation, the exchange of gifts for signatures, and Hobson's statement (translated by missionary Henry Williams) that, if the chiefs signed, the Queen would protect them, certainly impressed upon Māori the status of the Treaty as a thing of great power. Yet, as McKenzie argues, the fact that Māori remained a primarily oral/aural culture at this time would have suggested that, while the joining of their *mana* with that of Victoria through marking the parchment was a crucial step in establishing a relationship with the Queen of England, the details of how that relationship might work was up for negotiation as usual, through discussion and debate. The manner in which the Treaty was presented supported that view, being read out in Māori by its translator Henry Williams, after which the chiefs were invited to present their own observations and concerns. Many spoke strongly against the Treaty's terms, yet then went on to sign it. The missionary William Colenso recorded this reluctance, along with his own reservations:

> All being now ready for the signing, the Native chiefs were called on in a body to come forward and sign the document. Not one, however, made any move nor seemed desirous of doing so till Mr. Busby [. . .] proposed calling them singly by their names. [. . .] [The first chief then approached the table.] At this point I, addressing myself to the Governor, said, –
>
> [. . .] 'May I ask Your Excellency whether it is your opinion that these Natives understand the articles of the treaty which they are now called upon to sign?' [. . .]
>
> The Governor: 'If the Native chiefs do not know the contents of this treaty then it is no fault of mine. I have done all that I could do to make them understand the same, and I really don't know how I shall be enabled to get them to do so. They have heard the treaty read by Mr Williams.'
>
> Mr Colenso: 'True, your Excellency [. . .] It is no easy matter, I well know, to get them to understand – fully to comprehend a document of this kind; still, I think they ought to know somewhat of it to constitute its legality. I speak under correction, your Excellency. I have spoken to some chiefs concerning it, who had no idea as to the purport of the treaty.'
>
> (Colenso 1890: 33)

Following this exchange, a large number of the chiefs present nevertheless signed the document, including many who had spoken vociferously against it. It seems possible that the content of the Treaty, in their eyes, took second place to its importance as a *taonga* through which their *mana* and *tapu* would be fused with that of other chiefs including Captain William Hobson, the proposed *Kawana* or Governor, and Victoria, Queen of England.

Such treatment of written and printed documents as instantiations of chiefly *mana* was also evident in early land transactions. According to Anderson and Pickens, for example, the act of sale that conveyed title to much of the Wellington-Porirua district (now the site of New Zealand's capital city), was intended by the principal signatories 'to set the bounds of their *mana* over the harbour' (1996: 20) – what to European eyes appeared as an act of alienation was to Māori an assertion of chiefly efficacy and their ancestral ties to customary resources and land.

Taonga, personhood and exchange

So far I have explored how the Treaty of Waitangi and other written and printed documents were (and are) seen by Māori as *taonga*, things that, more than simply 'representing', 'signifying' or 'embodying' ancestral efficacy and power, *are* it in specific form. As Arapata Hakiwai has put it:

> Our taonga are not just wooden objects or aesthetic heirlooms, they speak and represent our origins, our beliefs, our very foundation on which we order our lives. We believe that our taonga possess a mauri or life force and wairua, spirit, all of their own.
>
> (in Cultural Conservation Advisory Council 1990: 116)

Returning to Mauss, such *taonga* are also the *hau* of the transactions through which they were exchanged, gathering together the *mana* and *tapu* of all those involved. In this view, the Treaty remains a living document, as relevant to contemporary Māori as the ancestors whose presence endures in its fabric.

In a similar sense the Wai 262 claim, like others to the Tribunal, might also be regarded as a *taonga*, the concepts it invokes instantiating the personhood of ancestors – and the promises they exchanged, generating relationships with others – in the present. Perhaps an analogy can be made here with Catholic relics, which bring the power of a saint to a point of focus, creating a nexus and site for supplicants to gain direct and physical access to an otherwise divine personality and power. Yet such comparisons can be misleading, as they mask very different assumptions about the nature of persons and things. In order to engage more fully with the concept of *taonga* – the subject and (I argue) substance of the Wai 262 claim – it is necessary to briefly examine Māori conceptions of personhood – a discussion inseparable from the dynamics of ritual exchange.

The alchemy of taonga

In Mäori, a person's *whakapapa* (often glossed as genealogy), makes them the 'living face' of their ancestors, an element in a network of ties of descent and other relationships whose vitality endures in *Te Ao Marama*, 'the world of light' through their identity and form (Salmond 1995: 26). The Wai 262 Statement of Claim identifies *whakapapa* as a key organising principle within what it describes as the Mäori 'world view'. As David Williams notes in a report commissioned by the Waitangi Tribunal for the claim, *whakapapa* 'is a great deal more than merely human genealogical tables of descent' (2001: 10). Not simply a static record of lineages, it is an inherently dynamic cosmological system for reckoning degrees of similarity and difference, determining appropriate behaviour, and manipulating existing and potential relationships to achieve desired effects. *Taonga* have long been crucial participants in this relational scheme.

I have argued elsewhere (Henare 2005: 121–5) that the Treaty of Waitangi may be understood as a chiefly gift exchange, whereby Queen Victoria 'gifted' to the chiefs of New Zealand *taonga* including *nga tikanga katoa rite tahi*, exactly the same rights as the people of England, while acknowledging their authority over their lands, their settlements and their own *taonga* or treasured possessions. In return, the chiefs agreed to *tuku*[5] to the Queen and her line forever *te Kawanatanga katoa o o ratou wenua*, the governorship of their lands, and *te hokonga o era wahi wenua*, the right to control the sale of land in New Zealand. Such occasions, whereby treasured *taonga* were exchanged in order to establish and maintain intra- or inter-tribal relationships, were already long established among Mäori, and have ever since been a central feature of Mäori life. They formed alliances between warring tribes, established new ties between strangers, and revitalised relationships that had gone cold. The kinds of *taonga* exchanged could include women and children, rights to land and resources, ancient weapons and greenstone valuables. Usually, however, *taonga* were passed down within kin groups, acting as (often tangible) instantiations of relationships extending across multiple generations. As Salmond has noted, such things played (and continue to play) a crucial role in bringing to a focus ancestral presence and effect:

> The alchemy of *taonga* [brings] about a fusion of men and ancestors and a collapse of distance in space-time. [. . .] the power of [such things can] give men absolute access to their ancestors.
>
> (1984: 120)

Writing of recent experiences among his own kin group, Paul Tapsell similarly notes how:

> The performance of taonga by elders effectively collapses time and reanimates the kin group's ancestral landscape, allowing descendants

to re-live the events of past generations. [. . .] This ability to collapse time, which becomes most apparent during tangihanga (death rituals, which normally extend over several days), allows ancestors and descendants to be fused back into a powerful, single genealogical identity.

(1997: 330).

Recognising the presence of whole ancestral lineages in a single *taonga*, as in a person, is crucial to grasping the significance of transactions in which important *taonga* were exchanged between kin groups to forge lasting ties across many generations. Thirteen years after the signing of the Treaty, for example, a large gathering of Mäori chiefs and colonial officials congregated at a school house at Otaki north of Wellington to bid farewell to Sir George Grey, third governor of the colony, who had held this position for the past eight turbulent years of the country's early colonial period. At the gathering, as Grey recorded in his despatches to the Colonial Office, an address signed by 'all the principal chiefs of this part of the country' was presented to him, together with two ancient *taonga* of the Ngati Toa and Ngati Raukawa tribes. Grey conveyed a copy of the address, together with these artefacts, to the Duke of Newcastle in London, along with a detailed account of their presentation, published in the *New Zealand Spectator*:

At eleven A.M., several of the principal chiefs [. . .] having assembled in the new School-house, Thompson [son of the late fighting chief Te Rauparaha] proceeded to read the address on behalf of the native tribes of the southern part of New Zealand [in front of a large, mainly Mäori, audience]. After which, a most interesting and affecting ceremony took place: Ranguira [*sic* – Rangiuira], the wife of Rangihaeta [*sic* – Te Rangihaeata], was led forward by several people, one of whom having cut the string by which a valuable green jasper ear-ring (a very old heir-loom of the Ngatitoa tribe) was attached to her ear, handed it first to Rangihaeata. The old chief then proceeded after the ancient Mäori custom of 'Hongi' to press the green stone to his nose, and pass it over his face in token of farewell, having finally parted with the precious heir-loom of the tribe as the most expressive mode of conveying to the Governor the assurance of his regard and esteem. The same ceremony was gone through by all the other chiefs present at the delivery, and was likewise performed on a Patu Paraoa, an instrument of war, also a very old heir-loom of Taratoa's tribe.

(*Correspondence*: 286–7)

The *taonga* that Grey was given on this occasion were indeed important valuables. Each bore its own name and had descended to the chiefs who presented them over many generations. That which was taken from the ear of Te Rangiuira was called Kaitangata, 'eater of men'. The *Spectator* recorded that:

It was first of all supposed to have been the property of Te Ngahue, a chief who came from Hawaiki, one of the Polynesian Islands, in his canoe, and having discovered the New Zealand islands, visited Te Wai Pounamu [the South Island] where he procured this jasper stone, which he called Kaitangata.

Te Ngahue then took the greenstone back to his homeland of Hawaiki, the place from where the ancestors of the Māori people emigrated to New Zealand. The *Spectator* continues:

Te Ngahue never returned to New Zealand; but his people, hearing of the fame thereof, embarked in two canoes, called Tainui and Te Arawa, and brought back with them here the Greenstone. From them, as the ancestors of the Ngatitoa tribe, it has descended through several generations.

(*Correspondence*: 286)

The *patu paraoa* or whale bone handclub given to Grey at the same time was Hine Te Ao, a maternal ancestor of the Ngati Raukawa tribe. According to the *Spectator*:

Hine Te Ao was born at Maungatantari [*sic* – Maungatautari]. She had a brother called Te Maihi, who was very nearly killed with this Patu Paraoa. It was in consequence seized and taken in payment for the offence by his sister, who gave to it her own name in remembrance of the painful event, and from her it has descended through six generations to the present time. It was presented to His Excellency by Taratoa in the name and on behalf of the chiefs and people belonging to his tribe, called Ngatiraukawa.

(*Correspondence*: 287)

After being passed down from generation to generation within their respective tribes, therefore, these precious and ancient *taonga* were presented to Grey as a representative of the British Crown, the inheritor of the promises made in the Treaty. Such prestations between Māori tribes and members of the royal family and their colonial agents have indeed continued over time into the present – Queen Elizabeth II, for example, wears a kiwi feather cloak she was given by Māori people at Rotorua on all of her visits to New Zealand.

Paul Tapsell, a museum anthropologist and young leader in the Arawa tribal confederation, has explained the significance of such transactions with regard to the recent return of tribal *taonga* to his own kin group, the Ngati

Whakaue people. In Māori, Tapsell notes, *taonga* are exchanged between lineages rather than individuals, and only the most valuable *taonga* are considered worthy of release to another kin group. The more valuable the *taonga*, 'the greater the prestige bestowed upon the receiver', and the heavier the obligation for future reciprocity (*utu*) (2000: 15; 1997: 337–8). The 'intention and result' of such prestations, as Metge has emphasised:

> was not to discharge the obligation between givers and receivers but to create and keep it moving from one party to the other, binding them in an on-going relationship. The expression 'tuia, tui, tuia' sums up this to and fro movement, 'stitching' the parties together.

> (1992: 66)

The *taonga* 'gifted' to Grey, then, like those exchanged in the Treaty, were intended to revitalise (and no doubt improve)[6] relations between the chiefs (as the concentration points of their kin groups' *mana*) and Grey as representative of the British Crown and thus of Victoria's line. In *hongi*-ing the *taonga*, the chiefs were mingling their own *hau* or breath of life with that of the ancestor-object, thus binding the intertwined lineages of the chiefs and that of Grey together, re-animating the promises of the Treaty and focusing their relationship in the form of their ancestor, the ancient *taonga*. As Tapsell notes, however, whereas within Māoridom, 'concern about the future well-being of [such] *taonga* was never an issue because the recipients understood their obligations as custodians', when a *taonga* was gifted into European hands, *utu* (the principle of equal return) was not always fulfilled. This created an imbalance which must be redressed, sometimes through the return of the *taonga* to the descendants of its former owners (2000: 15; 1997: 337–8). In the case of the *taonga* gifted to Grey, as with those exchanged in the Treaty, there was certainly an expectation among the Māori participants of an ongoing return. This would continue the relationship between Victoria's line and the chief's own descendants established in the Treaty, in which redress could be sought for the failure to make a sufficient return. The *hau* of the original gift lives on, requiring reciprocity through successive generations. This goes some way toward explaining the motivations behind the Wai 262 claim.

It is important to emphasise here that the gifting of *taonga* is not simply a feature of the past in New Zealand. Despite Māori being active participants in a predominantly anglophone twenty-first century society, such arrangements continue today; there are recent cases of children being 'exchanged' between tribal groups to balance historical conflicts or transactions, and valuable *taonga* continue to be 'gifted' to establish and maintain relations. The exchange of *taonga* in Māori has long been an integral part of the work of relating, and continues to be so in the present.

Taonga and objectification

The Wai 262 claim remains unresolved, and continues to excite controversy in New Zealand. While the claim follows and appeals to the logic of Māori gift exchange, some critics argue that it is holding up long-overdue reforms of intellectual property law, and thus deterring foreign investment, while the media represents it as yet another example of Māori gaining mileage out of postcolonial political posturing.[7] These arguments centre on an apparent paradox at the heart of the negotiations, which are presided over by the Waitangi Tribunal in an adversarial setting. Evidence is presented alternately by expert witnesses (many of them anthropologists) acting for the Crown, and by those working for the claimants. The stakes for winning a scholarly point are high, as the Tribunal has the power to recommend substantial financial reparations. The inferred paradox is this: if the basis of Wai 262 and other Māori claims is an appeal to tradition – the enduring salience of principles, practices and beliefs held in common with ancestors – then how can Māori claim special rights over things that are the commodified products of global capitalism? How, in other words, can they participate simultaneously in what appear as two distinct – even antithetical – cultural perspectives, one distinctively Māori, the other quintessentially Western?

It is not only those averse to postcolonial reparations who experience this as a contradiction. Anthropologists and historians, among them a number of Māori scholars, also struggle to reconcile the dynamism and vitality of Māori culture with assertions that a distinctively 'Māori world view', the parameters of which were laid down long before the arrival of European colonists, prevails among Māori in present-day New Zealand. Some attempt to resolve this through theories of strategic essentialism and neo-traditionalisation, sympathetically crafting commensurability out of political expedience and instrumentality (e.g. Hanson 1989; Levine 1991; Neich 1978; 1983; Sissons 1993; 1998). Others are more cynical, accusing the Tribunal of manufacturing history for present purposes (Oliver 2001), or charging some Māori and their supporters with cultural fundamentalism (e.g. Rata 2005). There is a common thread to all these stories, one which, I will argue, concerns objectification.

All the things that are claimed in Wai 262, including genetic resources, are claimed as *taonga*, a concept which, as already noted, is often glossed as 'treasured ancestral possessions', but which, I will suggest, may be understood here as particular kinds of objectifications – in Strathern's sense, as 'persons and things [. . .] construed as having value' (1988: 176). I am using the term 'objectification' advisedly here, building on Strathern's work and that of James Leach (2003a; 2003b), to describe a process that, while producing objects of a kind, does not necessarily invoke a subject (or at least the sort of subject that generally springs to Euro-American minds). Objectifications in the form of *taonga* are inherently productive, and reproductive, as they both arise from and are generative of relations. As distributed parts of persons, and as persons in their own right, *taonga* – whether in the form of people, knowledge, carved objects, the Māori language and even the radio spectrum – are a fundamental requirement of relationality. This is not to say that they give form and substance to something that would otherwise remain abstract, floating around in some sort of nebulous social ether, nor simply, to paraphrase Alfred Gell, that relations are a characteristic of the substantive world of people and things in which we live, rather than merely an attribute of an abstracted human sociality. It is that the very partibility and motility of *taonga* (see Holbraad, Chapter 9 of this volume), their 'thinginess' within a general state of flux, is precisely what makes them indispensable to the work of relating. Perhaps somewhat unlike the Melanesianists, therefore, I am using the term 'objectification' because I wish to emphasise the object-like qualities of *taonga* over their relational capacities, which is something I take as given.

This is no doubt a risky strategy, making it potentially harder rather than easier to convey the point, as it might be confused with certain arguments about the 'invention' of culture and tradition. Perhaps the thing to emphasise here is that the creativity in Māori modes of objectification is not a property peculiar to human beings. *Taonga* are not simply artefacts of individual subjectivity, nor of human agency in general; they are at once the product and fabric of dynamic relational matrices involving all manner of entities, that shift and transform over time. Foregrounding *taonga* as objects is neither a simple index of Westernisation, nor just a convenient analytic conceit. It is a way of approaching a concept that is not translatable in terms available to anglophone law or anthropology, a juxtaposition intended to throw into relief certain aspects of *taonga* that otherwise would be impossible to convey.

Objectification, anthropocentrism, and analyses of cultural change

Yet it is a commonplace in analyses of socio-cultural change, particularly those dealing with 'fourth world' societies or former colonies, that objectification – of one's self or one's culture – is a practice with a distinctively Euro-American pedigree. A side-effect of rejecting earlier anthropological tendencies that allegedly arrested 'primitive' cultures in an eternal ethnographic present (but cf. Sahlins 1999: 404–5), and of the resultant emphasis on the processual dynamism of culture, is that any effort to delineate and demarcate elements of culture, to reflect upon it, or foreground its continuities, is regarded as derivative of that earlier way of thinking. It is of course ironic (or perhaps something more sinister) that such a view has become endemic in the social sciences and humanities just as various minority groups, among them indigenous peoples, are attempting to assert their cultural distinctiveness on a world stage, often by appearing to deploy such strategies. (Whatever pronouncements they make on their own account, as Adam Kuper has recently argued, 'they do so in the idiom of Western culture theory' (2003: 395).) But I am more interested here in the theoretical implications of this kind of analysis, which seems to involve a degree of ontological projection.

The argument that peoples such as Māori are simply borrowing from the conceptual toolbox of anthropology (or of the West in general) for the sake (however laudable) of self determination obscures another possibility – that they are using the language of social theory in an attempt to articulate (untranslatable) concepts of their own. One reason why scholars might find it difficult to take their pronouncements seriously is not simply that the terminology deployed can appear somewhat dated – the often-used 'Māori world view' springs to mind – but that we are unwilling to acknowledge even the *potential* alterity of what is being put forward. As earlier mentioned, there is an idea about that incorporation into global capitalism and modernity involves a net conceptual loss on the part of the less powerful, resulting in a tragic though inevitable decline into inauthenticity, a kind of conceptual miscegenation. In this sense the very act of incorporating people into the *anthropos* – the 'family of mankind' – long regarded as the philosophical baseline of anthropology, entails deploying a set of assumptions built on specific notions of relatedness. Notwithstanding that such ideas have been thoroughly unpacked in 'the new kinship studies', or that terms such as 'race' have been largely rejected (at least in the academy), a residual biologism remains evident at the heart of contemporary anthropology. Assertions of a shared humanity are often based on the assumption of a universal (linguistically capable and reproductively isolated) subjectivity. (Among the most enduring elements in this scheme is of course the distinction between animate, agentive subjects and an inert and malleable materiality.) There are very good reasons for insisting on the authority of this conception, connected historically to the abolition of slavery, the rights of women and other moral and political imperatives. In insisting on an ontological apartheid between persons and things, however, it comes with a degree of hubris about the power and efficacy of some conceptions over others, a sort of philosophical 'survival of the fittest'. The strength of such moral convictions undermines analytic flexibility, preventing us from taking seriously other peoples' accounts of reality. What if, as I am arguing, there were other processes we might recognise as objectification in a certain sense? And what if such processes derived from quite different (and enduring) ontological assumptions?

I have argued that the *taonga* claimed in Wai 262, rather than being simply an example of the creative appropriation by Māori of European notions of property and ownership, are in fact distinctively Māori kinds of objects with a creativity of their own. Whereas it is common to juxtapose indigenous conceptions of property with those of the West in order to emphasise the fluid, relational character of the former in contrast to the alienating, divisive nature of the latter, however, I am interested in why Mäori might wish to highlight what I am calling the object-like qualities of *taonga*, the ways in which they are relevant to questions of ownership in a legal sense. This is not because I want to obscure the relational capacities of *taonga* – the ways in which they are valued for their capacity to generate relationships, which, as Leach (2003a) has recently argued (drawing on the work of Paul Tapsell) is fundamental to their operations. It is because the very different concepts of *taonga* and property have been brought together into a single sphere, in which one encompasses the other, in the Wai 262 'cultural property' claim.

Deploying the *taonga*-status of the Treaty as a 'living document', an instantiation of ancestral efficacy, the claim interweaves Mäori concepts with strands of legal discourse, in a pattern laid down many years ago. (New Zealand statutes have incorporated Mäori terminology since at least 1955.) Rather than simply deploying the idiom of Western culture theory, therefore, as Kuper and others would have it, Mäori are not only insisting upon but demonstrating the persistent salience and enduring vitality of their own concepts, and, by extension, of distinctively Mäori ways of being.

It thus seems that, instead of working from within a single perspective, Mäori are shifting between registers of value in a move enabled by the encompassment of one – that of commodities – by the other – that of *taonga*. This commensurability is consistent with Mäori notions of related-ness, in that, according to the workings of *whakapapa*, Mäoriness encompasses other identities without obliterating or diluting them – one may be Mäori *and* Irish, but even a majority Irish ancestry does not make one any less Mäori. The implications of this for analyses of cultural dynamism and the articulation of culture-based claims in postcolonial situations are significant and wide-ranging. If one can no longer assume that the effects of colonisation necessarily adulterate or demolish distinctive concepts, producing ontological hybrids, half-castes and cross-breeds, then it is neces-sary to acknowledge positions that may be wholly Mäori *and also* European. The creativity of *taonga* does not derive simply from the minds of individual subjects, but from a fabric of relations peopled both by objects that appear as people, and by people that appear as things.

Acknowledgements

The ideas explored in this chapter were developed through conversations with Manuka Henare, as well as discussions that took place during the interdisciplinary 'Artefacts in Theory' seminar which ran at the University of Cambridge Museum of Archaeology and Anthropology during 2003–4. These arguments were tested at the 'Thinking Through Things' conference hosted by the University's Centre for Research in the Arts, Social Sciences and Humanties (CRASSH) in October 2004. I am particularly grateful to

Fernando Dominguez-Rubio, Anita Herle, Daniel Miller and Maui Solomon for their insightful commentary on various drafts of the piece.

Notes

1 Ranapiri was a knowledgeable member of the Ngati Raukawa *iwi* or tribe. Mauss misspells his name as 'Ranaipiri' (in Best's original text it is correctly spelt as 'Ranapiri') (Best 1910: 438; Mauss 1950: 158).
2 The Mäori and English texts of the Treaty, as well as a literal translation into English of the Mäori text, are published as appendices in Orange 1987.
3 *Missionary Register* (September 1834), 418–19, cited in McKenzie 1985: 19.
4 Letter by William Puckey of 6 June 1842, cited in Parr 1961: 445.
5 Merimeri Penfold translates this term as follows: 'To tuku is to release something – a taonga, a wairua [glossed as 'spirit'] – from one sphere of influence into another. It will eventually return back into the whakapapa line.' From a discussion during fieldwork, 20 April 2000. See also Waitangi Tribunal 1997: 73–7, and Metge 1992: 72–97 for further discussion as to its import.
6 Grey had recently been instrumental in expropriating substantial tracts of Ngati Toa and Ngatiraukawa land, forcing their people into exile, and imprisoning one of their chiefs for 'rebellion' against the British Crown. See Anderson and Pickens 1996.
7 This attitude echoes the anthropologist H. B. Levine's argument that 'the widening and extension of the concept of taonga is a specific example of the elaboration of the [postcolonial] ideology of biculturalism' (Levine 1991: 445).

References

Anderson, R. and Pickens, K. (1996) *Rangihaua Whanui District 12: Wellington District, Port Nicholson, Hutt Valley, Porirua, Rangitikei, and Manawatu*, working paper: first release, Wellington, Waitangi Tribunal.
Beaglehole, E. (ed.) (1969) *The Journals of Captain James Cook on his Voyages of Discovery, Vol. II: the Voyage of the Resolution and Adventure, 1772–75*, Cambridge: Cambridge University Press.
Best, E. (1910) 'Mäori forest lore', part III, *Transactions of the New Zealand Institute*, 42: 438–41.
——(1900) 'Spiritual concepts of the Mäori', part I, *Journal of the Polynesian Society*, 9: 173–99.
Blank, A., Hënare, M. and Williams, H. (eds) (1985) *He Körero Mö Waitangi 1984*, New Zealand: Te Rünanga o Waitangi.
Clarke, G. (1903) *Early Life in New Zealand*, Hobart.
Colenso, W. (1890) *The Authentic and Genuine History of the Signing of the Treaty of Waitangi, New Zealand, February 5 and 6, 1840*, Wellington: George Didsbury, Government Printer.
Correspondence and Papers Relating to Native Inhabitants the New Zealand Company and Other Affairs of the Colony, 1852–54 (vol. 9, Colonies: New Zealand) (1972) Shannon: Irish University Press series of British Parliamentary Papers.
Cultural Conservation Advisory Council (1990) *Taonga Mäori Conference: New Zealand 18–27 November 1990*, Wellington.
Hanson, A. (1989) 'The making of the Mäori: culture invention and its logic', *American Anthropologist*, 91: 890–901.

Henare, A. (2005) *Museums, Anthropology and Imperial Exchange*, Cambridge: Cambridge University Press.

Kuper, A. (2003) 'The return of the native', *Current Anthropology*, 44(3): 389–402.

Leach, James (2003a) 'Owning creativity: cultural property and the efficacy of custom on the Rai Coast of Papua New Guinea', *Journal of Material Culture*, 8(2): 123–43.

—— (2003b) *Creative Land: Place and Procreation on the Rai Coast of Papua New Guinea*, Oxford: Berghahn.

Levine, H. B. (1991) 'Comment on Hanson's "The Making of the Maori" ', *American Anthropologist*, 93(2): 444–6.

Mauss, M. (1990) *The Gift: the Form and Reason for Exchange in Archaic Societies*, (trans. W. D. Halls), London: Routledge.

——(1950) 'Essai sur le don: forme et raison de l'échange dans les sociétés archaiques', in *Sociologie et Anthropologie*, Paris: Presses Universitaires de France.

McKenzie, D. F. (1985) *Oral Culture, Literacy and Print in New Zealand: the Treaty of Waitangi*, Wellington: Victoria University Press.

Metge, J. (1992) 'Cross cultural communication and land transfer in Western Muri-whenua 1832–1840', Waitangi Tribunal (Doc. F13), 8–26.

Milne, J. (2005) 'Māori want cut of research profits', *New Zealand Herald*, 27 February (downloaded from http://www.nzherald.co.nz).

Neich, R. (1983) 'The veil of orthodoxy: Rotorua Ngati Tarawhai woodcarving in a changing context', in Mead, S. M. and Kernot, B. (eds) *Art and Artists in Oceania*, Palmerston North: Dunmore Press.

——(1978) 'The Māori woodcarvers of Rotorua and their relationships with the museums of New Zealand – an historical approach', *AGMANZ News*, 9(2): 5–10.

Oliver, W. H. (2001) 'The future behind us: the Waitangi Tribunal's retrospective utopia', in Sharp, A. and McHugh, P. (eds) *Histories, Power and Loss: Uses of the Past – a New Zealand Commentary*, Wellington: Bridget Williams Books.

Orange, C. (1987) *The Treaty of Waitangi*, Wellington: Allen & Unwin.

Parr, C. J. (1961) 'A missionary library, printed attempts to instruct the Māori, 1815–1845', *Journal of the Polynesian Society*, 70: 429–50.

Rata, Elizabeth (2005) 'The rise and rise of the neotribal elite', paper presented to the Summer Sound Symposium, Marlborough Sounds, 11–13 February 2005, (downloaded from http://www.education.auckland.ac.nz).

Royal, T. C. (ed.) (2003) *The Woven Universe: Selected Writings of Rev. Māori Marsden*, Masterton: Estate of Rev. Māori Marsden.

Sahlins, Marshall (1999) 'Two or three things that I know about culture', *Journal of the Royal Anthropological Institute*, 5(3): 399–421.

Salmond, A. (1995) 'Self and other in contemporary anthropology', in Fardon, R. (ed.) *Counterworks: managing the Diversity of Knowledge*, London: Routledge.

——(1984) 'Nga huarahi o te ao Māori: pathways in the Māori world', in S. M. Mead (ed.) *Te Māori: Māori Art from New Zealand Collections*, Auckland: Heinemann.

Sissons, Jeffrey (1998) 'The traditionalisation of the Māori meeting house', *Oceania*, 69(1): 36–46.

——(1993) 'The systematisation of tradition: Māori culture as a strategic resource', *Oceania*, 64(2): 97–116.

Strathern, M. (1999) *Property, Substance and Effect: Anthropological Essays on Persons and Things*, London: Athlone Press.

——(1988) *The Gender of the Gift*, Berkeley: University of California Press.

Tapsell, Paul (2000) *Pukaki: a Comet Returns*, Auckland: Reed.

——(1997) 'The flight of Pareraututu: an investigation of taonga from a tribal perspective', *Journal of the Polynesian Society*, 106: 323–74.

Waitangi Tribunal (2001) 'Wai 262 Second Amended Statement of Claim on behalf of Ngati Kuri, Te Rarawa and Ngati Wai', 20 October 2001.

——(1997) *Muriwhenua Land Report*, Wellington: GP Publications.

——(1992) *Mohaka River Report*, Wellington: Brooker and Friend Ltd.

Williams, D. (2001) *Matauranga Māori and Taonga: the Nature and Extent of Treaty Rights Held by Iwi and Hapu in Indigenous Flora and Fauna, Cultural Heritage Object [and] Valued Traditional Knowledge*, Wellington: Waitangi Tribunal.

4

THE 'LEGAL THING' IN SWAZILAND

Res judicata and divine kingship

Sari Wastell

This contribution endeavours to push the proposed methodology of the present volume to something of an extreme. If the remit of this collection has been to suggest the ways in which a methodological attentiveness to 'things' can expose the outlines of disparate ontologies – formulations of the nature of reality where presumed divisions between subjects and objects, persons and things *emerge* from ethnography rather than precede ethnographic description – then the object of this chapter's attentions seems counter-intuitive. Law, and here very specifically the received law of the Kingdom of Swaziland (which is to say the rule of law system inherited from the country's colonial era), is often imagined as the most heady of abstractions, a monolith of analogies and formalism which the legal realists ridiculed as 'transcendental nonsense' (Cohen 1935; 1960, *passim*). Even where legal theorists advocated a return to empirical studies of law, verifiable concepts, and (legal) knowledge as experience linked to problem-solving (all hallmarks of the realist schools of jurisprudence), law itself was never couched in terms of a 'thing'. Indeed, where law equated quite strictly to the aggregate of rules which comprised a given legal system, the rules had to be administered and interpreted in order to earn the title of law; 'paper' rules remain ephemeral and count as law only once meaning is added through judicial interpretation. And the counterparts of these 'rule-sceptics' were the 'fact-sceptics', whose concern for the inherent uncertainty in law turned on the multiple meanings and interpretations which could attach to legal facts – a position which only further separated the immaterial character of law from the observable behaviours which animated it. In short, 'realism' in jurisprudence conferred no greater substantiality to an entity known as 'law', it merely re-focused attention onto those social interactions which concretised legal abstraction. And in such formulations, one can see the very meaning/thing divide which this volume has sought to reject.

That is not to say that there are no precedents within jurisprudence for addressing the 'thing-like' nature of law – i.e. *res judicata*.[1] In fact, one recent article by Lior Barshack (2000) will set the stage for much of the proceeding discussion. However, within anthropology, there has been a long tradition of treating the instantiations of legal, political and/or cosmological authority through law as visible expressions of hidden forces (although note that Riles, discussed later in this essay, sees this trend reversing (2003)). It is probable that the idea that law instantiated or articulated powers or forces external to itself was shored up from two directions – studies of Western rule of law systems which sought to understand whether law was a part of society or somehow an external reflection of it[2] on the one hand, and studies of customary legal systems (especially those of Africa) where the divine or charismatic authority that legitimates law is often transcendental in character and hidden from view in a variety of ways in legal proceedings[3] on the other. In both instances, law could only ever appear as a conduit for something else – its meanings always being sought from somewhere outside the law itself. However, the task of this essay is to work ethnographically from the practice of 'Western' law in an African country, bearing in mind those discussions within jurisprudence which seek to distinguish between law-as-activity (specifically, a normative activity) and law-as-thing (*res judicata*). What I will argue is that in some contexts, received law in Swaziland is approached not solely – in some instances perhaps not even primarily – as an activity centred on logic, rationale and argument through which meanings can attach to events brought before the law. Rather, the 'legal thing' in Swaziland is, at times, an entity through which an alternative formulation of power and efficacy is presenced, such that the law (in this case received law), emerges as a meaning-artefact, an entity whose very opacity, but simultaneously magical presence, makes it an amenable thing through which Swazis can both think and act.

What is striking when one begins to study law in Swaziland is the seeming contradiction between two thoroughly entrenched presuppositions. On the one hand, most Swazis will repeatedly assure you that one cannot expect justice from the magistrate's courts and high court which comprise the received law system. Criminals will always be let off, stolen goods will never be returned, and victimhood will always be translated into the peripheral role of a witness for the prosecution of a crime made against the state.[4] Whenever I spoke with a friend or neighbour who had been the victim of a theft or the like, the preferred recourse was to Swazi law and custom (the so-called 'customary law') or even to informal policing bodies such as the community police or local, hired security guards. A Swazi court president, a chief or your local security guard was best positioned to help you – they knew who the 'bad guys' were in the community and they had little truck for allowing lawyers to act out their perversions of justice in the name of a presumption of innocence. Most people with whom I spoke, some lawyers included, acknowledged the greater speed and efficiency with which Swazi law and custom dispensed justice. (And here it is important to note that the conciliatory strategies or restitutive measures enacted by community police and security guards were understood to be an extension of the workings of Swazi law and custom.) Western courts – as they are sometimes referred to in Swaziland – were seen to fail on every count.

Yet the contradiction is this. Swaziland is profoundly litigious – a place where the suspension of the rule of law in 2001 for a period of nearly three years was not viewed as an impediment to the lawyers' trade because, as one informant put it, 'Swazis will always want to drag things into court' (and here again, it was received courts specifically to which he was referring). I pressed several colleagues on this point. With some court decisions taken up to three years ago not being honoured because they displeased the king, would not legal activity diminish? Would people not eschew the considerable cost of bringing a case to court in light of the fact that they could not be certain a decision taken there would be honoured anyway? Many of my lawyer friends seemed nonplussed, and indeed, anecdotally at least, court-room activity seems to have thrived between 2001 and 2004. In fact, even challenges to the suspension of the rule of law were played out in a variety of ways within the courtroom.

During my most recent stay in the country in the autumn of 2004 the debate around the legality of the Macetjeni and Kamkhweli evictions (deriving from a longstanding chieftaincy dispute) came to a head when the government rescinded the 28 November 2001 statement, which had suspended the rule of law, and invited the evictees back onto their lands. Upon returning however, the evictees were turned away repeatedly by the police, despite the fact that Prince David, the Minister for Justice and Constitutional Affairs, confirmed that they had been free to return to their homes from 17 September 2004 onwards. The matter took on a particular urgency due to the fact that the Court of Appeal, a bench of judges drawn from Swaziland, South Africa and Botswana and representing the final level of appeal within the received law system of Swaziland, had just arrived back in Swaziland to sit for the first time since they disbanded in protest at the suspension of the rule of law in 2001. Assured that the decision by their court to return the evictees to their lands had finally been recognised, they had agreed to return, only to discover that the evictees had been driven from their homes after each attempt to re-settle. In an effort to apprise the returning Court of Appeal judges of the 'real' situation with respect to the rule of law in Swaziland, attorney Ben Simelane submitted an affidavit to the Registrar of the Court of Appeal on 15 November 2004 explaining the ongoing persecution his clients had faced throughout the autumn of 2004.

The affidavit looks much like many others I have come across. A cover page is followed by the point-by-point assertions of the deponent and is concluded by a notarisation by a commissioner of oaths. Each page is affixed with a 2 *emalengani* stamp (the local currency), and the filing notice clearly states the full address of the attorney who is presenting in the matter. The one curiosity of the document, however, is its deviation from form at the very top of the cover page. For affidavits are always filed with reference to a specific matter. For this reason, there is a space at the top to fill in which reads: CASE NO [. . .] /04. On the Simelane affidavit of 15 November 2004, this space is left blank. And where it continues 'In the matter between:', the author has simply inserted 'MACETJENI/KAMKHWELI EVICTION'. The point is, this affidavit does not actually pertain to any pending court matter. It is a completely redundant document. Where a court order has not been executed, one applies to the court to find whoever is obstructing the enacting of the court's decision in contempt and to issue a warrant of arrest. One does not go back to court to open a case about *why* the court's earlier decision has not been recognised. One can appeal against a decision; it is a nonsense to appeal in favour of one! But here we have an affidavit – like a protest made under oath – for submission to a court which is presently not sitting on any related matter.

My point in raising this example is simple. Clearly, given the cost of taking a matter to the received courts, most Swazis would only ever find themselves in such a court by means of a summons. So when I say Swazis are litigious, I must be referring in the first instance to a minority elite who can afford to pursue their concerns via court actions. And amongst even relatively affluent Swazis, I have innumerable examples of this – from low-waged waitresses suing for constructive dismissal with little illusion that their matter will be heard equitably, to well-heeled businessmen who keep their lawyers' numbers on their speed-dial so they can raise libel actions, a reflex which is popularly acknowledged as underscoring the actual 'truth' of the libellous statement (a point not lost on those who still choose to sue). When sitting in any of my favourite watering-holes in Mbabane, the capital – usually flanked by several lawyers unwinding after a long day of courtroom appearances and client meetings – one could be forgiven for mistaking litigation for a national passtime. The mobile phones around the table ring in a syncopated concert, abrupt consultations end with precise instructions to clerks to draft up documents overnight, and urgent applications follow in the morning. A disproportionate amount of discussion and speculation surrounds accusations made in the daily paper which *might* give rise to court action, and even seemingly trivial affairs are first contemplated in terms of court proceedings, when a simple phone call or small measure of compromise might actually suffice.

However, my larger point is that even those Swazis who are excluded from this frenzy of ongoing courtroom intrigue, exhibit a fascination for the (received) law. While most criminal and civil matters are dealt with through Swazi law and custom for the vast majority of Swazis, certain kinds of issues are played out almost exclusively in the various fora of the received law. And the type of case which will concern us here always turns on political debate around the contest between 'traditional' and 'modern' forms of authority and governance. The Macetjeni/Kamkhweli affidavit was a case in point.

There were any number of places where the failure of His Majesty's Government (very specifically at His Majesty's request) to abide by a court decision might have been voiced: the royal *kraal*, the parliamentary proceedings in Lobamba, the *toyi-toyi* protests of the labour unions taking place in the streets of Mbabane and in front of various government ministries. But an affidavit, a meticulously constructed narrative of the tribulations of two of the evictees,[5] was presented to the court – even in the absence of a case to which it might lend support. Such is the allure of the courtroom in Swaziland. Even where the power of the courts to enforce their decisions is rendered impotent, the received law court remains the arena par excellence for the negotiation of certain types of claims. Its effect appears almost mystical (although I will later come to argue that these engagements with the law are entirely pragmatic in nature).

While most Swazis will never have personal experience of these institutions, received law courts still remain the appropriate site in which to make certain kinds of challenges. So, for example, when violence and protests erupt on the streets over unilateral decisions taken by the monarchy, the nation's eyes will inevitably turn to see what the courts have to say on the given matter. The import of the Simelane affidavit was precisely that it was not meant to persuade the judges to decide a particular matter in a certain way. The matter was far too broad to be held within the scope of a single court action, and the judges were not the exclusive addressees to whom the document offered testimony. Indeed, they were only a part of the affidavit's intended audience – in fact a synecdoche for the real audience – the Swazi people. And more importantly, the document was both less and more than the narrative contained within its pages.

What I shall argue is that the Simelane affidavit indexes the extent to which Swazis reify ('Western') law as a particular kind of encompassing phenomenon – a phenomenon of a type with the divine kingship which organises Swazi sociality more generally. The law is approached as a civic totem of Western power (to borrow Barshak's phrase), where power is understood to be neither abstract nor a quality to be held, wielded or mobilised by a more concrete entity (see also Holbraad, Chapter 9 in this volume). One way to understand this conceptualisation of power[6] would be to see it as a direct corollary of how sovereignty is imagined and refracted through the prism of divine kingship in Swaziland, where the entirety of the Swazi nation is one in the person and body of the king. As such, 'subjects'[7] of His Majesty are not in a relationship of obedience to him, but part of the essence or enduring substance of kingship itself, a substance which is 'generative force' rather than exercises it. Thus, when Swazis engage with the civic totem that is 'Western' law, it is an alternative, non-Swazi form of this 'force' that Swazis understand as being presenced in the legal object.[8]

However, to pursue such an imagining of law-as-object, we need to begin closer to home. That is to say, it is first important to understand the ways in which scholars have already begun to think about the law as a unitary 'thing', largely in reaction to decades of scholarship which insisted on the fragmentary and intangible nature of the law. My difficulty with this new trend is a wholly anthropological one. In conceiving of the law as an object, what remains unexamined is what actually constitutes an object in the first place. Through a detailed examination of Annelise Riles' recent work 'Law as object' (2003), I hope to undermine *not* the conceptualisation of law as an object, but the presumed universality of 'objects' which might remain unenunciated in such an argument. Tacking between Riles' exploration of law in relation to Fijian identity politics and land claims in the colonial and postcolonial eras and my own work on kingship, law and sovereignty in Swaziland, I hope to demonstrate how disparate conceptualisations of sovereignty (if sovereignty is indeed the right word – see conclusion below) evoke distinct imaginings of the *kind* of object law might be.

Law as tool, law as a presenced essence

Already I am aware that there might be a great deal of unease in referring to such a thing as 'the law', as if such an entity self-evidently existed. As Annelise Riles so aptly noted, a lawyer (and Swazi lawyers account for many of the informants whose insights inform my rendering of received law in this chapter) would not recognise in their own engagements an 'interlocutor' which they could map onto my reified invocation of 'the law':

> Lawyers view their world as consisting of various phenomena and stances – rights discourse, constitutions, procedures, bureaucracies, doctrines, private norms, and dispute settlement processes. There is no impetus to put these together into a single actant, 'the Law', whose consequences can be evaluated as a whole.
>
> (2003: 190)

And certainly within jurisprudence and socio-legal studies, the reification of 'the law' is now held to be an error of past generations, not wholly unlike anthropology's great misgivings about our antecedents who once reified 'culture'. However, my argument here would be that in the Swazi context, the objectification of the law in this way is not a sleight of hand on the part of the anthropologist, but an artefact of the popular imagination.[9] This would contrast with Riles' discussion of 'law as object', insofar as her account, while compassing many of the same ends, explores the motivations and ramifications of *anthropology's* reification of 'the law'. Nonetheless, Riles' distinction between what she terms the 'expressive' and 'instrumental' genres of law exhibits both common denominators and some very salient differences with the practices I will be describing for Swaziland, and thus demands an abbreviated excursus.

Riles begins and ends her discussion of 'law as object' with an important observation about the uncomfortable parallels between law's capacity to create significations and anthropology's efforts to do the same. If at one point it was particularly fashionable to deconstruct the objectifications made by colonial law, the self-realisation that anthropology's own objectifications held too much in common with colonial legal practices was always in the offing. To put it rather bluntly, the presumption of an external subject position from which to create objects of knowledge – together with the concomitant presumption that the meanings and inter-relations of those objects were dissociable and required re-connection by law and/or anthropology – was a common ground which would ultimately turn anthropology's critique of law into auto-critique. Hence both anthropology's initial interest in law and its subsequent desuetude.[10]

However, this sense of law – a law which is exterior to the society over which it arbitrates – is only one of the two modalities of law Riles seeks to investigate.[11] She suggests that this 'expressive genre' of law captured anthropological attention up until the discipline's late-twentieth-century 'exhaustion with denomination and identification' (*ibid.*: 188), not least because it correlated to the discipline's (Foucauldian-inspired) preoccupation with those forms of knowledge generated by the colonial endeavour and its objectifications of the colonised (not to mention the ways in which such objectifications cycled back into colonial and indigenous knowledge practices alike). Here law, like anthropology, was predicated on meaning-creation. In colonial contexts, law-making was intimately tied to the delineating of social groups – in Riles' ethnography, Europeans from native Fijians, although her primary concern is with the so-called 'half-castes' who confounded a world so-ordered. Again, like anthropology, law in this expressive genre proves a reflexive entity, at once standing apart from the world and designating the relations between the various parts that comprise the whole (e.g. one law applies to the Europeans, another to the Fijians, thus not only distinguishing the two but also defining the nature of the relation of each group to the other) even as it draws attention to its own distinctiveness from that whole – rendered visible in its very ability to create such effects. Put another way, it is the very externality of 'the world' to 'the law' that allows for law-making. So it follows that law, in this expressive genre, not only objectifies social groups (among other things), but also the very act of law-making through which those social groups are constituted. Importantly, law working in this expressive genre becomes a site of contention – a place where significations outlive their utility or cease to map onto the objects of contemplation – a place, in short, in constant need of re-interpretation. If, to take Riles' example, property relations are objectifications created by law in its expressive form, these objectifications are fragile insofar as they can fall out of sync with historical and political contexts.

However, Riles contends that this genre of law is complemented by another – the instrumental genre – which has overtaken the expressive genre in garnering anthropology's attentions at the turn of the century. A primary difference between the two is the extent to which the latter is marked by a vacuity of meaning. Unlike the expressive genre, where law stands apart from the world and relates elements *in* that world through meaning-creation, law in its instrumental guise, *is* an object in its own right – an artefact in the world. Riles compares the two genres by contrasting how land features in each: where the expressive genre creates *objectifications* about property relations (connecting people to land, as disparate elements in the world, through idioms of ownership), the instrumental genre creates the *object* that is the land registration document. As she notes with respect to such documents, 'The instrumental genre fades into its target: Land registration documents, diagrams, and records become *instantiations*, not mere representations, of property rights' (*ibid.*: 204, emphasis mine). In the terms contemplated within this volume, land registration documents betray an indissolubility of meaning and artefact, insofar as there is nothing beneath the surface of the document, no latent meaning to be excavated and re-attached to the document – no idea or formulation about the world to be diagnosed from the formal aesthetics which characterise the document's construction. Rather the land registration form, like law in its instrumental form more generally, is a tool in the world which can be mobilised to a variety of ends. And as Riles concludes, 'To take the law as object in this sense is not to "know" law but to work through law' (*ibid.*: 209), an impulse which Riles feels characterises anthropology's engagement with law in the present moment.

So in this exploration of the instrumental genre of law, Riles has gone some considerable way towards restoring a sense of 'thinginess' to the law. In its instrumental mode, law is a 'thing' by negative definition. It is not abstract, not an idea *about* the world, but rather a 'tool' – her word – *in* the world through which to achieve a range of outcomes. And in all of this, one can hear many resonances with the general timbre of this contribution and its animus to breach the meaning-thing divide. But I might flag the implications of that word 'tool'. For in suggesting that these two genres create different forms of reifications such that 'legal knowledge is alternatively in the world and a reflection of it, alternatively knowledge and its own object' (*ibid.*: 206), one finds an ethnographic specificity to the practices she is describing.

In this geminate model of law, characterised by sequenced genres, law emerges as a technology, a contrivance, at once ideal and concrete, and due to its Janus-like character, a practicable instrument through which to effect the agendas of agents outside itself. Its reification confers a *certain* materiality – in the expressive mode law-*making* is objectified to the exclusion of the law and in the instrumental mode the two are conflated into a unitary object – but its force and potentialities must be directed and manipulated from outside of itself. But most of all, it emerges as a very finite medium – 'finite' because it is limited in magnitude, and 'medium' because it serves as an intervening substance through which to realise ends not intrinsic to the substance itself. And therein lies the ethnographic specificity – a modernist predilection for confining phenomena in the world to a subsidiary position vis-à-vis the world. What I want to explore is a context where the law is not a thing in the world, but a materialisation of the world itself.

So while I seize upon Riles' exposition in order to shift attention from a relentlessly abstract and conceptual sense of the law (the expressive genre) towards a more substantive and object-like understanding, I would be quick to point out at this juncture that 'things' themselves take on a variety of disparate forms. And the thing-like nature of received law in Swaziland is, if you will, a very different thing altogether. Let me sketch out some of the failures of correspondence with recourse to ethnography.

In Riles' discussion of the title documents produced by the process of land registration, she explored the extent to which the ordinances governing such matters concerned themselves with the minutiae of aesthetic forms. This preoccupation with the detail of how the titles are actually constructed had it own effects: 'These formalities drew the grantor and the grantee into a set of actions distinguishable in genre from others and expressly marked as distinctive in this way' (*ibid.*: 202). Thus, the object created by the instrumental genre of law is marked out as especially 'legal', operating at a register informed by a plethora of other social practices and relationships (*ibid.*: 203), but still held up as discrete by the formal features it engendered. This in turn activated a distinctive temporal idiom, one which collapsed the past into the present of the title document, eclipsing the multifaceted relations which were, inevitably, the document's precursors.

In Swaziland, aesthetic form is no less of a concern than in Fiji, but I suggest that its effects are geared in a different direction. As I mentioned before, the received law courts are widely mistrusted by the general public, and one of the most oft-cited reasons for this is that they are 'foreign' in nature. Like the bicameral parliament of the country, the workings of the court are not only recognised as part of the country's colonial inheritance, but their 'Western' character is the subject of considerable comment.

In both fora, the English language predominates. In the courts, it is the only language spoken. This might not seem odd altogether (and indeed simultaneous translation is available in the sittings of both the Senate and the House as debate moves in and out of siSwati as well as English), except that many in parliament simply cannot speak English at all, and the (received law) courts in Swaziland are probably the only place where siSwati is proscribed. But the language is only one facet of a supererogatory Englishness. The wigs and robes which characterise both parliament and the high court, the arcane language and formal gestures, the overmeasure of reserve and awe accorded the bench and the speaker of the house alike, are all not out of keeping with courts in many parts of the Commonwealth. And sufficient ink has already been spent explaining the purpose of the theatre and ritual of court proceedings elsewhere to rehearse those arguments here. Rather, I want to consider what might be unique to the Swazi context in this respect.

For what does appear different is the self-conscious efforts made to underscore these attributes as expressly non-Swazi. In particular, this is effected through evidencing the counter-position – that of kingly loyalty and what the Swazis refer to as 'the Swazi Way' (kuphilisana kahle singanyatselani – literally, living well and not treading on one another, invoked precisely because of the mantra's dissonance with the adversarial nature of the received courts and parliamentary procedures).[12] Women in particular, are called upon to 'presence' kingly respect; their heads must be covered at all times in parliament as in the courts, an act which, like placing one's left hand underneath the right forearm when shaking hands or receiving anything from the hands of another person, is understood to signal that the person in question is one in the body and person of the king – and hence, a Swazi.[13] The interesting point about the injunction to wear headscarves in parliament and in court, however, is that it was explained to me as compulsory precisely because these institutions are not 'traditional' fora of law and governance. Rather, they exist at the king's pleasure, and as the monarchy would have it, within the all-encompassing purview of his divine remit. Like all of my female colleagues, I too kept a headscarf in my handbag and a long skirt in my desk drawer (no trousers allowed either) in case I was unexpectedly called to hear a case put forward on urgent application. In point of fact, the guards checking those who would hope to enter the gallery would probably not require me to fashion a makeshift headscarf from toilet paper as a colleague was once required to do, but this was explicitly justified by the fact that I was not Swazi. Indeed, many a guard was slightly confounded and more than a bit amused by my insistence on wearing the headscarf and long skirt my colleagues were required to don, a point my friends put down to the fact that I was not playing the part expected of me.

Now, elsewhere I have considered at some length the variety of paradoxes inherent in the allegedly 'dual' legal system in Swaziland – a place where all judicial, as well as executive and legislative, authority is vested in His Majesty the King. The system is deemed to be dual in the sense that there exist two parallel legal codes, the received law, based on a Roman-Dutch common law tradition, and the 'customary' law, Swazi law and custom, each of which is administered in physically disparate spaces and through a distinct cadre of personnel.[14] One of the primary conundrums for me was the fact that there existed a law (within the received law system), which actually stated that the king was above the law.[15] Even before considering the place of the king in both the sensibilities and practices of most Swazi subjects, the very fact that the king can pass legislation of his own accord, that legislation generated from within parliament requires his assent to become law, that he appoints all high court judges personally, that he can dissolve the high court and parliament at will, and that he cannot be summoned to court or prosecuted by any court in the country, all suggested that a law declaring his supra-legal status would be redundant.

However, jurisprudentially, the law makes sense, when considered from the perspective of Swazi law and custom (hereafter SLC). Although SLC operates with little concern for its alleged circumscription within the received law (as spelled out in statute), and despite the fact that the popular understanding amongst most Swazis of the relation of SLC to received law is that the former trumps and encompasses the authority of the latter, received law is perceived as incommensurably 'other' in one respect. Its source – the very force of the law – does not emanate from His Majesty, as would be the case with SLC. And it is this sense of an alternative basis of power and efficacy, not simply a different way of achieving similar ends, which both necessitates the containment of the received law, but also proves it a dynamic arena for political improvisation on the part of the monarchy.

The reasons for this are complex and can only be adumbrated here, but involve the ways in which Swazi kingship is constituted through interactions with forms of power and potency which are deemed to be non-Swazi (Wastell forthcoming). Across the body of the nation, various classes of person have some capacity to negotiate that which is non-Swazi. But these abilities are a matter of gradation[16] and to the extent that a person exhibits such a faculty, the ability is understood to stem from one's relationship to His Majesty, in whom the well-being of the nation is physically embodied. In general, however, to be Swazi is to be consolidated inwards, towards the *siyanqaba* or fortress that is the Swazi nation-in-kingship. Only His Majesty is thought to have the exceptional capacity to breach the boundary of that fortress identity and engage fully with all that is non-Swazi. Indeed, it is in his ability to move outside of the limits of the Swazi way that his cosmological remit is made visible.

It is for this reason that the received law, whose force and legitimacy are clearly understood to derive from outside the Swazi nation, provides an arena for kingly engagements with non-Swazi forms of power. And in this sense, the law here is not a tool or something to be worked *through* at all. The better analogy, I would suggest, would be with sorcery (cf. Kapferer 1997), where a world is presenced, and the dissensions contained within that world are confronted and addressed.

Certainly the analogy with sorcery would not prove wholly counter-intuitive were one talking about SLC, where the work of diviners (*tangoma* or *tinyanga*) are intrinsic to much legal process in the family council (*ludsendvo*) and chiefs' courts alike (cf. Booth 1992). However, the sorts of technologies at work in those contexts proves a misleading correspondence. In fact, the occult practices associated with law (*umsetfo*, which can refer to both the received law and SLC) *are* akin to tools. For example, where one employs a *sangoma* to smell out a witch or to produce *muthi* which will cause a judge or chief to decide a case in one's favour, one is relying on the specialist knowledge which allows a *sangoma* to activate the agencies inherent in all things – animate or otherwise – in the world. This is a well established form of 'witchcraft' throughout southern Africa, and many anthropologists have explored its novel applications in contemporary circumstances (cf. Ashforth 2005; Moore and Sanders 2001).

However, the occult practices which better approximate my intended analogy with sorcery are those which involve the embodiment and manifestation of the world itself. One such example in Swaziland would be the *umdvutjulwa* or black bull which is integral to one of the most sacred rites of the *iNcwala*, or first fruits ceremony of the Swazis.[17] This annual celebration is a cleansing ceremony of kingship, intended to fortify and renew His Majesty for the coming year, and in so doing, ensure the health and wellbeing of the Swazi nation. During the ritual known as *kubamba inkunzi*, or literally holding/grabbing the bull, regiments of young warriors are called upon to catch a black bull and kill it with their bare hands. The bull has been doctored it is said, such that when it is released into the enclosure and sees the king, it will attack him in a frenzy and kill him if the regiments do not intervene – for what the bull is seeing is himself. Unlike the animation of an agency innate within the creature, *kubamba inkunzi* is a process of presencing the forces of Swazi kingship through the form of the black bull. In other words, it is an act of reification, insofar as 'kingship' is made material in the ill-fated beast. But just as the king is both a person and the encompassing nation that is held together within Swazi kingship (cf. Kantorowicz 1997), so too the bull takes on the full and immeasurable proportions of a world constituted through kingship's potentially infinite purview. Put another way, to presence the essence of what it is to be Swazi requires a medium as limitless as kingship itself. And this returns us to the distinction I made earlier between 'tools' as finite media manipulated by extrinsic forces versus the sort of 'modalities for presencing', which I would claim better correlate to Swazi engagements with the received law. The black bull, like the received law, is neither a thing in the world through which one can act nor a representation of the world. Rather, as Bruce Kapferer contends with respect to the practices of sorcerers more generally, both 'are not analogies to the world but materialisations of its dimensions and processes, and they are conceived of as being fully vital in the reality of human experience' (1997: 14).

However, it is important to remember that the analogy to sorcery is entirely my own; Swazis themselves do not speak of their engagements with the received law in idioms which would map onto their understandings of occult practices. In fact, when I essayed the comparison with the partner of an Mbabane law firm, he was mildly sceptical about the mileage I could hope to extract from the association of the two practices. What he said was telling and spurred much of the present work forward. He conceded that in some ways, lawyers could be equated with *tangoma* in the sense that they both have specialist knowledge to which only very few select members of Swazi society might have access. Equally, these abilities were morally freighted; the knowledge in question could be used for beneficial or nefarious purposes – the diviner/healer manipulates the same powerful technologies as the witch – so people's view of lawyers and *tangoma* alike is often ambiguous and hedged in with a certain degree of apprehension. But there the comparison ended, he suggested. For whereas *tangoma* were, in their own right, clearly activating, mobilising and re-directing agencies in the world to various ends, a lawyer was perhaps better understood as a *lincusa*, a liaison or intermediary.

The comment took me aback, and for a time it forced me to reconsider the tack I had been taking in my analysis of received law trials involving matters of Swazi governance. For a *lincusa* is not a person who has any particular specialist knowledge. Indeed, it is not a discrete role, such as a governor (*indvuna*), who might act as a *lincusa* between an aggrieved person and his/her chief. Rather, anyone can be a *lincusa*, in theory, though to be an effective *lincusa* requires one to have a certain degree of access and standing vis-à-vis the power or authority which is to be approached. For example, one does not actually have to have a *lincusa* to see His Majesty, but without one, or with a *lincusa* who is not a prince, a chief or trusted acquaintance of the monarchy, one would likely sit at the royal palace throughout the night and leave the following morning having never been received by the king.[18] More significant, however, is that while in theory a *lincusa* could refer to any sort of emissary who might announce or introduce two persons of differential status or power, its normal usage always refers specifically to that person who gives you access to the king. Other invocations of a *lincusa* are rare, and where they do occur, they are derivative of this iconic relation – the person who makes it possible for you to be in the presence of His Majesty, the *Ngwenyama*.

Presence and magic: thinking through *res judicata* in Swaziland

In the autumn of 2004, an anticipated day of lobbying in parliament with several colleagues was abruptly suspended with news of an urgent application to be heard in the high court that morning. The Coalition, a consortium of civic organisations including NGOs, church groups, labour unions and the Swaziland Law Society, had been working feverishly for some weeks to prevent the adoption and implementation of the country's new constitution, as it was seen to merely articulate the current (for some, unsatisfactory) state of affairs in the country. Now, word came through that an urgent application had been submitted to the high court to interdict the debate of the constitution that was set to begin in parliament that afternoon.

Representatives from the Coalition needed to be in high court to follow the proceedings.

So it was that I found myself in the gallery of the high court that morning, accompanied by a colleague from WLSA[19] (a local legal NGO) and the director of the Swaziland Federation of Employers. The application was already underway and Pheshaya Dlamini (then Attorney General) had already begun his decimation of the application. His attentions had just turned to his concerns over the *locus standae*[20] of the applicants, but having had no opportunity to source a copy of the application, none of the three of us could speculate on what his strategy would be. The lawyer presenting for the applicants was well known to us and a thoroughly competent practitioner, but the AG had a formidable reputation for finding holes in what seemed to be otherwise airtight applications. So what followed left me dumbstruck.

The AG's first observation with respect to the *locus standae* of the applicants was that one of them, PUDEMO, was a political organisation, expressly outlawed within both the constitutional framework and by royal decree, and therefore could not bring a case to be heard before any court in the land, much less one which sought to query the legitimacy of the country's constitutional process. I turned to my colleagues. This beggared belief. Having only a rudimentary understanding of law myself, the point seemed rather an obvious one and one which would not have been lost on the lawyers presenting in the matter. But my friends merely shrugged and continued to watch with evident enthusiasm. What was there to follow at this point? The application was moribund before it arrived in the courtroom as far as I could see, because the applicants could not even be recognised by the court.

Nonetheless, we spent the entire morning there until such time as the AG had summarised his main heads of argument and was ready to allow the applicants' lawyer his hearing. At this point, however, it was nearly noon, and the bench decided that it would be best to break for lunch and continue at 1 p.m. The applicants' lawyer interrupted, pointing out that the debate in parliament, which this case sought to interdict, was scheduled to *begin* at 1 p.m. Would it not be better to simply push on and allow the bench to hear as much of the argument as possible before that time? Chief Justice Annandale did not even consult his colleagues. He replied that he could not change the clocks in parliament, but that what happened in *this* courtroom would happen in its own time and that *this* court was now in recess.

In a somewhat desultory mood, my colleagues and I left the gallery and settled that we would head down to Lobamba to follow the parliamentary debate, which was obviously not going to be affected by the court proceedings. During the car journey, I pressed my friends on what had transpired. But surely it had been obvious to the applicants' lawyers that they could not hope to move an application forward in the name of an illegal organisation?

And had they really hoped to complete the entire process in the few hours available before the debate in parliament was scheduled to begin, thus rendering the application superfluous by and large? My consternation was met with indifference, and, half-teasingly, the only 'explanation' offered was: 'Sari, you must remember you are in Swaziland again!'

That night, I reviewed the morning's events up in the high court with several lawyers, most of whom were unaware that the application had even been lodged. One of them, himself a member of the executive of the Swaziland Law Society, assured me that the question of *locus standae* would not have been a blind-spot for the applicants' lawyer. 'Ah, they were never going to get anywhere with that application. But still, they do these things.' But if it was not the case that a legal error had been made, what was the point of airing an application which could never have proved successful? Or couched in the slightly larger terms which instigated the current essay: What was the impetus for those challenging monarchical authority to approach the received law when nothing decided within received law courts could be enforced against His Majesty's will?

There are a number of 'commonsense' answers to that question that I do not endorse. One line of reasoning might suggest that where one hopes to challenge the limits of monarchical authority, one would not be inclined to press the matter through 'traditional' legal structures, which are actually seen to be instantiations of divine kingly rule in the first place. Another rejoinder might tally nicely with the chief justice's invocation of the time of law and the extent to which the time of law is out of joint with the time of politics. Perhaps these un-winnable, unenforceable cases are meant to act as a record, testimony left extant in anticipation of a future day of reckoning when the monarchy will be held accountable (cf. Moore 1998). While I think that the discontinuities between 'legal time' and 'political time' are hugely relevant here, I cannot see that relationship in instrumental terms, not least because so little effort is made to actually keep a record of court cases in Swaziland. No law reports are published, transcripts and judgements are notoriously hard to track down even days after a case has been heard, and in the case of the urgent application discussed above, for example, the case never merited reporting in either of the country's two newspapers. No – time matters here, but it is not a linear chronological time of befores and afters, causes and effects.[21] Rather, the time in question here is the time of kingship and the temporal idiom of immanence.

I asserted earlier that one understanding of the monarchy's relationship to the rule of law might be to see it as a forum for visibly engaging with forms of power and authority which are not Swazi, thus displaying the exceptional capacities of the king. What I want to suggest here is that those who would challenge the immanent and all-encompassing authority of His Majesty are doing much the same. In repeatedly having recourse to the received law in order, ostensibly, to redress the balance of power in purely

Swazi matters, those who continue to agitate for multi-party democracy in the country are demonstrating capacities to negotiate non-Swazi forms of authority which should be the exclusive domain of divine royalty. My argument is that the reason why lawyers might often be associated with *lincusa* is precisely because the law is reified in the social imagination into a unitary entity which can presence the non-Swazi other, just as the black bull presenced Swazi kingship.

Lior Barshack, in an article addressing the totemic authority of rule of law systems (2000), anticipates such a possibility, although he is writing about Euro-American engagements with the received law. Drawing on the controversial distinction within anthropology between religion and magic, he follows Riles in suggesting that law works through two modalities. In a religious modality, one finds a focus on transcendence and the absence of the sacred Thing, and as with Riles' expressive genre of law, the authorising entity is absent, stands apart from and represents the world back to itself. However, in a magical modality, 'representation is replaced by immediate presence' (ibid.: 306).[22] Interestingly, Barshak hypothesises an explicit parallel between 'Western' law and divine kingship, arguing that 'by positing itself, the court posits law and order, like the divine king who by the mere fact of being alive sustains the kingdom and the world order' (*ibid.*: 307). For Barshack, the rule of law is always and everywhere a magical, reified mode of thinking, and one which defies the search for meaning, because the meaning of the law is simply the presencing of a civic totemic authority. It is this renunciation of meaning in favour of immanent presence which accounts for the character of legal formalism – a magical and 'fetishistic' mode of thinking in Barshack's account. And so it is that 'The magical enactment performed by the court is complemented by the fiction that the law exists' (*ibid.*: 309) – that the law actually is a meaning-artefact, opaque and of the same magnitude as the world itself.

In Swaziland, these two genres or modalities would have a particular resonance. For His Majesty displays a similar duality. He is at once, the king, a political suzerain, whose remit is circumscribed by the limits of his position vis-à-vis the people on whose behalf he acts. However, he is also *Ngwenyama*, the he-lion, whose purview extends indefinitely and in whose person, all former and future kings are conjoined with the totality of the Swazi nation. Swazis are explicit about this: An *Ngwenyama* is not merely a king. So it is not surprising that modes of presencing – just as the black bull presenced His Majesty as *Ngwenyama* rather than constitutional monarch – are familiar phenomena for Swazis. And these phenomena are necessarily – intrinsically – thing-like, collapsing object-in-the-world and world together.

Thus, when Swazi political activists approach the received law on matters pertaining to Swazi governance and the role of the monarchy, their actions are wholly pragmatic in nature – as is the case, I would argue, with all forms of magic. But this practical engagement is not best understood in terms of cause and effect and the calculable ends to which a legal decision might lead (cf. Holbraad, Chapter 9 of this volume). Rather, the engagement turns on presencing apposite, parallel forms of authority as if they were of a type with divine kingship. The subversive nature of such acts derives from the fact that it implicitly challenges the notion that the *Ngwenyama* has exceptional capacities to enact such boundary-crossings. By treating the law as a thing-in-the-world, a concrete and reified manifestation of Western totemic authority, Swazi political 'progressives' put themselves on a par with divine kingship itself, and in so doing, de-stabilise the axiological foundations of the monarchy's cosmological authority.

Umlomo longacali manga: the mouth that tells no lies

One of the most famous praisenames for the king – a 'name' that directly references the nature of kingship itself in Swaziland – is *umlomo longacali manga*, or 'the mouth that tells no lies'. This speaks to the Swazi understanding of truth and power in relation to their divine monarch, insofar as what His Majesty says, simply *is*. It is not the case that whatever he says must be obeyed, believed or affirmed in the face of various other formulations. Rather, 'the mouth that tells no lies' is the immanent entity that constitutes the world, in the moment of his presence, to be one way or the other simply by pronouncing it as so.

A Swazi colleague of mine once conceded that it would be easier to kill a king than to disagree with one, but when I laughed at the remark, he was quick to correct me. 'No, what I mean is that a bad king *can* be killed, but it is inconceivable that a living one could be wrong. If you disagree with a king, you harm the kingship.'[23] Indeed, another friend and informant, a close acquaintance of the king, had once been deeply troubled when the king said to him, 'The people do not want multi-party democracy, no?' His political leanings would have compelled him to disagree had the statement been said by anyone else, but his deep commitment to Swazi kingship made it impossible for the statement to be untrue. His only reply was '*Bayethe*', an exclamation which punctuates all intercourse with His Majesty and which can translate either as 'Hail!' or as 'agreement' – 'it is so'.

Thus, as indicated at the start of this essay, Swazis do not see their king as exercising 'power'. In no context would a Swazi say that the king *has* power (*emandla*) because it would suggest that he rules by entitlement. Even in the case of the controversial Macetjeni/kamKhweli evictions mentioned earlier, none of the many discussions I was party to were couched in terms of whether the king was entitled to evict the families from their homes. (He was said to have been compelled to do so.) And even in the high court, the one forum where debate over the limits of monarchical authority is routinely raised, argument centred not on what the king can and cannot do, but on the legality of how the act was executed.[24]

It follows then, from an ontological analysis of the king's power, that the king's purview, what He 'can' do so to speak, is imagined as limitless, the encompassing expanse of what it is to be Swazi and to have the Swazi way constituted through the substance of divine kingship.[25] Already, one can see that the algorithm which calculates the limits of sovereignty in terms of the decisions a sovereign might undertake makes little sense in a context where the king is seen not to decide what the world is but to constitute it as so. But now we are getting ahead of ourselves.

The question we began with turned on why certain constituencies within Swazi society might have recourse to the received law to arbitrate on the limits (or otherwise) of monarchical power, when any decision taken by the court that displeased His Majesty would never be acted on in any event. I have suggested that such a conceptualisation of power in relation to divine kingship is salient only in the context of the received law courts, which would account for why these cases continue to be brought forward. And throughout this piece, I have endeavoured to argue that while Swazis may be engaging with the received law with an eye towards a particular outcome, that outcome is not best understood by focusing on instrumental, cause-and-effect calculations which would yoke the outcome to the court's decision. Rather, the courts, I have argued, prove efficacious because they presence a Western civic totemic authority, a non-Swazi form of power with which only His Majesty should be able to engage. So 'decisions' do not feature here – only engagement, and more to the point, the issue of who has the capacity to engage. The question remains, why can 'power' be conceptualised differently in the received law courts and why are the received law courts alone seized upon as the obvious 'thing' through which to presence a non-Swazi essence?

The key to that question lies in the substitution of engagement for decision. For the emphasis on participation over and above closure/pronouncement/final adjudication has long been observed as a hallmark of SLC (and African customary law more generally). And SLC is understood to emanate directly from the Swazi king – indeed to be an instanciation of the nation-in-kingship. So in much the same way as Euro-American scholars have long indulged in a 'what if' scenario that posited 'customary law' as the analogue of 'Western' law, presuming that these might be two ways of doing the same 'thing' (law), I contend that Swazis treat the received law as a vehicle to presence a form of power or authority which they conceive of as 'of a type' with divine kingship. And to the extent that we cannot see a familiar form of engagement with the rule of law in my description of Swazi practices in this chapter, we might pause to wonder whether Swazis recognise their custom in Euro-American scholars' evocation of 'customary law'. But for present purposes, we will focus not on the Euro-American elision of custom and law into customary law, but on the Swazi counterpart.

So we are looking at an inversion. In certain instances, I suggest Swazis will treat the rule of law as if it were an analogue to their custom (SLC).

And just as one constitutes oneself as part of the nation-in-kingship through the very mobilization of SLC, so too does participation with the received law implicate an engagement with a non-Swazi essence. If the essence and infinite dimensions of Swazi kingship can be ritually presenced, so too, it is believed, can the essence of the non-Swazi, which is presumed to be as infinite in its materialisation as that of kingship. Contra Barshak, I am not suggesting that the received law courts in Swaziland or the 'Western' civic totem they presence are of a type with divine kingship, only that Swazis will treat them as such. What the Euro-American scholar (who believes custom is an analogue of law) and the Swazi activist (who believes the 'Western' legal object is presencing something of a type with divine kingship) share, is the conceit that their concepts (of power, of sovereignty, of the authorising force behind 'custom' and 'law' respectively) translate adequately. And that is where *res judicata* comes in.

The legal thing in Swaziland can never be the same sort of object as described in Riles' discussion of law-as-tool, nor the grander invocation in Euro-American jurisprudence of *res judicata*. The insufficiency of these renderings derives from the impulse to understand the Swazi *Ngwenyama* in terms of the concept of 'sovereignty', where the sovereign not only holds the monopoly over the power to punish, but can decide who is subject to the law and who is not. Where kingly authority is predicated, like 'custom', on participation and the isomorphic relation of the king and the nation, the very concept of 'sovereignty' appears as insufficient to understanding the nature (and extent) of the king's 'power'.

Following Agamben (1998), if we look for the sovereign in the exception – in the state of emergency – where will we find him in Swaziland? For the king does not *decide* what is normal and what is exceptional, as a judge would ruminate over the reasonableness of an action, or whether a context suggested that there were mitigating circumstances to be taken into account. If we embrace, as Eric Worby has so eloquently summarised Agamben's arguments of late, that 'sovereignty is revealed to be less about what is included in the protections afforded by citizenship, and more about *who decides* who is included, and who is excluded, from the protective (or violent) embrace of the law' (2003: 18), then the very concept of 'sovereignty' appears only to diminish any description of monarchical power. For the Mouth that Tells No Lies is incapable of making a decision, because everything that escapes his lips *already is the world*.

The king's ability to ignore a ruling, suspend parliamentary and court proceedings and dismiss judges from the bench all prove a red herring. While it is true that Agamben understands the definition of sovereignty as that figure which is both inside and outside of the law, 'having the legal power to suspend the validity of the law, [thus] legally plac[ing] himself outside the law' (Worby 2003: 15), it is the nature of this 'relation of exception'[26] (*ibid.*: 18) which fails in the Swazi instance. For the king can never place himself in a state of exception, subtracted away from the delimited jurisdiction of a Swazi nation over which he rules. The relationship on which Swazi kingship turns is one of encompassment, not exception (cf. Dumont 1981).

Thus, the legal object that this sort of authority would conjure, needs be, is different from the legal object invoked by a political metaphysics of 'sovereignty', a point underscored by Bruno Latour's recent exploration of *res judicata* (2004). He writes: 'When Roman lawyers intoned the celebrated adage "*res judicata pro veritate habetur*", they were declaring that what had been decided should be taken as the truth, which means, precisely, that it should in no way be confused with the truth' (*ibid.*: 109). In Swaziland, there simply is no difference between a 'truth' pronounced and a 'truth' which evades our capacities to disclose it, waiting to be discovered in piecemeal fashion through science or reason or even devotion. Where *res judicata* proceeds from a conceptualisation of power which is fundamentally about deciding – having the authority to declare something *as* truth, when in fact the truth (perhaps) *is* something else altogether, the 'legal thing' in Swaziland proceeds from the knowledge that truth is constituted by the power/essence in which one participates (be it Swazi or otherwise). Thus, to think through the legal thing in Swaziland is to recognise a double failing in our conceptual repertoire. When Swazis engage with the received law – in the context of a particular kind of claim, the limits of monarchy – as if the received law were an analogue to 'custom', we see the limits of understanding this legal object in terms of *res judicata*. But this only points to a further deficiency. For the kind of legal object one is witness to in these scenarios derives from the very conceptualisation of power and authority which underwrites the legal object itself. And in Swaziland, this force is so much more than a mere 'sovereign'.

My point here is not to suggest in any way that Swazis are 'mesmerised' by the rule of law or that their engagements with the rule of law are over-determined by their 'culture'. To argue as much would be to contend that Swazis could not act in any other way – that they can only incorporate this foreign formulation of power into their own terms of ontological refer-ence.[27] Nothing could be further from the truth. Swazis are consummate modernists, and Swazi lawyers accomplished practitioners of the rule of law in every respect. However, it is a matter of ethnographic fact that these pecu-liar cases, where engagements with the received law prove unanticipated, do exist. My argument is that one does not contradict the other. Rather, in cases involving the otherwise unthinkable question of the limits of monarchical authority, the rule of law is mobilised as if its workings were rooted in the logic of kingship. That Swazis can move between two seemingly incommen-surable conceptualisations of 'power' is an index of the ontological alterity of kingship. It is the capacity of the Swazi lawyer to either prosecute a case in a received law court in terms of the jurisdiction it enjoys in statute, or to materialize and engage with a non-Swazi essence through legal ritual, which begins to delineate the actual workings of their divine kingship. To insist they are somehow trapped in their 'culture' and only capable of one or the other would be to miss the point entirely – and with it, the (productive) conceptual failing posed by analysing Swazi kingship in terms of 'sovereignty' or the legal thing in Swaziland in terms of *res judicata*.

Acknowledgements

This contribution benefited from its earliest hearing in Amiria Henare's 'Artefacts in Theory' seminar, together with its presentation in a much revised form at a conference convened by Anne Griffiths and Franz von Benda-Beckmann. I gratefully appreciate both invitations to workshop the piece, as well as the many thought-provoking interventions offered by both audiences. I would especially like to thank David Nelkin and David Zammit for their comments both inside and outside of our session in Edinburgh. Additionally, the piece was given a most thorough reading by Beverley Brown, Kirsten Campbell, Eva Franz, Martin Holbraad, Musa Sibandze and an anonymous reader – all of whom moved the work forward in different ways. However, it was Ilana Gershon's comments, together with the many readings she suggested I return to, which made the most fundamental difference. All shortcomings in the work are, of course, very much of the author's making.

Notes

1 My usage of the term *res judicata* follows certain trends in legal philosophy rather than legal practice. In the latter, *res judicata* serves as a defence and denotes a matter which has already been heard and decided upon by the court and thus has the standing of a legal fact or a legal 'thing'. Obviously, this more black letter usage is not unrelated to broader jurisprudential debates about law and reification, but practising lawyers would not find the use of *res judicata* appropriate outside descriptions of specific matters brought before the law, rather than as a characterisation of the law as a particular kind of unity. The contrastive utility of this term is made explicit in the conclusion to the paper.

2 This was a debate which turned on whether law should best be understood as an autonomous realm of norms that existed 'outside' of society and therefore adjudicated over social relations distinct from its own ordering (the centralist or positivist position) or as a system – one of many – which made up the constituent parts of society and whose operations were inflected by incursions of other such systems (economic, political, educational, etc.) into its workings. For a rich ethnographic exploration in an African context, see Griffiths 1998, where she explores Kwena women's differential access to, and experience of, law dependent on their social situations, irrespective of the law's claims to legal equality.

3 Explanations for the invisibility of divine forces, where chiefs must be absent in the proceedings of chiefs, courts for example, go back at least as far as Frazer's discussion of the mortality of gods amongst so-called 'primitive peoples' (1996).

4 For a detailed discussion of Swazi understandings of 'justice' in relation to the received law, see the WLSA volume, *Charting the Maze: women in Pursuit of*

Justice in Swaziland (2000), a volume in whose research and writing I was also involved.

5 In point of fact, it was not just any two evictees, but the deposed chiefs themselves.

6 The more compelling approach would be to consider the insufficiency of the concept of sovereignty in relation to Swazi divine kingship and allow this inadequacy to prompt the production of a new, more apropos concept – a possibility only signalled, rather than consummately explored, in this chapter's conclusion.

7 The term 'subjects' might prove misleading here, and Douzinas' discussion of *subjectum* and *subjectus* (2000: 183–228) – as the paradoxical dyad which comprises the modern conceptualisation of the legal subject – is instructive in this respect. Following Balibar, Douzinas suggests that subject as *subjectus* is historically prior, and is 'a political and legal term signifying that someone is subjected to the power or command of a superior, a ruler or sovereign' (*ibid*.: 217). However, the modern subject is the product of the mutually constitutive, if seemingly incommensurable, re-combination of subject as *subjectus* and the subject as *subjectum* – a bearer of rights and responsibilities. That is to say, the modern legal subject is both the creation of the law and law's creator (*ibid*.: 216). No doubt, this concurs with a Western history of the subject and maps neatly onto the evolution of Western forms of law and governance, but it might equally account for why 'custom' repeatedly fails as an analogue of law and why the sovereignty fostered by Swazi kingship differs from descriptions of medieval European kingships in certain significant ways (to the point that talking about the Swazi king as a 'sovereign' might be a red herring entirely). My contention here is that Swazi sensibilities correlate more closely to the Greek *hypokeimenon* (from which *subjectum* – as opposed to *subjectus* – translates (*ibid*.)) or 'the permanent substance or substratum beneath an individual's properties, the underlying essence of a thing' (*ibid*.), where the 'individual' or 'thing' is actually the Swazi nation-in-kingship (following similar formulations by Dumont 1981). I am not suggesting that all practices of Swazi kingship in recent history have remained true to this formulation. But the fundamental failing of most assessments of the monarchy in Swaziland stems directly from the fact that the Swazi belief that one cannot distinguish the kingship from *bakaNgwane*/the nation, is rendered as a mere discourse of kingship at best or a contrived political ideology at worst. It is not. In Swaziland, both the conceptualisation of (what a Euro-American would equate to) the legal subject and the nature of sovereignty are products of the indissolubility of king and nation, and this has translated directly into the highly articulated governmental structure which predates the country's colonial era by more than a century.

8 In many ways, this argument is entirely confluent with that made by Sahlins in his book, *Islands of History* (1985), where the 'Other' (in his case, the arrival of Captain Cook in Hawai'i) is assimilated into pre-existing social templates or practices. The principle difference (aside from the fact that I am not pursuing anything like the structural-historical analysis offered by Sahlins) would be that in the Swazi case, this sort of encompassment also seeks to preserve the 'other' qua other, a dissimilarity my contribution also shares with Henare's chapter in this volume.

9 Although I would also qualify that claim by underscoring the fact that the analysis of that reification is very much my own.

10 Of course law is not alone in holding up a mirror to the contradictions inherent in anthropological knowledge production. Foucault's suggestion that 'discourse

creates its objects' was always both an enabling theoretical framework for anthropology and a damning indictment of anthropology's workings in equal measure.

11 Importantly for Riles' argument, both the expressive and instrumental genres are present in every act of law-making (*ibid.*: 205).

12 Indeed, one of the most striking things about the newspaper coverage of high court cases and parliamentary debates is the frequency with which proceedings are explained in terms of the rules of court or the rules of parliament. Although often ancillary to the substantive content of an article, the formalities which govern these proceedings are often treated as intrinsic to understanding what actually transpired.

13 Kings must be right-handed, and a left-handed prince, otherwise eligible for succession, is wholly disqualified solely by this feature. Bonner implies that this was a mid-eighteenth-century innovation to disqualify the young prince Magudulela (Bonner 1983: 47), who would have been the seventh Swazi king were he not passed over for his brother Ludvonga I, but the Swazi historian J. S. M. Matsebula suggests otherwise (as indicated in a footnote to his genealogical table of the Royal Dlaminis included in his book, 1988). Indeed, the story I was once told tallied better with Matsebula's account, namely, his mother, anxious to avoid the pressures of becoming a queen mother should her son ascend to the throne, had engineered his left-handedness by plunging the child's right hand into a boiling pot, such that the disfigurement caused him to privilege his left hand as he grew and developed. If true, this would mitigate against the idea that Magudulela's disqualification for kingship due to his left-handedness was an impromptu invention used to thwart his claims to succession – although it is impossible to say whether the story of the boiling beer vat was manufactured post facto to legitimate the justifications for his exclusion. In any event, right-handedness remains a direct reference to kingship in a wide variety of contexts. The Mavuso clan, who for historical reasons might have certain claims to kingship themselves, begin their praisename with *nkhosi* (king), *mavuso, mavuso waNgwane* (Mavuso of Ngwane – or descended from Ngwane from whom all Swazi kings descend), only then to qualify *ncele likhohlwa lemtimkhulu* (left-handed one from the big house).

14 The observation holds for the kingdom's governance structures, where a 'modern' (as the Swazis would describe it) bicameral parliament and governmental ministries exist in tandem with the 'traditional' system of chieftaincies and their governors (*tindvuna*) who maintain allegiance to His Majesty and the queen mother.

15 This state of affairs persisted throughout my fieldwork between 1998 and 2004, during which time the king's supra-legal status was put forward in the Constitutional Framework. With the adoption of the long-awaited constitution in late July 2005, this state of affairs has now been permanently entrenched.

16 In a variety of different contexts, it has been observed that the quality of kingship is often refracted in individuals and offices across a society, although in practice, such processes of refraction will vary. Sometimes all members of a society will have some measure of kingly power/essence, albeit the degree they exhibit will extend across a wide spectrum. In others, such diminutions of kingly 'substance' are exclusive to a small cadre of elite (see Quigley 2005: 2, for an abbreviated discussion in general and Drucker-Brown 2005 for a rich ethnographic case study in this respect). In the case of Swaziland, this phenomenon has been overstated in my opinion, leading to an emphasis on the stratified and 'aristocratic' character of the society (Kuper 1947) at the expense of a full consideration of how this stratification relates to the encompassing nature of Swazi kingship (Wastell forthcoming).

17 *INcwala* is a cleansing ceremony, which fortifies the person of His Majesty and ensures the fertility and health of the nation for the coming year. As such, it confounds a distinction between a 'positive' theory of kingship (one where the perfection of the monarch equates to the well-being of the nation) and the so-called 'negative' theories, which understand the king as a sacred scapegoat who takes on the ills of the nation and periodically expels them (cf. Quigley 2005: 10; and Scubla 2005), as the Swazi *iNcwala* clearly performs both functions. For an authoritative account of the ritual and its purpose, see Matsebula 1988.

18 His Majesty receives his subjects at the royal palace at Lozitha only through the night.

19 Women and Law in Southern Africa Research Trust.

20 *Locus standae* refers to an applicant's ability to be recognised by the court.

21 Particular thanks to David Nelkin who chased me on this point and articulated it in these terms, and more generally for the discussions he shared with me on the extent to which 'cultural sensibilities' at minimum inflect, or more strongly put, positively colonise the practice of the rule of law.

22 Barshack's discussion of the religious versus magical modalities of law exhibits numerous parallels with Riles' distinction between the expressive versus the instrumental mode, not all of which can be explored here. Most importantly for the argument put forward here is the fact that both see law as alternating between being a thing-in-the-world and an external position from which to observe and constitute the world in particular ways: 'In one of its facets, the law is a sacred Thing, a presence, while in another facet it is a word, reason and hegemonic system of representation that assumes the normative separation between subject and Thing' (Barshack 2000: 320).

23 The remark echoes the observation of many scholars that the phrase 'The king is dead; long live the king!' is an aphorism for the dual nature of kingship as both person and office.

24 For an extended discussion of the high court appeal case over the evictions, see chapter 7 in Wastell forthcoming.

25 Of course, the important corollary to this, as we shall see, is that Swazis go on to presume that the encompassing nature of the king's being – 'power' understood as an essence of which they are a part – is a shared characteristic of non-Swazi 'power'. While kingship is potentially infinite – capable of encompassing anything – it also defines itself against all that is non-Swazi. To be Swazi has little to do with blood quorum or any conceptualisation of 'ethnicity'. It is to be one in the body and person of the king. But equally, it is recognised that not everybody is part of the essence of Swazi kingship. Thus, the non-Swazis are imagined to part of another (non-Swazi) essence.

26 Agamben defines the 'relation of exception' as 'the extreme form of relation by which something is included solely through its exclusion' (*ibid*.: 18).

27 And here again is the salient difference between my account and that of Sahlins (1985).

References

Agamben, G. (1998) *Homo Sacer: sovereign Power and Bare Life*, Stanford: Stanford University Press.

Ashforth, A. (2005) *Witchcraft, Violence and Democracy in South Africa*, Chicago: University of Chicago Press.

Barshack, L. (2000) 'The totemic authority of the court', *Law and Critique*, 11(3): 301–28.

Bonner, B. (1983) *Kings, Commoners and Concessionaires: the Evolution and Dissolution of the Nineteenth-Century Swazi State*, Johannesburg: Raven Press.

Booth, A. R. (1992) 'European courts protect women and witches: colonial law courts as redistributors of power in Swaziland 1920–50', *Journal of Southern African Studies*, 18(2): 253–75.

Cohen, F. (1960) *The Legal Conscience*, New Haven CT: Yale University Press.

——(1935) 'Transcendental nonsense and the functional approach', *Columbia Law Review*, 35: 809.

Douzinas, C. (2000) *The End of Human Rights*, Oxford: Hart Publishing.

Drucker-Brown, S. (2005) 'King house: the mobile polity in northern Ghana', in Quigley, D. (ed.) *The Character of Kingship*, Oxford: Berg.

Dumont, L. (1981) *Homo Hierarchicus*, Chicago: University of Chicago Press.

Frazer, J. G. (1996) [1890] *The Golden Bough: a Study in Magic and Religion*, New York: Simon and Schuster.

Griffiths, A. (1998) *In the Shadow of Marriage: Gender and Justice in an African Community*, Chicago: University of Chicago Press.

Kantorowicz, (1997) [1957] *The King's Two Bodies*, Princeton NJ: Princeton University Press.

Kapferer, B. (1997) *The Feast of the Sorcerer: Practices of Consciousness and Power*, Chicago: University of Chicago Press.

Kuper, H. (1947) *An African Aristocracy: Rank among the Swazi*, Oxford: Oxford University Press.

Latour, B. (2004) 'Scientific objects and legal objectivity', in Pottage, A. and Mundy, M. (eds) *Law, Anthropology, and the Constitution of the Social: Making Persons and Things*, Cambridge: Cambridge University Press.

Matsebula, J. S. M. (1988) [1972] *A History of Swaziland*, 3rd edn, Capetown: Longman.

Moore, H. and Sanders, T. (2001) *Magical Interpretations, Material Realities: Modernity, Witchcraft and the Occult in Postcolonial Africa*, London: Routledge.

Moore, S. F. (1998) 'Systematic judicial and extra-judicial injustice: preparations for future accountability', in Werbner, R. (ed.) *Memory and the Post-Colony: African Anthropology and the Critique of Power*, London: Zed Books.

Quigley, D. (2005) 'Introduction: the character of kingship', in Quigley, D. (ed.) *The Character of Kingship*, Oxford: Berg.

Riles, A. (2003) 'Law as object', in Merry, S. E. and Brennais, D. (eds) *Law and Empire in the Pacific*, Santa Fe NM: School of American Research Press.

Sahlins, M. (1985) *Islands of History*, Chicago: University of Chicago Press.

Scubla, L. (2005) 'Sacred king, sacrificial victim, surrogate victim or Frazer, Hocart, Girard', in Quigley, D. (ed.) *The Character of Kingship*, Oxford: Berg.

Wastell, S. (2007) *The Mouth that Tells No Lies: Kingship, Law and Sovereignty in Swaziland*, Walnut Creek, CA: West Coast Press.

WLSA (2000) *Charting the Maze: Women in Pursuit of Justice in Swaziland*, Mbabane: WLSA.

Worby, E. (2003) 'The end of modernity in Zimbabwe? Passages from development to sovereignty', in Hammar, A., Raftopoulos, B. and Jensen, S. (eds) *Zimbabwe's Unfinished Business: Re-thinking Land, State and Nation in the Context of a Crisis*, Harare: Weaver Press.

5

COLLECTION AS A WAY OF BEING

Andrew Moutu

> The problematic of temporality is fundamental to the collecting process.
>
> (Baudrillard 1994: 15)

In her study of the nature of collecting in the European tradition, Susan Pearce identifies 'a need to open up the study of collecting to a range of interpretations, and to bring investigation of its significance into the mainstream, as part of our understanding of social life as a whole' (1995: 3). In focusing on the practice, poetics and politics of collecting, Pearce highlights the psychology of collections and the particular manner in which meaning and value are inscribed in the relationships between Europeans and the material objects they collect. Pearce (*ibid.*: 4) defines collecting as:

> a set of things which people do, as an aspect of individual and social practice which is important in the public and private life as a means of constructing the way in which [Europeans] relate to the material world and so build [their] lives. It is essentially an investigation into an aspect of human experience.

In taking up the call to open the study of collecting to a variety of interpretations, this chapter takes advantage of the English word 'collections', as it appears in a variety of ethnographic contexts, to advance the view that collections may be considered as a way of being. At the outset, I should clarify that this is not an ethnographic account about the English cultural experience of collections but rather one that is influenced by an appreciation of the knowledge practices of the Iatmul people of Papua New Guinea (PNG) with whom I carried out field research. The Iatmul deploy an epistemological scheme of juxtaposing analogies (Bateson 1958; Moutu 2003; Herle and Moutu 2003) in order to explain things to people. The discussion below will provide some examples of such a knowledge practice.

Museologists and other theoreticians often dwell on the intricate complexities that prevail in the relations between material objects and collectors (see

Baal 1994; Pearce 1992). A prime exemplar of such analyses is given by Baudrillard (1994) who interprets the 'system of collecting' in psycholoana-lytic terms, positing that the relations between a person and the collected object are sanctioned by the gaze and subjectivities of the individual subject himself. In defining collection as a 'discourse directed to oneself', Baudrillard's theory of collecting is grounded in a firm sense of individu-alism that is linked to a fetishisation of the object and marred by a vision of temporal continuity that is mediated through the objects which are collected. This chapter offers an alternative theorisation. While some physical objects are involved in the discussion that follows, the argument is not about collectible art forms of the kind one finds in museums, but rather traverses along the level of concepts and uses objects as a conceit to draw out the conceptual capacity of collections to organise and create the possibilities for re-conceiving meaning and reconfiguring social relations.

Consistent with the theme of this book, the 'things' that are discussed here involve an assembly of scenarios in which the notion of collections comes into play. The variety of ethnographic scenarios encountered is effectively a collection of sorts assembled here to 'think through' the idea of collections as a way of being. Whilst the ideas expressed in this chapter take their cue from reading a collection of essays in a book entitled *Cultures of Collecting* (Elsner and Cardinal 1994), the chapter also makes a critical departure from them. It thus mimics (albeit tangentially) the efforts of the editors of this volume who are required to assemble, organise – or as it were, collect the disparity of viewpoints canvassed in this volume in order to explicate the idea of 'thinking through things' (as opposed to 'thinking about things'). In the descriptions that follow, the scenarios discussed serve to exemplify and broach the idea of how one might approach collection as a way of being. Furthermore, these scenarios also highlight the way in which 'loss' is integral to the concept of collection advanced here. At the end, this notion of loss will be used to critique the manner in which Gell (1998), working in the paradigm of classificatory thought, has theorised about collectible art forms.

A collection of scenarios

Scene 1: the Aitape tsunami exhibition at the PNG National Museum

It is a familiar practice throughout Papua New Guinea that whenever a person has died or is afflicted with pain and illness, his or her relatives and friends gather to mourn for the deceased or to comfort and restore the rela-tives of the dead or the afflicted. As they collect and reconfigure themselves in the face of such contingencies, they also seek explanations as to why such an experience has befallen them. The date of 17 July 1998 is one that will be forever etched in the hearts and minds of the people of Arop, Warupu, Sissano and other smaller villages located along the northern coast of PNG.

On that fateful day, the people of these seafaring villages were over-whelmed by catastrophe. Triggered by geological processes beneath the sea floor, tidal waves rose to monstrous heights, crashed down on the shore like thunder and swept rapidly through the villages, engulfing all within reach of their cruel might before eventually retreating. Was it an act of retributive vengeance executed by ancestor spirits or was it an act of the Christian god? This was one of the many vexing questions articulated by the living victims of the disaster, their relatives and many other Papua New Guineans as they pondered the devastation.

Melanesians have a penchant for seeking the 'roots' (see Gell 1998: 58) of why tragedies such as the tsunami happen to them. The 'roots' of such misfortunes lie not in the way that scientists such as geologists explain events or physicians produce diagnoses. For Melanesians, the social and cosmic environment (see Narokobi 1983) is imbued with human and spiritual agen-cies which impinge upon one another in such a way that the motivations of such agencies are considered crucial in explaining devastating misfortunes such as this. Such questions arise not merely as a result of the incidental occurrence of misfortunes but from an assumption that these kinds of calamities carry teleological significance nested within wider cosmological notions of the world and man's place within it. The proclivity for this particular kind of causal reasoning on the part of the people of Aitape has meant that, despite the clarity of geological information we now have on the tidal wave, they are still asking whether the tragedy was an outcome of human or spiri-tual agency. In other words, a physical event must have been preceded by an intentional cause (see Gell 1998: 16–21). By such a cultural logic, the people of Aitape have reason to assume that an agent must have been responsible for the geological processes and the subsequent waves.

As 11 September is to Americans, so 17 July is for the people of Aitape, a date marked with the traumatic experiences of physical pain, emotional desolation, the demolition of homes and the destitution of persons and the loss of loved ones.[1] Homes were completely devastated and villages left in ruins. Well over 2,000 people were killed; others suffered injuries to their persons and their property. In the days following the tragedy, the villages and their people became the focus of international attention. Help and sympathy poured in from around the world. The survivors are now resettled and are, as it were, collecting themselves as a consequence of the events that have tran-spired since the tsunami.

Based on ethnographic collections made through fieldwork carried out in some of these affected villages, members of the Department of Anthropology within the PNG National Museum decided to stage an exhibition to recall the people and the villages that were claimed by the tide. The idea of the exhibition gained support and expanded to include both the disaster and the humanitarian efforts that were undertaken to restore the lives of those who were affected. International interest in the project meant that the museum was able to gain sponsorship for the exhibition, most notably from the Australian High Commission, local businesses, and media organisations in PNG.

The organisation of the exhibition was achieved through a collective effort involving staff from the museum, the University of PNG, the Australian High Commission and Caritas PNG, an organisation of the Catholic Church. This team assembled a collection of artefacts, predominantly photographs, newspaper articles and television clips, which showed the devastating results of the tsunami as well as the ongoing efforts to restore the lives of the victims. Some of the ethnographic objects and photographs in the exhibition had been collected before the event, while others were taken in its wake. The newspaper articles and video clips focused mainly on the aftermath of the wave, and care was taken in exhibiting photographs of human corpses and mutilated bodies.

Visual artefacts such as photographs and video footage captured a lot about what was going on not just after but also prior to the disaster. The photographs, in particular, brought into focus the relationship between the people of the affected villages and the Catholic missionaries established in the area. They also showed how people were trying to cope and readjust to the changes brought about by the tsunami. This was true not just for those who lost their loved ones, but also those who lost limbs, homes and possessions. Many had to re-establish their villages in new settings away from the beachfront.

One of the main speakers at the opening of the exhibition at the museum was the Chairman of the Aitape Rehabilitation Committee, Mr Balthasar Maketu, who works for Caritas PNG and was also involved in preparing the exhibition. Mr Maketu comes from Sissano, one of the villages badly affected, and lost his mother and several other relatives in the wave. As he was speaking one could see women from his area who were living in Port Moresby, and who were amongst the people who had come to see the exhibition, sobbing in tears. The atmosphere that prevailed in the gallery was very emotional. The exhibition not only provoked a deep sense of loss but also conveyed a message of hope for the future that lay beyond the experience and memories of the disaster.

The discussion so far has brought into focus several instances in which collections appear. For instance, the collection of artefacts that were assembled in the exhibition; the collection of people who gathered in the museum during the opening of the exhibition; as well as the people who collected themselves after the tsunami. Because the exhibition was a story of recollection and projection in the midst of devastating loss, despair and hope, it was inevitable that it would recall anguish and affliction, since the realities of such experiences could not have been denied or suppressed. It was a story the National Museum was able to reconstruct and tell through the collection of artefacts assembled through collective effort.

Moving on from this description of the tsunami wave and the exhibition, I will now consider how collections are involved in what I have described as a way of being. I suggest that this notion of collection as a way of being has to do with the place of time that is lurking within the alternating sequence of loss and projection which constitutes my concept of collections. In its act of devastation, the tsunami disrupts time by introducing loss and alteration into people's lives. As it runs through the villages it inflicts death and other kinds of loss which require people to re-group themselves and forge ahead. Hence one can say that the survivors of the Aitape tsunami are collecting themselves after the wave. But the museum exhibition on the tsunami appears like a collection within a collection, a story that is built upon that initial act of devastating loss, the ensuing process of re-settlement and a projection into the future. From the perspective of the tsunami as an agent of collection (the wave running through the villages claiming lives and possessions and forcing people to re-group themselves subsequently), one can see how collection interrupts the sequential flow of temporality, impregnates this interruption with loss, and then prompts people to reconfigure themselves in the midst of both despair and hope so that such a process of reconfiguration is itself an aspect of collection. Even if life must continue for the survivors of the tsunami, there is nothing continuous with the loss experienced except the memory of such a loss. While the story of the devastating tidal wave in Aitape is still in the mind of the reader, one might recall the Biblical account of the flood that God ordained in the days of Noah. (The reason why I am rehearsing the Biblical account of the flood will become obvious in the discussion below.)

Scene 2: Noah's ark and the collection of animals

The Biblical account of the flood resonates well with the Aitape disaster because they both make obvious the difference between the perception of physical and intentional causation, to recall Gell (1998:16). The Bible has it that heavy rain poured endlessly for more than a month and caused the excessive flood in the days of Noah, while scientists tell us that a geological fault in the seabed caused the Aitape tsunami. By analogy therefore, if the flood in Noah's time was caused by God, then the people of Aitape, who are also Christians, are left with a comparable situation of either assigning malevolent agency to ancestral spirits in the sea or being assured in a measure of faith that contemplates the benevolence of God. As noted earlier, they find themselves compelled to query the intentional roots of such a disaster.

In citing the Biblical account of the flood and the collection of animals in Noah's ark, Elsner and Cardinal (1994) identify Noah as the first collector. He collected a complete set of paired animals in order to ensure their salvation.

Noah's passion lay in the urge to save the world – to save not just single items as they chanced to occur but the model pairs from which all life forms could be reconstructed. Here is saving in its strongest sense, not just casual keeping but conscious rescuing from extinction – collection as salvation.

(1994: 1)

Noah's commitment to collect, they note, was motivated by the urge to preserve the species of animals which were facing an impending doom that God was executing. They also emphasise Adam's role in giving names to the animals which Noah later collected. Noting the connection between naming, labelling and ultimately classification, Elsner and Cardinal go on to argue that

> Classification precedes collection. Adam classified the creatures that God has made; on the basis of nomenclature, Noah could recollect these creatures in order to preserve them. Of course without the prior existence of the animals, they could not have been named; equally, without with their endowment with names they could not been collected.

(*ibid.*: 1–2)

In arguing that classification precedes collection, Elsner and Cardinal follow a Western epistemological scheme of thought that regards classification as a technique of comprehension which operates by way of discerning order and pattern in the diversity of collections. The complexity inherent in diversity is simplified or rationalised through the process of sorting collections. This conventional process of discerning order, pattern or regularities fits into a rational scheme of management, control and predictability. Such a process facilitates comprehension and understanding, which are the epistemological ends of classification. Because it is used as a technique of conventionalising distinctiveness, classification appears as an epistemological midwife at the call of order, management and control. It is through the need for epistemological sensibility that collection is rendered classificatory or that it is deducted as such from an initial mode of being-in-the-world. Elsner and Cardinal then go on to extend this classificatory scheme of thought to embrace a much wider dimension of human social existence:

> Collecting is classification lived, experienced in three dimensions. The history of collecting is thus the narrative of how human beings have striven to accommodate, to appropriate and to extend the taxonomies and systems of knowledge they have inherited. And the world itself, certainly the social world, has always relied on its appointed collectors [here they refer to different kinds of collectors such as tax, rent, refuse, etc.] [. . .] The social order is itself inherently

98

collective: it thrives on classification, on rule, on labels, sets and systems. Notions such as caste, class, tribe and family, priesthood and laity, privileged and poor, prescribe a grid into which actual people and objects are allocated. If the people and the things of the world are the collected, and if the social categories into which they are assigned confirm the precious knowledge of culture handed down through generations, then our rulers sit atop a hierarchy of collectors. Empire is a collection of countries and populations; a country is a collection of regions and peoples; each given people is a collection of individuals, divided into governed and governors – that is, collectables and collectors.

(*ibid.*: 2)

Contrary to Elsner and Cardinal, I contend that their broad conceptualisation of collection as 'lived experience in three dimensions' can be turned on its head. Rather than viewing collections as a reflection of a prior epistemological scheme of classification, I suggest that collections can be considered as a way of being. Let me elaborate on this. In the citation above we find that people are known by names with particular kinds of histories, roles and identities which allow them not only to be distinguishable from others but also provide the grid and matrix by which they enact their social life and function through time. Elsner and Cardinal associate collections with classificatory schema primarily because of their view that classification is prior to collections. Such a position makes obvious the presumption that knowledge is intricately bound up with the process of collections. However, the fact that people are divided into groups with particular types of identities does not necessarily mean that this or that set of identities implies the enactment of a classificatory scheme of lived experience, which is then instantiated in the form of collections. Contrary to Elsner and Cardinal, I argue that collection is not necessarily an enactment of a classificatory scheme of thinking but rather that the enactment of social relations necessarily summons differentiation. Let me elaborate on this with the following ethnographic observations.

People are obviously different from one another, but this difference does not necessarily posit a mode of classification. The Iatmul people, for instance, with whom I did ethnographic fieldwork, are divided into different totemic and ritual moieties with different clans, sub-clans and lineages, etc. Clans are exogamous and one can only take a spouse from a clan other than one's own; men from one ritual moiety will initiate the children of the other moiety; clans which form one men's house can 'eat together' from a common fishing lagoon; etc. This is the way in which the 'structure' of social life is organised for them, and one may sort them into different classes or groups of people for purposes of understanding how Iatmul differentiate between and amongst themselves. Such a procedure is fine insofar as this is a rational attempt to deal with them for analytical purposes. However, the Iatmul

themselves do not employ a classificatory mode of thought to provide explanations either of themselves or of other phenomena in the world of their
experiences, as we shall see from some vignettes below. Rather they provide
explanations of all kinds of things through juxtaposing analogies (see
Bateson 1958: 266). Some ethnographic vignettes from the Iatmul might help
to elucidate this argument.

When I came across the widespread appearance of Iatmul *wasari*[2] or
same-names – for instance the name Kamangari is the name of men in
Kanganamun, Parimbe, Kaminimbit and Nangusap villages – I asked the man
from Kanganamun about the significance of same-names. Employing an
imagery similar to Bateson's metaphor of the rhizome, he explained by
pointing to shoots of sago palm which were seen sprouting out from a stem
which lies buried beneath the sub-soil. Alternatively, he turned around and
pointed to small banana shoots growing around a matured banana plant
standing on a mound beside the sago palms. He said the system of *wasari* is
like shoots which stem from a common origin. To explain the relationship
between people who have the same-names amongst the Iatmul, my interlocutor used the imagery of how shoots from the sago palm and the banana
tree were standing side-by-side since they emanate from a common stem. As
Iatmul mythico-historical narratives go, clans have a common origin, but after
a process of schism and fission comes into play, they split apart and reconfigure themselves in separate villages. The *wasari* serve as an onomastic link to
their story as members of one clan. Same-names are relatives who belong to
the same clan, but the clan is distributed throughout different Iatmul villages.

In another instance when I probed my interlocutors about the kinds of
names they give their children, one of them told me that: 'stories are very big
things to us. Villages sit on stories and they are like canoes which are
fastened to poles on the banks of the Sepik River which prevent them from
drifting away.' These stories are like mythico-biographical charters that
contain personal names which are bestowed on people. The man then went
on to say that ideally a name that is bestowed on a person must 'match' the
bearer of that name. When I queried the notion of 'matching', he pointed to
the pair of boots I was wearing and said 'just like those pair of boots must
match your feet; so it must be with names that we bestow on people'.

On another occasion I found a group of men playing sacred flutes one
night in a place reserved only for initiated men. As the time on my watch was
nearing 12 a.m., the musicians stopped and one of my interlocutors told me
to just listen to all of the sounds of the night. On the stroke of midnight two
wild-fowl in the nearby bush began singing a duet, whose subsequent hourly
repetition provided interludes of musical antiphony until dawn. One man
asked me: 'Did you hear that?' When I replied in the affirmative, he said:
'The two birds you have heard are like the two birds which are singing here.'
He was explaining to me how flutes were conceptualised as metaphorical
birds.

The three vignettes described above show how Iatmul provide explanations of all kinds of things through juxtaposing sets of analogies. The person who is presented with these analogies must apprehend the internal relation contained in the analogies in order to catch what his or her interlocutors are trying to explain. It comes as no surprise to find that Bateson's classic ethnography, *Naven*, is structured by a logic of juxtaposition, with chapters deliberately laid side-by-side in such a way that the reader is supplied with a set of images intended to facilitate an apprehension of explanation itself, rather than having ethnography presented as a problem that needs an explanation (Bateson 1958: 266). Following from what we have seen thus far, one might say that if apprehension is the epistemological end of juxtaposition as it is practised among the Iatmul, then classification serves a function of comprehension amongst its practitioners as epitomised in scientific practice. This contrast between classification and juxtaposition leads me to argue that knowledge appears to be a different order of engagement than living a life in a world which is 'classified' into different kinds of clans or moieties, let alone nations and empires, collectors and collectibles. To think of collections as the living enactment of classification is to impose an epistemological view on social life. The field of social life and experience is one that necessarily requires differentiation, and I argue that such differentiation is not an enactment of classification but a necessary axis of social relations.

To return to Elsner and Cardinal's argument, we find that in dividing the process of collection into sets of collectors and collectibles, they sustain a binary logic that undercuts the classificatory mode of thought. The basis of their argument, that Noah collected after Adam classified, derives solely from the chronological sequence of Adam preceding Noah in Biblical history. In my reading of this Biblical account of the flood, however, I would argue that Noah was not a collector. He simply answered God's call and built the ark according to instructions. It was God who summoned and collected the animals, which Noah subsequently paraded and brought into the ark. Noah's response to this can be taken as the enactment of his personal relationship with God based on faith.

Contrary to Elsner and Cardinal, who hold that Noah collected out of an impulse for conservation, I would argue that it was Noah's relationship with God that caused him to obey God despite the apparent absurdity of building an ark on a mountain far above sea level. Noah aided the process of collection not because of an urge to rescue the species of animals from the ensuing devastation, but because of his willingness to abide by the word of God. This should not be taken as the urge to collect for the purpose of salvation. Ultimately, it was God's intention that preceded the collection, and not a classificatory scheme as such. Whether intention is itself classificatory is a question I will return to in the latter part of this chapter when we see how collecting is bound up with classification.

In the discussion above I have used the stories of the Aitape tsunami and the Biblical account of the flood in Noah's days to advance a critique of the way in which Elsner and Cardinal have conceptualised collections as an enactment of a classificatory scheme of thinking. Initially, I take their argument as a theoretical position that exemplifies my proposed argument that collections instantiate a way of knowing, a position which assumes an epistemological conception of social life and experience rather than as a way of being. I then offered a description of Iatmul knowledge practices based on juxtaposition in contrast to their way of life which is enacted around moieties, clans, lineages, etc. The contrast between knowledge practices based on juxtaposition and a way of life governed by moieties and clans is not based on a classificatory scheme of thinking but on how Iatmul differentiate amongst themselves, and it is proposed here that this differentiation should not be interpreted in classificatory terms. This ethnographic example was aimed at debunking both the argument that collections necessarily enact a classificatory paradigm of thought and the associated epistemological view that sees social life as 'classification lived'. We now proceed to a consideration of other kinds of collections.

Scene 3: mixed scenarios of collection

Every Friday evening during term time in Cambridge, there is a seminar held in the seminar room of the Department of Social Anthropology. Promptly at 5 p.m., lecturers, fellows and graduate students of the department collect together for this seminar, which lasts about and hour and a half. In the usual run of 'seminar culture' (see Gell 1999), the attendees of the seminar retreat in a motley of small groups to the bar at Kings's College where they iron out their differences, discussing and expressing support or dislike for the seminar just ended. In one such Friday seminar, a member of the audience raised a perceptive question to a speaker who had just finished giving a paper. The speaker was taken aback momentarily by the question and had to collect himself before he could provide a response to the question. In this example we find a collection of people classified as anthropologists sitting inside a seminar room. In my view, the gathering or collection of anthropologists (or people from other disciplines) inside a seminar room amounts to a way of being in which people of a kind or category[3] relate to themselves or others in very specific ways.[4] It is difficult to determine which came first, the discipline of anthropology or the seminar.

Pressing on after the seminar ended, we find that the presenter is asked a question which puts him in a position of temporary loss. This experience of momentary loss and the need to respond allows the presenter to collect himself before responding. Although it occurs in a different context under a different kind of psychological condition, this moment of loss and response is similar to the experience of the tsunami in Aitape, where people suffered loss and then had to re-gather themselves. Figuratively, a question can be as devastating as a tidal wave, which first drowns the speaker and then allows him to make a comeback. What collection reveals in this context is the movement back and forth in time. The question interrupts the flow, causes the speaker to retrace his steps and then allows him to respond. The movement of thought between loss and the response, the moment of displacement and re-conceptualisation, is where time becomes constitutive of collections. Through the momentary displacement, time enfolds itself and springs forward, collection picks itself up and strides on after the lapse.

In another familiar situation, we hear of a graduate student (from one of those Cambridge colleges) who was on her way to Sainsbury's supermarket, where she was intending to collect some food. After getting off her bicycle, she tried to lock it and then suddenly realised that her keys were missing; she remembered that she had left them in the door to her room. She had to return to her room in college to collect them. In thinking about the girl's trip to the Sainsbury's where she is to collect some food, my mind recalls the Iatmul women of Kanganamun village who make daily trips to fishing lagoons to collect fish trapped in their nets. On mornings that followed a heavy rain in the night, some of the women would find that a lot of water had collected in their canoes and they were thus forced to empty the rainwater out of their canoes before undertaking the trip.

The scenarios just mentioned above might seem mundane and to add little value to the argument. However, in a Heideggerian version of phenomenological ontology, the ordinary aspects of human existence – such as collecting keys, or food from a shop or lagoon – provide an immediate entry into thinking about how one's sense of being-in-the-world unfolds through daily existential chores and concerns. The keys and canoes reveal our entanglement with a world of equipment, and it is in these kinds of contexts – such as a missing key or a wet canoe – that the nature of one's being-in-the-world becomes expressed as a concerned orientation with equipment. Writing in a different context, but providing a sage explanation concerning this interaction with equipment, Weiner (2001: 6) explains that the world of human experience is 'oriented not by an attitude of detached contemplation but of practical circumspection':

> The view in which equipmental contexture stands at first, completely unobtrusive and unthought is the view of practical circumspection of our practical everyday orientation. 'Unthought' means that it is not thematically apprehended for deliberate thinking about things; instead, in circumspection, we find our bearings in regards to them.
> (Heidegger 1962: 163, cited in Weiner 2001: 6)

Thus it follows that if we consider the images of the Cambridge student who has to return to college to collect her bicycle keys, or the Iatmul woman removing water that has collected in her canoe, one might see collection appearing as a process of purposive engagement with a world of equipment, which is a basic condition of our being-in-the-world in Heidegger's view of ontology. In Heidegger's scheme of ontology, the concerned orientation with things displaces the dichotomy between subjects and objects and reveals *Dasein* phenomenologically in terms of a successive series of time horizons branching out into future dimensions of possible choices, actions and outcomes. However, as we shall see, such a vision of temporality is based on a sense of continuity, a view that is here ruptured by the ontological work of collections. In collections we encounter momentary loss, a returning and a projection towards the future. It is not continuity but loss that reveals the ontological work of collections.

Whilst our minds are still with the Iatmul, Gregory Bateson once remarked on how the anthropologist sets out to 'collect an exceedingly complex and entirely foreign culture in a few months and upon his return, he discovers shocking gaps in his fieldwork' (1958: 257). In this rendition, collection imbues ethnographic material with a sense of tangibility comparable to ethnographic objects that are collected and taken to museums. In other sections of his ethnography, Bateson uses the notion of collections in the vein both of an epistemological scheme of knowing and also as a way of being-in-the-world-with-others. Thus for instance, he refers to the gathering of data as a collection of information (*ibid.*: 3); to a group of men of a particular clan who have collected to perform a particular mortuary ceremony (*ibid.*: 47); as well as to the collection of ethnographic objects such as a pair of secret flutes.

During his fieldwork, Bateson was intent on buying a pair of Iatmul secret flutes. After purchasing two from a particular village, he had them wrapped and brought to the village in which he was residing. On arriving in the village he 'unpacked them solemnly in the ceremonial house and the natives eyes lit up when they saw the carving and shell work with which the flutes were ornamented'. The Iatmul men who had gathered in the men's house congratulated him for 'buying something worthwhile at last and remarked that all the rest of [his] collection was nothing but firewood' (Bateson 1936: 161–2). The Iatmul men were happy and praised Bateson for collecting the flutes, which were part of the men's ritual paraphernalia. Bateson tells us that after 'it was dark the two best musicians in the village came to try the flutes. Fascinated by its ability, one of them exclaimed, "This bird sings of itself without me blowing it" and soon the two musicians became so entranced that they played on in the ceremonial house till dawn' (*ibid.*).

However, after the thrill of acquisition and the bliss of musical ecstasy, a sudden moment of gloom sets in. A concern about loss became apparent when the faces of the men in the ceremonial house fell that morning. When Bateson queried their worried faces, they asked him: 'What are you going to do with the flutes? Are you going to take them away with you when you go?

Will they sing anymore? [. . .] Will women see them? Who will play them in your country? Can white men play the flutes?' (*ibid.*: 62). The Iatmul men were worried not about losing the metaphorical birds but about the capacity of the two birds to continue singing. It was not enough to collect an object that is more than firewood; one also has to collect the knowledge and the appropriate kind of relations and protocol that are necessary to animate the life of the flutes as musical birds. This Iatmul concern over the relations necessary to animate the pair of flutes resonates well with the reasons as to why God made Noah collect a pair of animals. The internal relation contained in a pair of animals is necessary for the reproduction of the species. Such an internal relation of paired necessity is fundamental to the animation of Iatmul flutes. The Iatmul considered that Bateson must also collect the necessary relations that could continue to animate the flutes, otherwise they cannot sing on their own. In response to their concern, Bateson appeased them by asking the Iatmul musicians to teach him how to play the flutes so that when he returned to England, he could teach another white man and they could play the flutes in a duet (*ibid.*).[5]

The imagery of Bateson unpacking the flutes resonates well with the philosopher Walter Benjamin's unpacking of his library (Benjamin 1999). Benjamin, however, utilises the narrative of this event to provide 'some insight into the relationship of a book collector to his possessions, into collecting rather than a collection' (1999: 61). Benjamin reckons that there is a prevailing sense of disorder in collection, a kind of chaos that loses its temper, making it necessary for order to come into existence in the form of shelving or cataloguing. For Benjamin therefore, 'there is in the life of a collector a dialectical tension between the poles of disorder and order' (*ibid.*: 62). If order subsumes an epistemological scheme of classification, then it has to be created out of an initial condition of chaos. For the Iatmul on the other hand, the order is already there as a kind of necessary presence instantiated in the form of paired flutes and paired musicians. Such an orderly situation does not require the contingency that Benjamin suggests as he reflects on unpacking his books. For Benjamin, collection emerges out of chaos, whereas for the Iatmul, it seems, collection presupposes a necessary order. Despite unpacking his library, Benjamin hasn't yet read the books, his books are unorganised and he is trying to shelve them into an order of one sort or another, because the 'counterpart to the confusion of the library is the order of its catalogue' (*ibid.*).

Commenting on this account of collecting and the unread books, Cardinal (1994: 69; cf. Schor 1994) observes that 'Benjamin makes the case for the bibliophile as one who never reads his books.' Seen in this light, one might think of Bateson as someone who collected but did not play the flutes he collected from the Iatmul. For the Iatmul, it seems, what is important is to collect and not to lose the relations that animate collections because such relations generate and structure the life of musical birds as well as of humans.

Scene 4: when collections can become not a collection

On the night of 19 May 2003, thieves broke into the public gallery of the PNG National Museum in Port Moresby and stole a total of fifty archaeological and ethnographic objects that were on display in the museum. This is an account of what happened. Soon after midnight a gang of fifteen men armed with knives, metal rods and homemade guns held up the security officers at the museum. The thieves caught the security officers by surprise, held them at gunpoint, and forced their way into the gallery. They used a pinch bar to open the glass door, smashing the locks on the museum's interior door before entering the gallery. The lights had been turned off for the night leaving the gallery pitch dark, so the thieves had to light old newspapers to find their way around. After entering, they went straight to two particular exhibition areas within the gallery where objects were on display and removed fourteen stone artefacts – mainly mortars and pestles – and thirty-six ethnographic pieces comprising mainly of body adornments. These objects come from different parts of PNG. The ethnographic objects were in a glass case which was smashed and the objects taken out. The entire episode lasted less than fifteen minutes and the thieves left the museum premises as fast as they had entered. Judging by the information that the security officers provided, it was a well planned and executed criminal operation.

The museum carried out an investigation into the robbery by sending some of its staff, including myself, to nearby squatter settlements. Within a week it was established that an expatriate art dealer was involved in commissioning the operation. A total of K10,000 (£2,000) was paid to the youths who were involved once they delivered the stolen objects to the dealer. As soon as they received the money, some of them fled Port Moresby for their home provinces. However, disagreements over the distribution of the money soon threatened the gang as a collective, as complaints were made by some of the members. Word soon spread in the squatter settlement, leading the museum's officials to a member of the gang. The gang member willingly gave some information about the theft but fell short of supplying the identity of the man who had commissioned the crime. Following these developments, however, the gang member became reluctant to cooperate further and remained elusive for some weeks until he was shot dead by police for a different crime. After his death, the museum's officials were unable to contact other members of the gang, and so the entire investigation foundered. The objects are still at large, probably in the hands of an art connoisseur overseas, and the identity of the dealer remains unknown. On this account, an old adage seems to hold sway that if one man's loss is another man's gain then the stolen collections became another man's collection.

As a curator with daily responsibilities over the artefacts on display in the museum's public galleries, I myself suspected that the theft was motivated by commercial interest in the objects. This view was based on the fact that the objects stolen did not seem like a random selection. Following a week of investigation, this view was confirmed when we discovered the organised nature of the crime. When the thieves entered the museum, all of its public galleries were open to them but fortunately they only collected objects from specific sections of the galleries, while the rest of the collections were left untouched. The thieves seemed to have been restrained from taking other objects from the museum by a prior act of selection that specified which objects were to be taken and which were not. This prior act of selection would indicate (in this example) that classification precedes collection. The gang collected only what was classified as suitable by the art dealer. Such a process of prior classification was necessary for the thieves to know what to take and what to avoid. Furthermore, what seems to have motivated the classification was the monetary value that the art dealer must have seen in the objects. Taking such a scenario to the extreme, one might see that classification functions as the operational scheme of motivation. However, this leads us back to the question of whether the motivation to collect is itself classificatory – so that collection functions as the enactment of the prior mental act of classification – or whether collection is inescapably a process that discriminates between what is and what is not collected. In this example, we find that collection is an enactment of a classificatory process because the knowledge one derives from classification is necessary to implement the desires that motivated the classification in the first place.

In the Biblical account of Noah's ark, I argue that it was not Noah who collected, but God himself who collected through Noah's willingness to follow his instructions. This implies that God must have predetermined what he wished to collect. However, such a suggestion carries the problem of reducing God to the role of a simple classifier. That is, God is often understood to be a higher order of being, and to associate him with the role of a classifier would be to relegate or even deny his ontological status. As the Biblical account goes, Noah had been seeking to convert the people around him for well over 100 years, but they refused to hear him and in their refusal, they earned the wrath of God. The people that God did not allow to enter the ark were people who by their actions refused to be obedient to him, unlike Noah and his children. In the story of the Aitape tsunami we find the tidal wave rushing through villages and collecting what it did at its own discretion, and it is difficult to ascertain whether what was collected, destroyed or lost through the wave was predetermined. What was collected by the tsunami is a loss to the surviving relatives of those who perished, and what was destroyed by the Biblical flood was what Noah did not collect. In the theft of collections at the PNG National Museum, we encounter an instance of classification that precedes collection which binds collection effectively with knowledge. Such a knowledge is necessary for fulfilling the purposes which motivated the organisation and execution of the crime in the first place. This final example suggests that collection is classificatory only when it is tied to a need that requires the knowledge of types for its execution.

Conclusion

In this chapter, I have assembled a series of scenarios through which collections may be apprehended as a way of being. These instances show how collections appear either in a person's mind; in a collection of museum objects; as a process of gathering together in a seminar room; in a men's house on the Sepik river; as a group of men who constitute a criminal gang; or in the members of a team working together to present an exhibition at the PNG National Museum. I would think of scenarios such as anthropologists gathering in a seminar room; Iatmul men gathering together as a clan to perform a mortuary ceremonial; a bunch of museum attendees looking at a collection of artefacts in an exhibition; or indeed any collective unit doing something in concert, as instances which exemplify the notion of collections as a way of being. This conception of being is tantamount to saying that a collection is greater than the sum of its parts (see Baal 1994: 99; Pearce 1992) by which I have in mind a synergistic conception of being whereby the interaction between two or more people, things or agents gives rise to a combined effect that is greater than individual persons or things could effect on their own accord.

The way in which collectivities enact their way of life is structured within a particular nexus of relations which allow people involved to define themselves differently in different moments. To think of collections appearing either in the form of collectivities or in terms of individual life and experience in classificatory terms is to approach social life and experience mainly as an epistemological attitude, which obviates a more subtle ontology that lies buried beneath layers of social relations and the orientation or comportment towards the world of equipment. And by an epistemological attitude I mean a detached reflection as opposed to a pre-reflexive analysis. The Iatmul epistemological scheme of explanations is pre-reflexive in the sense that the explanations were given by my interlocutors without reflecting on whether their explanations constituted an epistemology. If the Iatmul juxtapose analogies, the task of the analyst is to catch the internal relation contained in such analogies. Collections serve an epistemological function when they are bound up with classification. I have also argued critically that classification is a kind of epistemological midwife that facilitates management and control over inherent diversity in collections.

The discussion has also implicated the manner in which time is involved in the constituting of collection as a way of being. This appears most visibly in scenarios such as the speaker who gives a seminar to anthropologists. A question prompted the speaker to collect himself before he could respond to the charge laid against him by a member of the audience. In this instance of collection and response, the speaker is made to go back and retrace his steps and the logic of his arguments before reasserting his position or taking on the insights offered by such an exchange. It is in this moment of loss and projection that, I think, the temporal life of collections as a way of being is made most visible. The movement of thought from the initial point of shattering (or devastation) to a reply or the re-gathering of 'pieces' is a temporal experience. In this process, collection assumes a synthetic behaviour of piecing together temporal moments, and in so doing it contrives a sense of continuity that is predicated upon a condition of loss. Loss, therefore, has a productive role in the temporal constitution of collections.

To explicate this, I have tried to retain pride of place for the sense in which loss is integral to the temporal character of collections. This sense of loss is evident in cases such as the museum exhibition which recalled the loss of life caused by the tsunami; the seminar presenter; the student who forgets her keys and has to return to her room to collect them; Bateson's discussion of the anthropologist who discovers shocking gaps in the information he has collected from his field research; the Iatmul women who empty water that has collected in their canoes before undertaking their errands; the Biblical account of flood and the collection of animals in the face of impending loss; or the collections that were stolen from the PNG National Museum.

Against this background of descriptions of loss, I find a problem in the way in which collections have been depicted as a narrative of sequential evolution with a continuous thread through which human experience unfolds (Cardinal 1994: 68). The sense of loss described in the scenarios shows that loss (cf. Kirsch 2001; Weiner 1995) is integral to the constitution of collections, since this kind of loss seems to imbue collections with a temporal life and efficacy. The affinity between classification, continuity and collection becomes clear in contemporary anthropological writing on collectible art forms, such as the ones described by Gell (1998: 156–8; 221– 58) in his theory of art and agency. Gell's rendition of the phenomenological notions of retention and protension – which are derived from a Husserlian conception of time consciousness – does not accommodate the sense of loss which we have encountered here.

Gell used the notions of retention and protension to describe how an oeuvre of art works, such as those of Marcel Duchamp, behaves in ways analogous to a phenomenological scheme of perception and time consciousness. The notions of retention and protension serve a function of continuity which ensures that impressional contents of perception are integrated into a continuum which allows someone to refer to past experiences and future hopes and expectations. Along this line of thinking one might see Gell's books such as the *Anthropology of Time* (1992), *Wrapping in Images* (1993) and *Art and Agency* (1998) as an oeuvre, with each of them anticipating and recapitulating previous works. A sense of continuity threads through these pieces. Working under the spell of Husserlian phenomenology, Gell uses such a model of time to explain how the art of perception operates as a series of constant 'nows' with each piece serving as a temporal moment that encompasses the past and the future moments and brings them into a consciousness of the now. On this score, Baudrillard (1994: 17) provides a telling commentary relevant to Gell's oeuvre, as we find in the following observation:

> The man who collects things may already be dead, yet he manages to literally outlive himself through his collection, which originating within this life, recapitulates him beyond the point of death by absorbing death itself into the series and the cycle.
>
> (original emphasis removed)

Despite death, continuity thrives. However, the scenarios described in this chapter uncover a sense of loss which the analytical narratives of continuity in collections often overlook. Gell's theory of an extended mind (see Gell 1998: 221–58) represents just such a preoccupation with continuity associated with collectible art forms. In this account I have tried to show that there are collections which are sometimes lost or reconfigured elsewhere, like Iatmul clans, and at other times a collection can be no longer a collection because it is lost forever, like the stolen pieces from the PNG National Museum or the lives lost in the tsunami. It is in loss that the temporal life of collections is constituted.

Acknowledgements

I am extremely grateful to the editors of this volume for all their time, help and stimulating discussion; to Marilyn Strathern for her customary incisions, and other friends including Anita Herle and Manpreet Janeja for comments on earlier drafts. I alone am responsible for all the weaknesses of this argument. A version of this paper was written in Rabaul, Papua New Guinea, while I was on a research trip, and I am grateful to Nick Lyons of Rabaul Metal Industries, who allowed me the use of his computer and email to send a draft off to colleagues and the editors in England.

Notes

1 The tsunami that hit PNG was located along the coast directly east of Indonesia and had a magnitude of 7.0 on the Richter scale, while that which devastated lives in countries such as Indonesia and Thailand on Boxing Day 2004 had a magnitude of 8.7 and claimed several thousand lives compared to the lesser toll of the PNG tsunami.

2 Iatmul *wasari* are like nicknames but their version of nicknames or same-names, as I call it here, stems from a common totemic denominator bound up with cosmological understandings which inform their system of personal names (see Bateson 1958; Moutu 2003; Wassmann 1990; 1991).

3 The sense of collection deployed here conveys the impression of that which is greater than the sum of its parts (see Baal 1994: 99, 106). My account here does

not address the issues of class and membership, etc. such as we find in set theory for instance. But collection as a logical activity appears in Cantor's theory of sets where he defines class as 'a collection into a whole of definite objects of intuition' (Cantor 1962: 282, cited in Grossman 1983: 204).

4 This is an anthropological rendition of the Heidegerrian notion of *Dasein* as 'being-in-the-world and being-with-others' (Heidegger 1962). Such a rendition may run contrary to Heidegger's intention to reconcile the meaning of 'Being' (Heidegger 1962). In a critical response to Sartre's psychological theory of imagination, and because it betrays the ontological sense of otherness, Heidegger explains that this conception of *Dasein* in terms of 'being with and being oneself' (1962: section IV–V) was never intended to be 'an incidental contribution to sociology' (Heidegger 1978: 221). I am, however, proposing that one might import and apply the Heideggerian notion of being-with-others in a way reminiscent of the anthropological notion of relations (cf. Weiner 2001). In a manner akin to people gathering together, collections behave in ways similar to the phenomenological comportment of 'relations' (Strathern 2000), which bring together disparate elements within its reach to make meaning possible. It is in such a gathering that collection is instantiated as a way of being.

5 See Herle and Moutu (2003) for a recent ethnographic exhibition of Iatmul art objects.

References

Baal, M. (1994) 'Telling objects: a narrative perspective on collecting', in J. Elsner and R. Cardinal (eds) *The Cultures of Collecting*, London: Reaktion Books.

Bateson, G. (1958) *Naven*, Stanford: Stanford University Press.

——(1936) 'Music in New Guinea', *Eagle*, 48(214):158–70.

Baudrillard, J. (1994) 'The system of collecting' in J. Elsner and R. Cardinal (eds) *The Cultures of Collecting*, Cambridge MA: Harvard University Press.

Benjamin, W. (1999) [1970] *Illuminations*, trans. H. Zorn, London: Pimlico.

Cantor, G. (1962) *Of Men and Numbers*, New York: Dodd, Mead.

Cardinal, R. (1994) 'Collecting and collage-making: the case of Kurt Schwitters', in J. Elsner and R. Cardinal (eds) *The Cultures of Collecting*, London: Reaktion Books.

Elsner, J. and R. Cardinal (1994) 'Introduction', in J. Elsner and R. Cardinal (eds) *The Cultures of Collecting*, London: Reaktion Books.

Gell, A. (1999) *The Art of Anthropology*, Oxford: Berg Publishers.

——(1998) *Art and Agency*, Oxford: Oxford University Press.

——(1993) *Wrapping in Images*, Oxford: Clarendon Press.

——(1992) *Anthropology of Time*, Oxford: Berg Publishers.

Grossmann, R. (1983) *The Categorical Structure of the World*, Bloomington: Indiana University Press.

Heidegger, M. (1978) *Basic Writings*, ed. D. F. Krell, London: Routledge.

——(1962) *Being and Time*, trans. E. Robinson and J. Macquarrie, Oxford: Blackwell.

Herle, A. and A. Moutu (2003) *Paired Brothers: Revelation and Concealment in Iatmul Ritual Art from the Sepik, Papua New Guinea*, Cambridge: Cambridge Museum of Archaeology and Anthropology.

Kirsch, S. (2001) 'Lost Worlds', *Current Anthropology*, 42(2): 167–98.

Moutu, A. (2003) 'Names are thicker than blood: concept of persons and ownership amongst the Iatmul', unpublished Ph.D. dissertation, University of Cambridge.

Narokobi, B. (1983) *Melanesian Way*, Port Moresby: Institute of Papua New Guinea Studies.

Pearce, S. (1995) *On Collecting*, London: Routledge.

——(1992) *Museums, Objects and Collection*, Leicester: Leicester University Press.

Schor, N. (1994) 'Collecting Paris', in J. Elsner and R. Cardinal (eds) *The Cultures of Collecting*, London: Reaktion Books.

Strathern, M. (2000) 'Emergent properties', Robert and Maurine Rothschild Distinguished Lecture, Department of History of Science, Harvard University.

Wassmann, J. (1991) *The Song to the Flying Fox*, Port Moresby: Institute of PNG Studies.

——(1990) 'The Nyaura concepts of space and time', in N. Lutkehaus, C. Kaufmann, W. E. Mitchell, D. Newton, L. Osmundsen and M. Schuster (eds) *Sepik Heritage: Tradition and Change in Papua New Guinea*, Bathurst NSW: Crawford House Press.

Weiner, J. (2001) *Tree Leaf Talk: a Heideggerian Anthropology*, Oxford: Berg Publishers.

——(1995) *The Lost Drum: Myth of Sexuality in Papua New Guinea and Beyond*, Wisconsin: Wisconsin University Press.

6

SEPARATING AND CONTAINING PEOPLE AND THINGS IN MONGOLIA

Rebecca Empson

The concept of 'fortune' (*xishig*) permeates many aspects of Mongolian social life. It motivates practices that involve separating (*avax*, *salgax*) a piece from a person, animal or thing at moments of departure or transition, and then containing (*xadgalax*) it in a different form. In this chapter, I use the concept of fortune to think about things that are either displayed on top of or concealed inside the chest kept in every Mongolian household. Thinking about the Mongolian concept of fortune through these things will allow us to question what kinship is, or looks like, in Mongolia. It reveals that the containment of a part, when separated from a whole, is essential for the maintenance of different kin relations. Furthermore, the invitation to 'see' kin relations through these things elicits the realisation of different relations at a single moment in time. When viewed together, they can be said to reveal a person made from each of the parts. Examining the means by which a thing is contained and the access people have to it, as well as its intended audience, will show how kinship is constituted through the separation of people and attention to things. In conclusion, I suggest that in the absence of people, the *doing* involved in making things visible or invisible makes relations. In this sense, 'vision' becomes the tool by which relations are created.

Anthropological approaches to Mongolian kinship have tended to emphasise agnatic relations, based on the idea of clans that preserve the 'shared bone' of patrilineal ancestors (cf. Vreeland 1954; Lévi-Strauss 1969). Moving away from these structural analyses, recent approaches to kinship in anthropology have emphasised a relational approach, whereby people are able to shift between different modes of engagement depending on context. Here, relations themselves exist prior to the position of the person with whom the relation is held and it is people who are able to move between them (Strathern 1990; Viveiros de Castro 2004). In such a way, Strathern has emphasised that: 'a performance is always a reduction: a single act created out of composite relations' (Strathern 1994: 248). The aim of this paper is to explore how such an approach, which acknowledges shifting relational perspectives, might inform the way in which relations in Mongolia are created through the separation and containment of things. It does not require any great leap of the imagination to find that people and things are interchangeable in Mongolia in different ways. Objects in Mongolia often command the same respect as would be shown to human beings. This is not because these things 'stand for' people. Rather objects, like humans, contain another dimension of the visible world and something of the essence of the person is thought to adhere to their belongings. Chabros states that in Mongolia: 'Analogies of form perceived between quite different and unconnected objects may result in the qualities of one object being attributed to the other' (Chabros 1987: 270).[1] The tendency in Mongolia to perceive analogies, to see one thing as another, to discover relations between visible and hidden things, is the focus of this chapter.

Mongolians use the very general term 'thing' (*yum*) to refer to made or found things, but things do not always have to be material artefacts.[2] Mongolians distinguish between visible things (*xaragdax yum*) and invisible things (*xaragdaxgüi yum*), so that things can also be events and matters. I suggest that things, placed on top of and inside the household chest, together act as a site that absorbs aspects of people's relations and draws attention to relations in the absence of people. These things can be viewed as vessels that remain in place and act as the 'ideal kin group' or person, as people necessarily move away from the house and shift different ways of reckoning relations. They allow for the continuation of certain relations that cannot be enacted in shared place. In all cases, the thing is viewed as a piece that has been separated in order to be contained, and is held to be a powerful essence or composite part of a person. Given this similarity, I will proceed to use the term 'thing' to talk about actual artefacts as well as pieces of people. It is suggested that the separation of people, or the ability to reflect on social relations through the containment of some part, is essential for the growing of kin relations in Mongolia.

The concept of fortune

It is important to stress that pieces, which are contained when something has been separated, are not simply visual substitutes, icons or proxies for absent people (cf. Weiner 1985). Instead, relations come into existence through the creation of these things. Mongolians hold that, in order for certain relations to continue, multiply and grow, people, animals, or things have to be separated so that a necessary aspect of them can be contained and a liveable version of a relationship becomes possible. This general concept is grounded in the cosmological idea of *xishig* or fortune. As an abstract quality, it is difficult to generalise about the principles of fortune. The concept can be understood on various levels, applying to many aspects of social life (cf. Holbraad, Chapter 9 of this volume). Primarily, *xishig* refers to the concept of a life-force or animating essence that can be understood through actions that involve attending to a part or portion that fuels a whole. Because it is mobile, the exact place or property of this animating essence is difficult to locate. The uncertain residence or property of fortune means that people take daily precautions so as not to lose it or let it slip away unnoticed to outsiders. For example, when a cow has been sold and is about to be separated from the herd, a woman will silently wipe the inside of her coat across the muzzle of the animal and detach a piece of its tail hair to keep safely contained in the house (cf. Montell 1934: 109). Because the fortune that allows cattle to reproduce and prosper may be contained in just one cow, actions that involve keeping back a piece ensure that the animating life-force, essential to the whole herd, does not depart with that single animal. When something is separated, be it an animal, a family member, or some thing, precautions that involve keeping a piece back ensure that the essence, or fortune, is retained to support the whole.[3]

In response to my enquiries about the Mongolian idea of fortune during fieldwork with Buryat nomadic herders in Northeast Mongolia, people referred to practices, or described scenarios, that would illustrate an aspect of this concept. It seemed as if fortune could only really be understood if thought about through actions that involved attending to things. Frustrated at my inability to grasp the fluid nature of fortune, one friend finally presented the following scenario:

> Rebecca, if you want to understand what fortune means, imagine a brick building. If you take just one brick out, the whole building might fall down. You may try to find a single brick you can take so that the building still remains. Maybe your whole life you cannot find this brick, so instead you take precautions. You decide not to take a whole brick out but just scrape away a little at a time from different bricks. In this way you ensure you always keep a little back in order to maintain the whole: it may contain the fortune.

In tracing the origin of the Mongolian word, Chabros (1992: 155) suggests that *xishig* primarily refers to the idea of 'portion'. The term is used in 'The Secret History of the Mongols' to refer to the selected bodyguards (*xishigten*) that protected Chinggis Xaan (cf. Lessing 1960: 460).[4] Later, Chabros (1992) explains, the word came to be associated with wider notions of favour, good-fortune and benefit. It came to encompass broader meanings, including that of an individual's share or portion of the vital energy that forms a lineage. Understanding fortune as an energy or vital portion, which animates the kin group and is passed on to each of its individual members, is fitting for my analysis. In this general sense, fortune is seen to increase the kin group's life-potential as a kind of sacred essence or source, fulfilling a common desire to increase one's domestic herds and have numerous children.

Like Mauss's (1972: 133–49) famous description of Melanesian *mana*, fortune in the wider Mongolian sense can be used as an adjective, noun and verb. It is divisible yet whole, a force, being, action, quality and state. The idea of fortune can be viewed as a series of fluid notions. For example, while it is possible to exchange an object or animal that may contain fortune for something else, this exchange does not demand a return. In turn, while wealth may be the result of accumulative fortune, fortune does not generate profit in the sense of monetary value. But fortune does not simply dwell on its own. Whether it resides in a herd of animals or a single piece of cloth, it is attached in a relation to a person, or a group of people. Often irreducible to a single meaning, the Mongol term *xishig* is frequently used to refer to different things when paired with a second term. It can be a rare gift received from a highly esteemed person (*buyan xishig*), or from one's animals (*malyn xishig*), without the giver expecting returns. Such pairing intensifies the good-fortune, vital-essence sense rather than modifying it. A story someone tells you or some crucial information accidentally overheard can be fortunate (*amny xishig*). A sweet given by a child after they have received blessing (*myalaax*) or an object that has brought about fortuitous events (*xishigtei yum*) can also contain fortune. A person or family can have it (*xishigtei xün, ail*) when their health and work go well and animals and food are plentiful.

Using fortune to think about things

We have seen that Mongolians think about fortune in multiple ways. Fortune can change location, disperse, and suddenly emerge again in an interaction. In this section I suggest that the concept of separating in order to contain fortune can be transposed analogically to ideas about kinship, and specifically to the idea that the creation of kinship in Mongolia is achieved through the separation of bodies. Given this similarity, I shall use the idea of a (separated) portion that animates a whole, to think through practices that involve separating yet containing relations through things. This is of great importance for Mongolians because the separation and assemblage of kin members at different seasonal places means that maintaining a connection with a person, place, or thing is essential. Because movement is an inherent aspect of Mongolian kinship, I will show that relations based on affinity, which involve the separation and incorporation of difference, are the necessary, yet invisible, background that support the visibly fore-grounded relations based on consanguinity, containment and sameness. The things that I focus on can be found inside most Mongolian households. I shall argue that the ways in which they are displayed parallels the concealment or display of different ways of reckoning kinship. When viewed together, these things could be seen to provide an ensemble of multiple ways of reckoning kinship in Mongolia. They allow the viewer to apprehend him or herself as an exemplary person made from several severed parts.

Drawing on Gell's (1998) idea that material objects can act as indexes that appear to abduct agency, things kept inside and on top of the chest come to stand for, and act as, instruments of social agency and relatedness. While these things do index certain current relations, viewing or attending to them also initiates the possibility of new relations. These things can thus be viewed as tools or instruments that index certain ideas that produce an effect, such as a motivation or interpretation, on behalf of the recipient who views or uses the thing. For example, we will see that photographic montages are a way for agnatic kin groups to reveal their infinite networks to outsiders. I should make it clear that while I do draw on Gell's (1998) wider point that objects have an effect (in this chapter, kinship is the effect), I do not use his extensive abduction thesis to explain how things appear to have agency. However, it is important to note that some of the things discussed in this chapter do have a kind of agency in themselves. For example, when a person leaves their natal home, pieces that are left behind ensure that they are able to continue these relations, but for the person who remains and attends to these pieces, the objects have a kind of agency in that their containment is seen to increase the life-potential of the kin group. In this sense, the thing can have an effect or a type of agency depending on whose perspective we take. The things which I look at can also be viewed as distributed extensions of a relation or parts of a person. This is not a mystical idea of the person. It is imperative for Mongolians, who are nomadic herders, that people are able to manifest themselves, via things, in different spatio-temporal locations, beyond the confines of a single bodily form. In this way, people are not just where their bodies are, but in many different places simultaneously (cf. Strathern 1994; Gell 1998: 21). By exploring the kind of technology that reveals or conceals relations, we will see that objects do not just commemorate past relations, they also initiate relations that make up current kin.

Understanding kinship through things

Agnatic kinship, based on the idea of shared bone (*etsgiin töröl, yasan töröl*), permeates much of Mongolian life. Virilocal residence is expected, and property, mostly in the form of animals, is traditionally distributed among sons. The youngest son of a family inherits the bulk of his father's livestock, including the family hearth that is held to represent the continuity of patrilineal descent. Nevertheless, throughout the year, wooden houses (*baishin*) as well as Mongolian felt tents (*ger*), and the people who inhabit them, move over the landscape. As the physical shell of a house reconstitutes itself in different places, the people who inhabit a house also change seasonally. Throughout the year, people move from a house to different locations with different networks of people, in order to attend school, work, hunt, marry, or trade. While summer encampments gather together extended relatives in order to help with the preparation of milk products, winter encampments are often only inhabited by a few family members. During the autumn and spring, children attend school in district centres and younger family members may move away from the household to engage in temporary work, trade, or hunting. Although virilocal residence is expected, and agnatic kinship is held to dominate kin relations in Mongolia, throughout the year different forms of sociality are enacted in different places. People have to move to different locations, activating other types of relations, while still being tied to their agnatic household. This section will focus on the way in which the movement of people and place is managed through different things that are kept in the household chest.

Both wooden houses and Mongolian felt tents are prevalent in the countryside, and throughout the year people interchange kinds of residence. For example, a family may live in a wooden house at their summer pasture, but occupy a felt tent at their winter, spring and autumn pasture. When fixed in a particular space, the house (be it a wooden house or a felt tent) is made a container for storing valued possessions, meeting with visitors, sleeping and eating, and for moments when one needs to sit for a long period to fix or sew something. As a one-roomed, open-plan space, there are no personal areas inside a Mongolian house. Instead gender, hierarchy and status define the interior. This adaptability allows for the incorporation of different configurations of kin members, as well as outsiders, at any given moment. For example, an elderly female guest will know in exactly which part of the house to sit as she enters an unknown person's house. Mongolian kin terms also allow for the incorporation of outsiders. While most terms between kin are fixed and categorise people in terms of hierarchy and gender, some terms are both classificatory and un-gendered.[5] For example the term 'younger sibling' (düü), used for people younger than the speaker, does not specify gender or type of relation. Terms such as these are not ambiguous for Mongols. It is only because their range of meaning is different from anything we are familiar with in English that they may, at first, seem ambiguous to us. In addition to fixed kinship terms, Mongols need these shifting and flexible terms in order to be able to incorporate people who come in and out of the house whom they sometimes want to treat as kin. In turn, while away from relatives, people are able to establish sibling-like relations with others through the use of such terms.

The seasonal movement of people, and the places they inhabit, creates the continual need to relocate both physical and relational boundaries. This can give rise to the feeling that there is no fixed place in which to situate people when trying to define kin relations. For Mongolians, however, the separation and incorporation of people and place is not unsettling or difficult.[6] They overcome this movement by ensuring that certain things remain contained inside the house as people and houses move location. These things act as sites for containing particular aspects of people's relations in the absence of people. Instead of people constituting a home, in Mongolia, valued things inside the house remain in place and stand for relations that are attached to it. This idea is also extended to the landscape surrounding the house, which is marked with stone cairns, sacred trees, buried placentas and tethering posts that invoke a sense of inhabited space in the absence of houses and people.

To avoid an ahistorical account, before I begin to explain how people maintain relations through the containment of things, the genealogy of revealing or concealing relations in the house should be placed in brief historical perspective. During the socialist period, Buddhist icons and shamanic implements were prohibited from being placed on view, but statues of Lenin and posters depicting, for example, strong industrious cooperative workers or joyful rosy-cheeked pioneers were openly displayed. Genealogical diagrams (*ugiin bichig*), going back over seven or eight generations through agnatic lines, were either burnt or hidden in the bottom of chests. Differences, especially of an ethnic or class kind, were thought of as politically polluting and people were forced to use their father's name as a surname instead of their clan name (cf. Humphrey 1973: 477). The Buryats, an ethnic Mongolian group on the northern Mongolian-Russian border with whom I did my fieldwork, migrated to Mongolia from Russian Buryatia in the early 1900s. They experienced extreme forms of political persecution during the socialist period, to such an extent that during mass purges in the 1930s, almost all the male members of the community were killed or taken away. Turning people away from their kin networks, and the distinctions that these create, has concealed the diverse ways in which Mongols actually reckon kin relations and conceive of the person.

As a general introduction to ideas about kinship in Mongolia, Mongolian procreation beliefs hold that an infant has to be separated from the spirit world, which makes it vulnerable as a human. After this vulnerable stage, the shared substance of 'bone' from the father is emphasised. But while agnatic kinship may be the foundation for many kin relations in Mongolia, these relations coexist with other ways of conceiving kin. Ideas about lay-reincarnations (*irgej töröx*, *daxin töröx*), blood relations (*ekhiin töröl*, *tsusan töröl*) based on movement, links with one's birthplace and the deceased, as well as age-sets also form lasting kin or 'kin-like' relations. This multiplicity allows for people to be other things, while at the same time being defined by their bones and ethnic identity.[7] A focus on things kept inside the family chest allows us to explore the ways in which agnatic kinship coexists with, and is indeed dependent on, these other modes of kinship, through the way in which these relations are contained in different things that are deliberately displayed or concealed from view. To paraphrase Strathern; these 'deliberate provocations to vision' become a way for Mongols to instantiate different networks of relations (cf. Strathern 1994: 243).

The things on which I focus pivot around two distinct ways of reckoning relatedness. First, the relations that are visible on the chest's surface, in the distribution of family property, through communal ritual, and in formalised language are based on the idea of shared 'bone' from one's agnatic forefathers. Such relations exemplify an ideology of patrilineal descent and the continuation of relations over generations. They are, however, dependent on a second mode of relatedness, involving the separation and incorporation of people. For such groups to exist, people have to move, establish links with other groups, and incorporate non-kin outsiders. These mobile relations are based on the idea of 'shared blood' from one's mother. This provides an 'umbilical relation or communication' (*xüin xolboo, tsusan xolboo*) that is passed between a woman and her children, and between siblings. Blood relations are given anew each time a person is born and are drawn upon at different periods in a person's life as people are necessarily separated from each other in different locations. Such relations are not made visible in particular sites. Rather, they are hidden in parts that are kept inside the household chest. I turn now to examine how these relations are maintained, through an analysis of things kept in and around the Mongolian household chest.

Analysis of the household chest

Relations that are visibly displayed

In the northern, rear part of the Mongolian house, in the most honourable section (*xoimor*), opposite the door as one enters, stands a painted wooden chest (*avdar*). The chest may be covered in embroideries or painted with inter-locking patterns (*xee*). The things that I am going to discuss can all be found around or inside this large chest. On the chest's surface, visible prized possessions that indicate wealth and prestige are displayed. These include objects such as radios, clocks, batteries, perfume and so on. In the centre stands a large mirror. Surrounding this mirror on either side, or attached to the wall above, are two large frames containing a montage of three-quarter-length, portrait-style photographs (*jaaztai zurag*) of kin members on both the mother's and father's side. This montage creates a pile, or layering, of different images over time, as old photographs are concealed behind new ones.[8] Above the mirror, religious icons and images can be found that comprise a small shrine (*Burxan*) on which religious books (*sudar*), pictures of consecrated animals (*seterlesen mal*) and daily offerings of milk libations (*Burxandaa idee tavix*) are placed. Above this shrine, on the wall behind the chest, hang large painted portraits of deceased patrilineal relatives (*jaaztai taliigaachiin xörög*), shrouded in ceremonial silk scarves (*xadag*). These portraits occupy a high position, comparable to the sacred Buddhist images. They emphasise agnatic dominance in the household (cf. Sneath 2000: 224). Around this fixed display, embroideries (*xatgamal*), sewn by daughters-in-law, are hung, depicting their views on different family relations. Guns, used by men for hunting, are placed at its side. Things kept inside the chest are never revealed to guests and are concealed from general view.

Young daughters-in-law, separated from their natal homes, and elderly female household members are in charge of maintaining this very visual display. They feed it with offerings and attend to and change its form. In turn, visitors to a household are expected to respond to it. As one enters a house, after greeting the host, one is expected to go to the chest and, while bowing down towards it, knock one's head (*mörgöx*) against its surface three times and turn a prayer wheel or offer some money or sweets to the religious icons, or to a portrait of the host's deceased relative. In so doing, a visitor pays respect to their host by honouring the fact that they are a part of a wider network of people who respect their elders and the ancestral spirits of the landscape. In addition, because the mirror is at the centre, when attending to or viewing this display a person may catch a glimpse of themselves at the centre of these different imaginings of kinship. The display allows the viewer to respect their host while at the same time to imagine themselves as placed, albeit fleetingly, within this web of relations as a potential part of the network that they are honouring.

What kind of relations does the viewer and attendee honour through responding to these things? I suggest that photographic montages of living kin members, displayed in frames above the household chest, can be viewed as a modern take on the traditional Mongolian practice of recording genealogies. While Buryats in Mongolia are interested in maintaining genealogical records, their genealogical diagrams were often burnt during political purges in the 1930s. During the socialist prohibition of recording genealogies, Mongolians embraced the medium of displaying photographs to represent their kin. Unlike anthropological kinship diagrams, Buryat genealogical representations do not define age groups in hierarchy from the top to the bottom of the page, over generations. They depict kin relations in the form of a cluster of male descendents expanding outwards from a single founder in the middle or top half of the page. Given the increasing interest in tracing one's genealogical background, do these photographic montages provide a new technology for recording genealogical relations based on agnatic kinship?[9]

Photographic montages mirror some of the compositional forms used to represent relations in traditional Buryat genealogies. The photograph of a patrilineal elder is often placed, with his wife, in the centre of the frame. They are surrounded by their siblings and children, whose images extend outwards towards the periphery of the frame. Such composition mirrors Buryat genealogical diagrams and represents a centric view of kin relations that expands outwards from a patrilineal founder.[10] Deceased patrilineal kin members' portraits are hung above the photographic displays. The photographs can be seen to mimic the style of these portraits and thus enforce the dominant patrilineal ideology that they imply. On closer inspection, however, we see that what links people together in photographic displays differs from the agnatic links that join people together in genealogical diagrams. Photographic montages of kin members reckon relations through both the mother's and father's side. They also include photographs of school friends, people from one's summer pasture, work colleagues, and groups of people at other special events. Information such as ethnic background, class and status can be 'read' by viewing the locations in which the images have been taken, the clothes people are wearing, and the type of events celebrated. Viewing the display, visitors are able to infer their host's relation to other kin members, as well as friends and colleagues. The networks of relations depicted in these montages are an expansion of those found in traditional genealogical descriptions. Alongside relations based on the shared blood and bone from one's mother and father, other relations are also emphasised. Photographic montages thus replicate Buryat genealogical diagrams in their form, but extend their content to include other types of relations.[11]

Like genealogical diagrams, the montages also construct a 'portrait-chronicle' (cf. Sontag 2002a; 2002b) of previous connections, and remind one of kin members who are absent. In so doing, they depart from a single person's perspective and provide a memory-map in which past and present relations are imagined to exist at once. In Mongolia, having one's photograph taken involves posing front-on for the camera. To this extent all photographs are reproductions of each other; what makes an image 'good' to look at is that it looks at you. Instead of freezing individual characteristics or gestures, we see a replicated pose of motionless groups of people looking at us (cf. Bouquet 2001). As a person is able to quickly glean information from a genealogical record, so too is the viewer able to abstract information about crucial networks and relations from the montage. This view of several groups of people, looking out together from the display, dazzles the viewer with the multiple relations available to the people of that household. In this sense, the groups of people in photographic montages 'reach out to the consideration of others' (Humphrey 2002: 69, italics in original).[12] By drawing attention to the infinite networks available, the montage confuses the viewer as to who is and who is not kin.[13] Viewing the photographic montage in this way, people are not depicted as mobile individuals. Rather people become replicable members of static groups, with potentially infinite links to other groups.

Photograph montages, portraits of deceased elders, and shrines that honour the spirits of inhabited places (*baigaliin lus savdag*) outwardly display relations, with infinite connections, given through agnatic relations in a visible form. Such fore-grounded relations may subside at different periods in a person's life but they can always re-emerge and be drawn upon again. These images are not about person-to-person relations, but replicate relations between groups. For example, if a man decides to spend the spring building wooden houses and needs help tending his herds, he may turn to his brother who will assist him without expecting anything in return. For the person who attends and adds to the display, there is a sense that, although they move to different seasonal places, the chest's visible surface remains as a fixed site inside the house that increases over time. We can draw a parallel here with points in the landscape such as stone cairns (*oboos*). People make piles of offerings to these throughout the year and during communal ceremonies. The comparison is not just analytical: small pieces from these offerings (usually pieces of rice) are retained and stored in a bag (*dallagany uut*) at the family chest. These places anchor meetings between people in a fixed visible form. This technology is meant to be seen. Its efficacy, as I will show, acts as a shield against those relations that are concealed.

Concealed relations in hidden things

Things displayed on top of the chest, which are visible as soon as one enters the household, provide a site for preserving agnatic relations and extend these to include relations between wider groups of people. These connections are inherited; one is never fully separated from them. They increase or decrease according to where one chooses to locate oneself. Inside the chest, concealed from general view, are hidden things that have been detached from people at moments of separation and transformation. Such things are individually wrapped in blue ceremonial silk scarves and are carefully placed at the bottom of the chest among winter or summer clothing, as if they have the *potential* to move but must be contained. The things hidden in the bottom of chests that I focus on comprise of actual parts of people's bodies, such as pieces of umbilical cords and children's hair from the first hair-cutting ceremony. They are very rarely handled or exposed for view. I turn now to the way in which these things are produced and concealed in relation to ideas about 'shared blood'.

Like relations based on the idea of 'shared blood', things found in the bottom of chests are not passed on over generations. They are the products of the separation and movement of people between groups and are created out of alliance and exchange in one's own lifetime. The concept of 'sharing the same blood' is linked to the movement of women across agnatic kin groups.[14] Such relations are not contained in any particular visible location or site, such as a stone cairn. Instead, they are realised through a special type of relational communication (*xüin xolboo, tsusan xolboo*, literally: umbilical communication, blood communication) that allows people to have anticipations, feelings and premonitions about each other (*sovin tatax*, literally: premonition is pulling at me), even though they may be separated in terms of place. For example, if a person falls ill or suffers some accident while away from home, a mother or sibling will begin to feel pain in their body, have bad dreams and sense that the absent person is in danger. As children grow and leave the home, relations between a mother and her children, and between siblings, do not cease.

Equally, it is imperative that people who have this type of relation are physically separated from each other. This is because relations based on 'shared blood' or 'umbilical relation/communication' are considered to be too close to live with. For example, it was suggested to me that when a child is first born, the mother and child merge into and become one another so that the mother's body becomes child-like (*eejiin bie nyalxardag*, literally: a mother's body becomes wet and like an infant), expectantly craving sweets and gifts from visitors and strangers (*goridox*). The ritual cutting of the child's first hair creates a necessary distance between a mother and her child, separating their shared physicality. Similarly, twins are considered to have an intense form of umbilical relation. If one twin falls ill or suffers, the other will do so too. In order to lessen the effects of such a relation, twins go through a ritual whereby a piece of red rope, tied between their wrists, is severed. We can begin to see here that it is held to be necessary to detach oneself from the physical intensity of umbilical relations based on shared blood. By creating a physical distance and by giving a part of oneself away, a liveable version of the relation is formed. It is because of this that, when people are physically separated from each other, a part is produced during the act of separation. This part is carefully retained in order to maintain the relation in a separated form. Containing a part of a person's body at their natal home can be analytically compared to the concept of fortune, and the practice of separating yet containing, in three distinct ways.

First, by containing a piece of hair from the child's first haircutting ceremony, parents separate off and contain a part of their child at a point at which they are introduced to agnatic kin. The haircutting ceremony is seen to mark the point at which a young child, having fully rejected the temptation to maintain contact with difficult un-reincarnadted spirits, is secured in the human world. By keeping a part of this hair, which has been severed from the child at a point at which departure from relations with others and acceptance in the kin group is celebrated, children are formally bound to 'relations of bone'.[15] Second, in retaining a piece of the umbilical cord at their natal home, relations between a woman, her children, and between siblings, all of whom may later disperse, are maintained. It allows women, who move between groups and never fully belong to their groom's or father's agnatic kin, to maintain a partial connection with their natal home. This is exemplified in the term used for a bride as a 'person with an umbilical cord and an engagement' (*xüitei-süitei xün*), indicating that she is someone who is about to move to her groom's family, but still has continued relations with her natal home. Although people have to be physically separated, due to the intense aspect of these relations, people do draw upon them at different times throughout their life.[16] For example, a married female friend of mine, after having experienced a series of miscarriages attributed to spirit and human curses, drew on her natal family fortune by making offerings to their sacred tree. When the situation became worse due to intra-household feuds, she was able to return, albeit for a brief period, to her natal home. The umbilical cord is both an actual part of a person achieved through separation and an expression of a relation that, through separation, can reappear: its containment is achieved through departure, but it remains in order to allow for the possibility of return.

Finally, by retaining these pieces in her married house, a woman is able to solidify relations with her children even though she lives with her husband's family and is regarded as belonging to another group. It allows her children, who ultimately belong to her husband's kin group, to maintain a lasting tie of relatedness with their mother, their siblings and their place of birth, regardless of where they happen to be. Women often use these pieces as magical remedies for their children and as an aid for fertility. They both protect a person in a situation of crisis, and facilitate the possibility of future kin. By carefully hoarding a piece of the umbilical cord or pieces of the child's first hair in the family chest, the mother-child relationship (*ekh üriin xolboo*) is maintained as a possible relation, regardless of people's physical location. Through focus on objects in and around the household chest, we see that certain aspects of people's relations are safely contained and hidden from view, precisely because they are created when that part of a person, determined by gender and birth-order, separates, moves, and changes.[17] In this way, the contained and hidden parts become the visible manifestation of relations that are concealed from general view and are not displayed openly in daily life or through communal rituals.[18]

The practice of separating off a part at moments of transformation is also present at Mongolian rituals of death. Here, the giving away of pieces severs relations with the living in an acceptable way. When a person is about to be separated from their body, the dying person gives away their belongings in order to break attachment to people and things and free the soul (cf. Humphrey 2002).[19] Death can be seen as an extreme form of separation that does not allow for the possibility of return. While people create kinship through the accumulation of things, at death these things have to be disposed of, thereby cutting off further relations. It should be noted that deceased people's things are not kept in the household chest. Death is, thus, an extreme kind of separation that Mongolians have to manage in relation to ideas about the separation or containment of things. But it is not just at death that 'detachment from a person [is] achieved by giving something [of oneself] to them' (Humphrey 2002: 71). We have seen that living people also practise this form of detachment. Movement of people away from the house, in marriage for example, demands that people are separated on the condition that a part, or thing, is kept back.

The value of separation

Parts, hidden inside the chest, provide a vessel for what are otherwise location-less connections. These vessels are the outcome of relations that are volatile and uncertain, but they anchor people in relations that transcend a person's physical location and form. Traversing relations that are located in visible sites according to agnatic groups, invisible or hidden things, achieved through separation, allow for people to cross boundaries of agnatic relations. In this way, the parts do not simply contain or stand for relations but actively create and facilitate them. The point is not that these are somehow illicit connections.[20] Instead, relations based on separation and departure are necessary for sustaining the visibly enacted relations based on agnatic kinship. In turn, it is important to note that things contained in the bottom of chests are not about 'possession' in the Western sense. Instead, liveable relations come into existence through the creation of these things. Although they are highly valued, they are intrinsically tied to their original producer and cannot be used in exchange for something else (cf. Weiner 1992). They become material parts through movement and, in so doing, create a lasting connection to the person they were once attached to. The thing is, thus, never a full replication or replacement of the person, but a part that is necessarily different from its original form.[21] They also suggest a difficult connection with a relation that one must be separated from. Instead of viewing these things in terms of a resource, value is given to the exchange in the perspective that they allow. When viewing kin relations through these things, we make what is considered the periphery the centre. Through these parts of persons, difficult relations are maintained as open possibilities. By keeping and retaining a piece, an anticipated return to a possible version of the relationship is created (cf. Weiner 1985: 221).

Although these things could be viewed as icons, in that they are held to contain some part of a person in their absence, they are not passed on over generations. Instead, we have seen that they preserve the possibility of current relations between living people. Because they cannot be exchanged or substituted for another form, they could be viewed as 'hyper-personal objects' (Humphrey 2002). They are comparable to what Humphrey (2002: 67) has termed 'a refuge thing' (*xorgodson yum*), in that they have a hyper-identification with the person they belong to (or have been detached from). The spirit or soul (*süld, süns*) of a person is believed to be attached to such an object and they have to be looked after with care. When people move away from the household, such a piece (either an umbilical cord or a piece of hair) is retained at the moment of transition, and kept back by the people who remain. The 'hyper-personal' aspect of these things means that they have to be detached and separated from the person they are indexing. Once separated, they are carefully cared for by someone else, in part, because they provide vessels that accumulate fortune for the whole family. For example, several umbilical cords in a house are held to attract fertility and the possi-bility of more children. Instead of merging relations between people into groups and then making them visibly static, as with photographic montages, these things separate bodies and maintain a link with the person they were detached from. They can be seen to act as channels for living person-to-person relations.

Having used the concept of fortune to think through things in and around the household chest, certain ideas about Mongolian kinship emerge from our analysis. It has been suggested that relations based on agnatic networks are visibly foregrounded as immobile centres from which people reach out to different connections with other groups. These group relations are, however, dependent on the separation and incorporation of others. Relations from which one must be separated, in order to support the possible growth of this centre, are concealed from general view. For example, inside the chest a piece of hair is kept that has been detached from a child, ensuring that it trans-forms from semi-human outsider to agnatic kin member. These hidden pieces intercept and move away from the visible group relations. Through this movement these transformations also support the possible growth of the centre (cf. Empson 2003). By maintaining a part, they facilitate the possi-bility for relations to continue in a liveable form. Using the idea of 'separating in order to contain', the analysis can be extended further to focus on invisible things that emerge and make themselves known in people. Lay-reincarnations, which are common among Buryats in Mongolia, scramble any linear idea of shared substance and bring deceased relatives from either the father's or mother's side into the kin group.[22] While relations with the deceased are not contained in visible artefacts, they do continue through lay-reincarnations. Here a person's body becomes the vessel or container for a deceased person that moves, over time, to different bodily containers.[23] It is, then, important to note that it is not always material pieces that remain when people are separated and move. With lay-reincarnations, people make themselves visible in another bodily form (cf. Empson 2006).

The difference between things

The Mongolian concept of fortune provides a conceptual window through which kinship ideas can be discerned. Things, viewed as parts that are retained to sustain the whole, command our attention to different domains of connectedness between groups or individuals that extend beyond ideas about 'shared bone'. In this way, a corporal presence is not always necessary for maintaining relations (cf. Telfer 1999). In photographic montages, indi-vidual people are dislodged to reveal infinite connections between groups. These connections can be understood as immutable chains that are passed over generations. Parts, hidden inside the chest, provide temporary vessels for future meetings between people. When focusing on these pieces and attending to their containment, they seem to burst out from behind the static groups and draw attention to people's mobility. Although people may not visibly enact these relations in one location or site, the containment of particular parts, inside the household chest, anticipates alternative meetings between people.

In his seminal work on place, Casey (1998: 301–8) draws on Deleuze and Guattari's distinction between 'smooth' and 'striated' space. Striated space refers to a landscape with distinct points or sites that mark its surface, and can be identified and specified. Rather than residing in place, people move *through* striated space from one point or location to the next. In contrast, smooth space has indefinite extensions. People move *in* this space rather than to fixed points along a trajectory. Smooth space is filled with multiplicities. It has a non-limited possibility of localities that resist exact concentration or reproduction. I suggest that the distinction between striated and smooth space can be used to highlight the ideas concerning Mongolian kinship that I have presented so far. With striated space, containment, permanence and renewal over time are paramount. Within the household different sites, such as photomontages and portraits of deceased patrilineal elders, echo this idea. Like visible places in the landscape, such as *oboo*s which pile high on mountaintops and sacred trees which emerge with fluttering ribbons from dark ravines, people ensure these sites visibly accumulate and grow in order to allow for people to attend to networks that may be drawn upon in various configurations throughout a person's lifetime. Attending to these places, we find that people merge into groups that are fixed, passed on and contained over generations.

In contrast, people also have to negotiate an inevitable series of movements and transitions as they move about in an absolute passage without a fixed centre. Here, we find that people never return in the same way. The things hidden inside the chest provide temporary vessels or places where relations based on the premise of separation and movement may temporarily reside. Like the concept of fortune in Mongolia, these relations have the potential to extend to unlimited places. They are uncertain because they do not guarantee prolonged residence in any fixed place over time. With such varied and unpredictable residence, we find dispersal of these relations is a constantly impending possibility.[24] The varied location of animal fortune and the in-between position of incoming women and young infants allows for their extension to, and partial placement in, any given space as they emerge in varied relations at different moments in time. Given these multiple ways of containing past and present relations, the idea of 'commemoration' in the Western sense, seems inadequate. In the West, relations with the deceased are often maintained through commemorative sites and living people need the physical presence of each other for relations. In Mongolia, relations between living people are created via the careful containment of dynamic and variable things, but relations with the deceased are maintained through the site of a person's body (cf. Empson 2006). I suggest that instead of acting as sources in which people locate the memory of an absent person in a communal place, the things inside the chest work as channels that allow for relations to continue with people who are dispersed and separated. We have seen that these channels allow for spatio-temporal flexibility, whereby people do not need to be confined to relations within particular spatial coordinates (cf. Gell 1998: 222).

Revealing the whole through vision

Although people and animals move across the landscape in Mongolia and there is a sense of unbounded vastness, the household and domestic encampment is desired as a fixed centre that reconstitutes itself in different places. We have seen that the chest acts as this site, gathering together different aspects of people's relations. In this section I would like to clarify what happens when people actually view and engage with the display. First, I will examine the set of kinship perspectives present in the display. I suggest that they are dependent on each other, but only ever appear independently. Second, I show how the two perspectives can, at certain points, simultaneously reveal a whole. This is achieved when: (1) a person observes an exemplary person through their own image in the display; and (2) when an observer views a person looking at himself or herself through the chest's mirror. Finally, I explore the role of the mirror in Mongolia and examine its capacity to reflect or deflect knowledge.

Let us return to the chest, which stands on the ground at the back of the Mongolian house with various objects contained inside and displayed on top of it. The way in which these objects are displayed can be taken as a template according to which Mongols view the person. Photographic montages outwardly depict the person as a replicate member of a whole group with links to other groups. When we switch perspective to the hidden parts that are usually delegated to the periphery, however, relations based on movement and transformation momentarily become a different kind of centre (cf. Wagner 1987). In order to understand how these two perspectives are dependent on each other, I divert briefly to examine the Rubin vase-profile illusion (cf. Arnheim 2002: 223). The Rubin vase-profile illusion, developed in 1915 by the psychologist Edgar Rubin, is an image that most of us are familiar with. In this image, we either see two black profiles facing each other, in front of a white background, or a white vase on a black background. Rubin developed this image to illustrate the dynamic nature of subtle perceptual processes. Because one of the contours of the image is shared with the other, it is difficult to perceive both images simultaneously. Instead, our vision fluctuates between the vase and the profiles. As one image becomes the background, the other becomes the foreground and vice-versa. The ability to see one image, and then the other, but not the two simultaneously, is referred to as 'contour rivalry' (i.e. we shift attention between the shape or the contour). The reversal of images that the observer perceives in the vase-profile illusion is due to their individual tendency toward biasing either the shapes or contours, making one interpretation stronger than the other. With regard to the chest, we have seen that things displayed on top of or inside the chest allow us to switch perspectives between different ways of imagining kinship in Mongolia. When first viewed, agnatic relations are foregrounded on top of the chest, and the actual chest, as well as its contents, serve as a physical as well as a relational background for these relations. When we switch perspective to the parts contained inside the chest, however, we see that people have to transform and separate so that agnatic relations can continue. Through the Rubin's figure-ground reversal, we can see how Mongolians alternate between a set of relational perspectives that are dependent on each other.[25]

I would like to push the analysis beyond the idea of alternating constituent perspectives and suggest that, at certain moments, the two perspectives can be revealed simultaneously. While each aspect of the display mirrors a different way of tracing relations between kin, together they form an ensemble of the different relations that make a person. In the centre of the display stands a mirror, so that while standing in front of it the viewer sees a reflection of themselves looking back at them. Through this mirror reversal, the display allows us to simultaneously gaze at ourselves, while constructing a figure that stares back at us with our own eyes (see Figure 6.1).[26] The display structures our vision so that a very particular image of ourselves becomes visible. In this sense, looking at the display always involves looking at and making ourselves visible in a particular form (cf. Sobchack 1992: 51). The chest structures our vision, gathering together these different

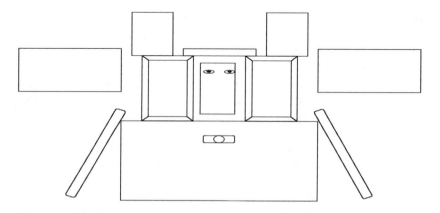

Figure 6.1 The Mongolian Household Chest. In viewing the display the parts come together to form a person.

aspects of the person into a single image, allowing us to draw out the different relations through our gaze (cf. Strathern 1994).

While viewing each of the separate parts prompts a different reflection of the person, viewing the display in full, and seeing oneself through it, makes all of these relations visible at once. In turn, if we bring in the perspective of an observer who views a person looking at themselves through the display, the chest can be said to reveal a person as constructed out of all the parts. While the viewer's gaze simultaneously looks at and is looked back at, the observer and the viewer see a figure constructed out of all the parts. Here, the chest is foregrounded as a figure due to the viewer's gaze which acts as a necessary background.

I am not proposing that the concealed parts are suddenly physically revealed when people look at themselves through the chest. Rather the chest, as a whole, becomes visible as a site that is able to foreground agnatic relations due to the support (or background) of those relations based on movement and transformation. The invisible, hidden parts, generated through separation, support the possibility for the visible parts that constitute agnatic relations. When viewing the display in full, a person is revealed as constituted by all these things through their own gaze. Each of the things that we have focused on make parts of people's relations visible at different moments in time, but when we view ourselves through the display, the parts appear together to form a site that reveals a person made possible through each of them.

At the beginning of this paper I suggested that the creation of kinship in Mongolia is achieved through the separation of bodies. The separating, merging and remaking of bodies has been an underlying theme throughout this discussion. While much attention has been given to the necessity of separating people through the containment of parts, by viewing the display in full and seeing a person through it, what flashes into view, as one glances at oneself at the centre of this display, is a calling into being of the person who views it. Viveiros de Castro (2004), in a chapter concerning, among other things, Piro concepts of the person, argues that the production of (consanguineal) relatives requires the intervention of (potential affine) non-relatives, and this can only mean the counter-invention of some relatives as non-relatives. Among the Piro, what distinguishes consanguineal relatives from affinal relatives are their bodily differences. If the body is the site of difference, then a difference is required in order to make bodies by means of other bodies (cf. Viveiros de Castro 2004: 7). Kinship is thus in a state of reciprocal dependence whereby non-relatives are needed to make relatives and vice-versa. The discussion concerning the two constitutive perspectives resonates with this point. The figure that is revealed through the display also establishes a similar type of perspectival difference. As a person is revealed in the display the chest becomes the site and instrument of this bodily differentiation (cf. Viveiros de Castro 2004: 8). In this sense, perception, or vision of self, is dependent on this instant of reciprocal gaze, whereby the detached pieces form a whole that can be looked at, in order to be able to see ourself. I am not referring to the separate parts here. I am referring to the image that is produced through the chest as a whole. One result of experiencing this duality of looking at and being looked back at is that the person we encounter, in the context of the mirror, is not a person as an exact replication of our self, but rather a prototype of a person that can only be seen through its separation.[27] In such a way, the chest transfigures and refracts the visible world, rather than merely duplicating it. It allows the viewer to see a transformed image of himself or herself. The chest thus provides a vehicle for recognising a type of exemplary personhood. It should be noted that I use the term 'exemplary' because the perspective that is revealed through the chest is impossible for a living person, who although a mother, daughter-in-law and daughter, cannot visibly enact all these relations at a single moment in time. The figure that is revealed can be said to crystallise the multiple relations necessary for kinship in Mongolia.[28]

It should be noted that there are restrictions on the type of vision that allows us to view a person in this way. The Buryats in Mongolia place limits on who can look at the mirror and when it is possible to look at it. For example, infants should not look in mirrors because they may see their reflected image as that of a stranger and have bad dreams.[29] In general, people do not look in the mirror at night (or if it is damaged), because the image that is revealed is distorted. When there is a full moon, people cover the mirror in cloth, or turn it around so that it faces the wall, ensuring that the round image of the full moon, which enters through the smoke hole (*toono*), does not appear in the mirror and illuminate the inside of the house allowing bad spirits to enter. In Mongol culture mirrors are used in two distinct ways. They reveal things that are otherwise not known, or they deflect things. In such a way, the mirror has the double capacity 'to both gather in and deflect at the same time' (Humphrey with Onon 1996: 226). In shamanic performance, for example, the mirror is used to deflect, or cast aside, evil spirits. But when used for divinations, vodka is poured on the mirror to reveal and confirm links of causation. A Mongolian friend explained to me that the double capacity of the chest's mirror means that it is like an eye (*nüd-shig*). It must be regularly cleaned because the mirror may 'see' bad things. These should not linger and accumulate on its surface as the mirror may redirect these back in the house. In its double capacity, the mirror is 'an instrument not only of containment and absorption but [it is] also [used] for breaking out of the world into another state which reflect[s] the hitherto unseen truth' (Humphrey with Onon 1996: 226). It should be clear that because mirrors in Mongolia have the capacity to reveal that which is not known, the perspective afforded through the chest is not a perspective that a living person can embody. Not unlike the shaman discussed by Humphrey with Onon (1996: 226–2), the image that appears through the chest is one that catches the fragmented aspects of the person and reveals a unity of form to the viewer.

I have suggested that when a person looks into the mirror at the centre of the display an exemplary person is revealed. It is important to emphasise, however, that the import of vision does not have to rest solely on the presence of a mirror at the centre of the display. Elkins (1996), in a fascinating book on the nature of seeing, explores relationships established between objects and observers. Elkins examines the ways in which observers are altered by objects, or fused with them, through acts of seeing. His point is similar to that which I have made about the mirror's capacity to reveal an exemplary person to the viewer. Through looking at the display, the chest and the observer merge into an in-between state, lost in the field of vision. In such a way, vision is not a passive activity involving a discrete viewing subject and a viewed object: seeing alters the thing that is seen and reveals a metamorphosis to the seer (cf. *ibid.*: 11–12). Siding with Elkins' point, Mongols would argue that it is not just the mirror that reflects or deflects different perspectives; other things also send back our sight. In this way, one could equally make the point about any object in the display. Indeed, the arrangement of things in and around the Mongolian household chest differs between Mongolian groups. For example, among Xalx Mongols, a photographic montage is sometimes placed above the mirror, or the mirror may be in a different location entirely and a single Buddhist image may be displayed on the chest.[30] In these cases, viewing the display also instantiates kinship in the same manner (through separation, concealing, enclosing and revealing differing aspects), there is just a difference in the details of what people view according to their different ideas about what makes a person. This variation reflects the different ways in which Mongolian groups make kinship differently through similar means. Notwithstanding variations between different Mongolian groups, the household chest needs a corporal presence to be seen as a person made from the different parts. In this sense, vision, situated in another person, is necessary to create this perspective.

I should like to point out why it takes a certain type of relation to the thing being viewed to be able to see the container as an image of our self. That is, I would like to explain why a visitor to a household will not recognise the 'body' configured when viewing themselves through the chest's parts, as something recognisable as themselves. I suggest that in these cases, a visitor may guess and speculate as to the chest's contents and various parts but they cannot fully see themselves as constituted through them. This is because the means by which they see an image of themselves does not relate to any aspects that they are familiar with. For visitors, the image that is revealed can only ever be a replication of themselves in a singular form. The concept of 'reciprocal vision', that one has to be looked at in order to be able to look (i.e. that the gaze creates a relation), is also fundamental to the concept of fortune. If we recall the example of the cow presented at the beginning of this paper, something has to be given away in order for it to be kept back to support and increase the whole. In this sense, separation is an ontological precondition for the possibility to retain and increase fortune for growth of the family and its herds. Similarly the separation of people, or the ability to reflect on social relations through the containment of some part, is essential for the growing of kin relations in Mongolia. In turn, a person is only able to see their multiple aspects as an exemplary figure constructed in the display through their own gaze. In this way, we could conclude that Mongolian kinship relies on the separation and transformation of people in order for sameness, or consanguinity, to continue. The necessity of separation, in order for sameness, seems to be a theme that underlies many, if not all, social relations in Mongolia.

We have seen how various things, inside and on top of the household chest, are made to stand for relations that are reflected through the gaze and interpretations of others. Through looking at ourselves looking at the display, each of the visible and hidden parts dissolve as separate channels and present themselves as a single form. The things that I have discussed can be seen, in their parts, to reference different kinship perspectives and points of transformation. When viewed together they appear as a whole. Thinking through these things has highlighted relations outside of relations based on agnatic kinship. It has shown that agnatic kinship survives due to these different relations. The visible and invisible aspects of people's relations are mutually dependent on each other. We have seen that the ways in which these relations are contained in things mirrors the ways in which these relations are realised in people's interactions.

Conclusion

In conclusion, I should like to make some suggestions about why it might be necessary for Mongolians to index relations in things, and why this is tied to the idea that a person has to extend beyond their physical or spatial location. First, due to the practice of nomadic herding, it is necessary in Mongolia for people to reckon relations with people who are physically absent. When people are dispersed across the landscape, things contained in the household can be seen to allow for the containment of certain relations that cannot be enacted in shared place. We have seen that through the use of photographic montages, far- reaching kin terms, and the spatial layout of the house Mongolians construct flexible ways in which to incorporate outsiders. These technologies act as potential ways of reckoning kinship that are drawn upon to activate wider networks in the absence of kin. Underneath these visible means, however, we have seen that ways are found to distinguish bodies and create different relations.

The theme of retaining relations in the absence of people is something that seems to permeate the need for locating Mongolian kinship in different forms. While people may be necessarily absent, due to the constraints of nomadic herding, historical pressures of migration, and political persecution, relations can be imagined and contained through the construction of different sites. Focus on the display of these relations in households brings to the fore some of the ways in which objects and people are mutually constituted by processes of objectification (Humphrey 2002: 83). These things are the products of relations that, in turn, allow people to make further relations when they are viewed or displayed. The things discussed all transform the typically temporal aspect of people's kin relations into a contained visual site. With the continual movement of both people and place, I suggest that viewing the household chest as a container or site is necessary for the imagining and creating of Mongolian kinship.

Acknowledgements

I am grateful for insightful comments from those at the London School of Economics Anthropology Research Seminar when I presented an earlier version of this paper, and from those at the Thinking Through Things workshop at CRASSH, University of Cambridge. Versions of this paper were also presented at St Andrews University and Manchester University Social Anthropology Research Seminars. I am very grateful for comments and suggestions during these seminars, some of which I have not been able to take up in this chapter, but which I hope will be addressed in an extended form. I also thank Martin Holbraad, Caroline Humphrey, Andrew Moutu, Marilyn Strathern, Aparecida Vilaça and Rane Willerslev for their important comments and ideas on earlier drafts of this paper. I thank Routledge's two anonymous readers for their helpful suggestions. Naturally, none of these people should be held in any way accountable for any of my deficiencies, which are wholly my own responsibility. Writing this paper has been made possible due to the support of the British Academy Postdoctoral Fellowship Award (BA PDF 2003/145).

Notes

1 Chabros (1987) states: 'It is difficult to consider the material culture of traditional Mongolia in isolation from non-material or spiritual aspects' (270).
2 Often, if the 'thing' has been made, the intention of the maker or the person who owns or uses it is held to be part of it. If the 'thing' has been found, or appears, the way in which it makes itself visible to someone is held to indicate the intention of the thing it stands for.
3 Practices that involve 'separating-yet-containing' the fortune of animals include: to make sure fortune does not leave when giving away a container of cream or milk, the giver pours the contents of their container into the recipient's container which is placed on the ground. When the recipient's container is full, the giver places their own container on the ground and pours back a little of the cream or milk into their

own container so that the sacred portion (*deej*), containing the accumulative fortune of one's animals, is retained.

4 'The secret history of the Mongols' is an account of the ancestry and life of the Mongolian leader Chinggis Xaan, more commonly referred to in English as 'Ghengis Khan'. Onon (2001) estimates that this account was probably recorded in 1228.

5 Specific kin terms draw attention to agnatic and non-agnatic kin by differentiating relatives on the father's side (*avga axlegch*), or mother's side (*nagats axl egch*). Male heads of two families, related through the marriage of their children, have classificatory terms (*xud*), as do female heads of two families related through the marriage of their children (*xudgui*). Grandparents distinguish their grandchildren as coming from either their daughter (*zee*), or son (*ach*, also meaning favour, grace and benefit). See Vreeland 1954; Pao 1964; and Park 1997 for extensive information on kinship terminology in Mongolia.

6 See Humphrey with Onon (1996): 'The Mongols do not take over any terrain in the vicinity and transform it into something that is their own. Instead, they move within a space and environment where some kind of pastoral life is possible and "in-habit" it' (135).

7 The Mongolian concepts of 'blood' and 'bone' should not be confused with Western essentialist concepts of these terms (à la Gil-White 2001). Through the concept of fortune, this paper proposes that although much Mongolian kinship is 'given at birth' through the inheritance of substance, Mongolian kinship is also made in practice throughout life. While classical anthropological accounts (cf. Vreeland 1954; Lévi-Strauss 1969) and Mongols alike may hint, through the use of specific terms, at ideas that seem essentialist, in practice we see a multitude of ways of being related.

8 It is not just individual portrait-style photographs that are displayed in such frames. Groups of people such as a family member's class-mates, a pair of brothers preparing to leave for hunting, or a family visit to a historic site all provide occasions in which the moment can be captured in a photograph and displayed along with more formal portraits.

9 Increasing interest in recording genealogies is, in part, due to the fact that people have to record their clan name on identity cards. For information concerning variations in eighteenth- and nineteenth-century Buryat genealogies in Russian Buryatia, see Humphrey (1979).

10 This circular representation can be found in many other Mongol forms, such as circular offerings at stone cairns (*oboo*) and to the family hearth (*gal golomt*).

11 Bouquet (2001) makes a similar point in relation to photographic displays: 'photographic reproduction [is revealed] as a powerful means of establishing and cutting genealogical relationship[s]' (110). See also Bouquet (1996) for the limits of analysing kinship through anthropological kinship diagrams.

12 Humphrey (2002) has drawn attention to the twofold way in which, when displayed by their owners, personal possessions reach out to the consideration of others: while they may be displayed to signal social status or vanity, they equally stand for the need for acknowledgment or recognition by other living people (cf. Humphrey 2002: 69).

13 For a similar idea, see Gell's (1998) discussion of Trobriand prow-boards that dazzle exchange partners to surrender their valuables.

14 For further information concerning ideas of separation from people and place, see Stafford (2003), and for information concerning the movement of women in Chinese patrilineal kin groups see Stafford (2000: 110–26).

15 The hair-cutting ceremony marks the child's entrance into social life (see Humphrey 1974: 479).

16 The umbilical cord is held to stand for a child's life-power or soul (*süns*), and the loss of their first hair at the hair-cutting ceremony represents the incorporation of a child into the world of people (cf. Galdanova 1992). See also Humphrey (1973: 22): 'Buriat women preserve the umbilical cords of the children, since it is thought that the cord is somehow "a line of life" whose magic power would be broken if the cord were to be thrown away. [It is] associated by the Buriat with female descent and thought of as complementary to patrilineal essence' (Humphrey 1973: 22).

17 See Chabros (1987), who explains that certain things within the family containing magical properties are regarded with the same respect as people. It is equally important not to keep things which have been owned by outsiders. Seen to contain a part of that person, they have the potential to cause pollution.

18 The concept of revealing and concealing different aspects of people's relations can, of course, be extended outwards. A case in point would be restrictions placed on the daughter-in-law in terms of language. Uttering personal names in Mongolia draws attention to the hierarchical relationship between the speaker and the person the name refers to. Daughters-in-law are tabooed from uttering the names of senior male affines and must find suitable substitute words to refer to them, even in their absence. For further information concerning name taboos and the suppression of attention, see Humphrey (1993).

19 Humphrey (2002) states: 'It is believed that the spirit or "soul" (*süns*), even after death, remains emotionally attached to one particular object which was much used in a person's lifetime' (67).

20 They are not illicit, but the relation indexed in the thing remains the same as at the point at which it was separated.

21 The idea that things originating from one source are similar, but not the same as each other, could be applied to naming practices in Mongolia. It is not uncommon that children of one household share a name that has a similar part but a different ending, i.e. *Bibish* (Not-me) and *Terbish* (Not-them), or *Batchimeg* (Bold-decoration) and *Battsetseg* (Bold-flower), etc. Here, a part of the name is shared, but it is modified each time to be slightly different.

22 It is difficult to determine if all children are held to be lay-reincarnations. Sometimes, parents hold that their child is a reincarnation of someone, but do not voice this opinion to others. In turn, parents may fight over who the child actually is a reincarnation of. When they are older, children may inquire about who they were held to have been a reincarnation of, and the answer to this is often embedded in who the parent longed to have been reborn in their child. The ethical dilemmas faced by parents when children want to find out about their reincarnated past can be compared to the ethical problems faced in Euro-American kinship thinking when children want to know about their birth parents' genetic history (see Strathern 2001).

23 It should be mentioned that relations with the deceased do not just make themselves visible though human bodies. For example, it is considered dangerous to bury many family members in the same location because they may start to call on the living to join them.

24 Exactly the same practice concerns domestic animals. A drawing of a horse or cow is often placed at the altar representing an animal that has been consecrated. This animal is allowed to run freely and will never be ridden or milked (*seterlesen mal*); it thus provides a container or vessel that accumulates fortune for the whole herd. Inside the chest, however, are pieces of tail hair from individual cattle and horses that have been gathered at points of separation and departure.

25 By this I mean that the two perspectives only make sense in relation to each other.

26 A similar shift in perspective can be noted in Levin (1988). Levin, drawing on the work of Jean Paris, examines the history of Western painting as a transformation of human vision whereby the seer gradually becomes a part of what is being seen in the painting. In Byzantine mosaics the viewer is an object that the gods look at. But in Renaissance art, due to the gazes in the paintings being cast in different directions, the viewer is afforded the possibility of becoming part of the scene (cf. Reed 1999).

27 For a similar practice see Willerslev (2004: 639–41):
'Under normal conditions, a person's body is not presented to him as an object in the world, a thing that he can encounter or straightforwardly observe. Rather, it is an object only from the perspective of another, in the same way as another's body is an object from the perspective of ego.'
See also Humphrey with Onon (1996: 225): 'What you see in the mirror is yourself and not-yourself. It is a depersonalised, two-dimensional, image which you do not spontaneously know, but have to recognise.'

28 Furthermore, the figure that is revealed through the chest shatters our own anthropological understandings of 'blood' and 'bone' as the foundation of kinship in Mongolia, allowing us to see beyond these ideas.

29 The soul of an infant is held to be unstable and can easily be 'dislodged', finding another bodily container to inhabit. Many things, including fear of strangers, may cause the soul-loss of young infants.

30 Among Tuvinian groups, umbilical cords are placed in separate cloth pouches and are sometimes prominently displayed above the chest (C. Humphrey, personal communication).

References

Arnheim, Rudolf (2002) [1954] *Art and Visual Perception: a Psychology of the Creative Eye*, the New Version, Berkeley: University of California Press.

Bouquet, Mary (2001) 'Making kinship with an old reproductive technology', in Sarah Franklin and Susan McKinnon (eds), *Relative Values: Reconfiguring Kinship Studies*, Durham NC and London: Duke University Press.

——(1996) 'Family trees and their affinities: the visual imperative of the genealogical diagram', *Journal of the Royal Anthropological Institute, Incorporating Man*, 2(1): 43–66.

Casey, E. S. (1998) *The Fate of Place: a Historical History*, Berkeley and Los Angeles: University of California Press.

Chabros, Krystyna (1992) *Beckoning Fortune: a Study of the Mongolian Dalalga Ritual*, Wiesbaden: Otto Harrassowicz, Wiesbaden Press.

—— (1987) 'The decorative art of Mongolia in relations to other aspects of traditional Mongol culture', in *Zentralasiatische Studien. Des Seminars fur Sprach – und Kulturwissenschaft Zentralasiens der Universitat Bonn*, no. 20: 250–81, Wiesbaden: Otto Harrassowitz, Wiesbaden Press.

Elkins, James (1996) *The Object Stares Back: on the Nature of Seeing*, New York: Harvest Harcourt.

Empson, Rebecca (2006) 'Enlivened Memories: Recalling Absence and Loss in Mongolia', in *Ghosts of Memory: Essays on Remembrance and Relatedness*, edited by Janet Carsten, Oxford: Blackwell Publications.

——(2003) 'Integrating transformations: a study of children and daughters-in-law in a new approach to Mongolian kinship', unpublished Ph.D. thesis, Department of Social Anthropology, University of Cambridge.

Galdanova, G. P. (1992) 'Zakamensky Buryats', in L. P. Potapov and K. M. Gerasimova (eds), *Historic and Ethnographic Articles (Second Half XIX Century–First Half XX)*, Russian Academy of Science, Siberian Department, Novosibirsk: 'Science' Press.

Gell, Alfred (1998) *Art and Agency: an Anthropological Theory*, Oxford: Clarendon Press.

Gil-White, Francisco J. (2001) 'Are ethnic groups biological "species" to the human brain? Essentialism in our cognition of some social categories', *Current Anthropology*, 42(4): 515–54.

Humphrey, Caroline (2002) 'Rituals of death as a context for understanding personal property in socialist Mongolia', *Journal of the Royal Anthropological Institute, Incorporating Man*, 8(1): 65–87.

——(1995) 'Chiefly and shamanist landscapes in Mongolia', in E. Hirsch and M. O'Hanlon (eds) *The Anthropology of Landscape: Perspectives on Place and Space*, Oxford: Oxford University Press.

——(1993) 'Women, Taboo and the Supression of Attention', in S. Ardener (ed), *Defining Females: the Nature of Women in Society*. Oxford: Berg Publishers Limited.

——(1979) 'The uses of genealogy: a historical study of nomadic and sedentarised Buryat', in L'équipe écologie et anthropologie des sociétés pastorals (ed.) *Pastoral Production and Society*, Cambridge and Paris: Cambridge University Press and Maison des Sciences de L'Homme.

——(1974) 'Horse brands of the Mongolians: a system of signs in a nomadic culture', *American Ethnologist*, 1(3): 471–88.

——(1973) 'Some ritual techniques in the bull-cult of the Buriat-Mongols', the Curl Lecture 1973, in *Proceedings of the Royal Anthropological Institute of Great Britain and Ireland*, no. 1973: 15–28.

Humphrey, Caroline with Onon, Urgunge (1996) *Shamans and Elders: Experience, Knowledge, and Power among the Daur Mongols*, Oxford: Clarendon Press.

Lessing, F. D. (ed.) (1960) *Mongolian-English Dictionary*, Bloomington: Mongolian Society, Indiana Press.

Lévi-Strauss, Claude (1969) *The Elementary Structures of Kinship*, revised ed, trans. James Harle Bell and John Richard von Sturmer, ed. Rodney Needham, Boston MA: Beacon Press.

Levin, David Michael (1988) *The Opening of Vision: Nihilism and the Postmodern Situation*, New York and London: Routledge.

Mauss, Marcel (1972) *A General Theory of Magic*, trans. Robert Brain, London and Boston MA: Routledge and Kegan Paul.

Montell, Gösta (1934) *Våra Vänner På Stäppen: Genom Mongoliet till Torgoterna vid Etsingol* (Our Friends on the Steppe: through Mongolia to the Torgots by Etsingol), Stockholm: Lars Hökerbergs Bokförlag.

Onon, Urgunge (ed. and trans.) (2001) *The Secret History of the Mongols: the Life and Times of Chinggis Khan*, Richmond: Curzon Press.

Pao, Kuo-Yi (1964) 'Family and Kinship Structure of Khorchin Mongols', *Central Asiatic Journal. International Periodical for the Languages, Literature, History and Archaeology of Central Asia*, 9(4): 277–311. The Hague/Wiesbaden: Mouton/Otto Harrassowitz.

Park, Hwan-Young (1997) 'Kinship in post-socialist Mongolia: its revival and reinvention', unpublished Ph.D. thesis, Department of Social Anthropology, University of Cambridge.

Reed, Adam (1999) 'Anticipating individuals: modes of vision and their social consequence in a Papua New Guinea prison', *Journal of the Royal Anthropological Institute Incorporating Man*, 5(1): 43–56.

Sneath, David (2000) *Changing Inner Mongolia: Pastoral Mongolian Society and the Chinese State*, Oxford: Oxford University Press.

Sobchack, Vivian (1992) *The Address of the Eye: a Phenomenology of Film Experience*, Princeton NJ: Princeton University Press.

Sontag, Susan (2002a) [1971] 'In Plato's Cave', in *On Photography*, London: Penguin.

——(2002b) [1971] 'The image-world', in *On Photography*, London: Penguin.

Stafford, Charles (2000) *Separation and Reunion in Modern China*, Cambridge: Cambridge University Press.

Stafford, Charles (ed.) (2003) *Living with Separation in China: Anthropological Accounts*, London and New York: Routledge Curzon Press.

Strathern, Marilyn (2001) 'Children in an information age', unpublished paper delivered at Brunel University conference, 'Children in Their Places', June.

——(1994) 'One-Legged Gender', in Lucien Taylor (ed.) *Visualizing Theory: Selected Essays from V.A.R. 1990–1994*, New York and London: Routledge.

——(1990) [1988] *The Gender of the Gift: Problems with Women and Problems with Society in Melanesia*, Berkeley and London: University of California Press.

Telfer, Jon (1999) 'Relationships with no body? – "adoption" photographs, intuition and emotion', *Social Analysis, Subjectivities in Material Worlds* (ed. Anne Meneley), 43(3): 144–58.

Viveiros de Castro, Eduardo B. (2004) 'The gift and the given: three nano-essays on kinship and magic', in Sandra Bamford and James Leach (eds) *Genealogy Beyond Kinship: Sequence, Transmission and Essence in Ethnography and Social Theory*, Oxford: Berghahn Books.

Vreeland, Herbert Harold III (1954) *Mongol Community and Kinship Structure*, Human Relations Area Files, New Haven: Behavior Science Monographs.

Wagner, Roy (1987) 'Figure-ground reversal among the Barok', in L. Lincoln (ed.) *Assemblage of Spirits: Idea and Image in New Ireland*, Minneapolis: Minneapolis Institute of Art.

Weiner, B. Annette (1992) *Inalienable Possessions: the Paradox of Keeping-while-Giving*, Berkeley: University of California Press.

——(1985) 'Inalienable wealth', *American Ethnologist*, 12(2): 210–27.

Willerslev, Rane (2004) 'Not animal, not not-animal: hunting, imitation and empathetic knowledge among the Siberian Yukaghirs', *Journal of the Royal Anthropological Institute* (n.s.) 10: 629–52.

7

TALISMANS OF THOUGHT

Shamanist ontologies and extended cognition in Northern Mongolia

Morten Axel Pedersen

Based on fieldwork in Northern Mongolia, this chapter examines how certain sacred paraphernalia employed in shamanist rituals make visible a social ontology otherwise hidden to ordinary people.[1] Heeding Edward Hutchins' call for an anthropology which addresses how cognition takes place 'in the wild' (1995), my analysis rests on the theoretical premise that Darhad Mongolian shamanic knowledge is embedded in different religious artefacts, such as the shamanic costume, whose intricate design triggers peoples' momentary conceptualisation of social relationships which otherwise remain unseen, and, for the same reason, to a large extent unknown. Darhad shamanist ritual, in that sense, constitutes a distinct 'cognitive platform', which, by temporarily situating its participants within a tabooed assemblage of artefacts, provides access to deeply esoteric thoughts.

In addition to providing fresh material from a little-known ethnographic region, the present chapter also aims to accommodate two quite different theoretical approaches concerned with how people think through things, namely, on the one hand, the 'distributed person' approach spearheaded by Melanesianists such as Roy Wagner (1991) and Marilyn Strathern (1988), and on the other hand, the 'extended cognition' approach advanced by cognitive scientists like Andy Clark (2003) and Steven Mithen (1996). This reconciliation attempt must be seen in continuation of Gell's study of the abductive social agency of art objects (1998), which has proven to be so productive for anthropology (see Pinney and Thomas 2001; Layton 2003). Gell here suggested that the Trobriand Kula exchange system, for instance, constitutes 'a whole *form of cognition*, which takes place outside the body, which is diffused in space and time, and which is carried on through the medium of physical indexes and transactions between them' (1998: 232, original emphasis). For Gell, then, certain art objects do not serve to represent a corresponding body of social and cultural knowledge; rather, the very materiality of this object is itself a vehicle of such knowledge.

In what follows, I want to contribute further to this anthropological exploration of 'how thought [can] conduct itself in art' (Küchler 2001: 57) by considering the socio-cognitive properties of shamanic material culture in Northern Mongolia. In so doing, I also aim to provide new insights into the animist ontology into which these talismans are known to offer special access. Following Viveiros de Castro (1998a; 1998b), I shall thus suggest that the shamanic costume affords the shaman with a multiple, extra-human body, which, by inducing a momentary transformation of his or her corporal gestalt, enables the shaman to attain otherwise unattainable points of view. The Mongolian shamanic costume, therefore, does not only constitute a powerful 'talisman of thought' which enhances peoples' abilities to think (through) certain things, it also represents a highly potent 'ontological tool' inasmuch as it is perceived to imbue shamans with the magical capacity to crosscut the boundaries between human and nonhuman beings.

The active externalist challenge

What, then, do I mean by 'thinking through things'? A good way of embracing this question is to consider the recent critique of the hitherto dominant paradigm in cognitive science, which has been raised by different philosophers, anthropologists and cognitive scientists. Matthew Day (2004: 110), in his attempt to rethink the impact of material culture on religious cognition, takes issue with evolutionary psychology's so-called 'Swiss army knife' model of the mind, which, paraphrasing Hutchins (1995), 'may be guilty of attributing the right information-processing properties to the wrong system'. Day's concern is that much recent cognitive science suffers from an overly mentalist bias. By focusing on the modular architecture that allegedly governs the perceptual (and, more controversially, also conceptual) processing of mental inputs (see e.g. Fodor 1983; Sperber 1996; Fodor 2000), the dominant representational approaches severely underestimate the cognitive impact of what Day calls 'external task-environments' in human thinking.[2] The time has come, then, for cognitive science to take rather more seriously the findings from anthropology as a unique form of 'outdoor psychology' (as Geertz once defined the subject). For even on the debatable assumption that the human mind since the Pleistocene Age has evolved into a kludge of only partly interconnected 'mental organs' (Sperber 1996: 123–34; Cosmides and Tooby 1994: 89–98), this does not mean that much of our cognitive processes are not *actively* embedded in the world. After all, as Clark and Chalmers put it in their influential article on 'The extended mind' (1998),

> if as we confront some task, a part of the world functions as a process which, *were it done in the head*, we would have no hesitation in recognizing as part of the cognitive process, then that part of the world *is* (so we claim) part of the cognitive process.
>
> (1998: 11; original emphases)

In fact, recent research carried out by both neuroscientists and cognitive psychologists shows that, while the massive modularity thesis 'remains strongly underdetermined by the available evidence' (Day 2004: 110; see also Fodor 2000: 55–78; Sterelny 2003: 177–210), Clark and Chalmers' active externalism is supported by a growing body of controlled experimental data, for instance with respect to the unsolved mystery of human change-blindness (see e.g. Noë forthcoming). Based on their own as well as others' experimental findings regarding the use of spatial indices in (for example) visual imagination, Spivey *et al.* reach the conclusion that 'the objects of thought, the very things upon which mental processes directly operate, *are not always inside the brain*' (2004: 178; emphasis added). According to this study, then, the 'very things' which augment human cognition should not be regarded as decoupled objects requiring detached mental computations, for they are as much part of the cognitive processing system as the naked brain is, and therefore constitute the active vehicles, and not the passive inputs or outputs, of what some cognitive anthropologists refer to as 'cultural representations' (2004: 179–82). To be thinking through things, then, here amounts to the form of biological cognition where humans (as well as many animals and, of late, certain robots) use the world as its own model, as it were, for instance when finding their way by constantly probing their *Umwelt* for relevant 'affordances' (Clark 1997: 35–51; cf. Von Uexküll 1921; Gibson 1979).

Now, defenders of a more internalist position might object that the above picture of human cognition, even if true, only involves so-called low-level cognitive processes. In defence of the massive modularity thesis, Sperber for instance notes that 'once a certain level of complexity in modular thought is reached, modules can emerge whose function is to handle problems raised, not externally by the environment, but internally by the workings of the mind' (1996: 133). This is plausible enough, but does not necessarily imply that many such higher-order thought processes (or, in Sperber's own terms, 'metarepresentations') will not benefit from, so to speak, *re-externalising* themselves into the world. In fact, as is often argued, humans are apparently unique in having the capacity to perform 'off-line cognition' (i.e. contemplating imaginary scenarios beyond the experimental limitations of the here-and-now). But it is also true that humans have a propensity to translate complex internal 'off-line' tasks into less complex externalised 'on-line' ones, that is to say, into materially embedded conceptual operations involving 'the strategic use of non-biological artefacts to scaffold and augment biological modes of computation' (Day 2004: 112). The use of calculators to augment algebraic computations is an often-cited example of such 'cognitive scaffolding', as indeed is the invention and the tools of writing itself.

In fact, some cognitive archaeologists now believe that our widespread use of cognitive technologies is not just a product of human evolution, but was actually a *precondition* for its most recent stages (e.g. Mithen 1996). According to this theory, some of the most archaic material culture (like, say, hunting traps) has had an impact on human evolution 'similar to that of language in terms of creating networks of minds, disembodying minds, and exceptionally increasing the range of conceptual spaces available for exploration and the manner in which this could be undertaken' (Mithen 1998: 181; see also Dennett 2000). Far from having only an impact on a limited range of 'low-level' cognitive processes, then, the human activity of thinking through things on this active externalist perspective is regarded as essential to our extraordinary success as a species, because, as Clark puts it, it is only due to our propensity to 'dissipate reasoning' that we have come to 'use intelligence to structure our environment so that we can succeed with less intelligence' (1997: 180; see also Sterelny 2003: 234–40).

The central tenet of the above argument is echoed in recent work by cognitive as well as developmental psychologists, phenomenological philosophers and art theorists, as well as artificial intelligence (AI) and robotics researchers (see, for example, Clark 1997; Chrisley and Ziemke 2002; Sutton 2002). However, objections have been raised against the far-reaching philosophical ramifications of the active externalist approach, notably with regard to the concept of the self. Clark and Chalmers themselves submit that one radical implication of their theory is a notion of an *extended self*, with all the 'increasingly exotic puzzles' which this idea entails ('is my cognitive state somehow spread across the internet?' (1998: 20). Nonetheless, they defend the notion of a 'fuzzy set for mental contents' (Spivey *et al.* 2004: 179), but they do so by strictly limiting the cases in which a given artefact of extended cognition belongs to an actual mental state of the thinking subject. Clark and Chalmers thus operate with the notion of 'extended beliefs', denoting a certain type of non-occurrent beliefs which reside *outside* the human brain (in an Alzheimer's patient's notebook, for example), but whose causal and logical status are nonetheless 'functionally isomorphic' with the same beliefs were they the result of a person's introspective thinking (cf. Clark 1997: 217–18). Crucially, the notion of extended beliefs only applies to those artefacts, or assemblages of artefacts: (a) without consulting which people would never undertake the relevant actions; (b) whose information is directly available; (c) whose information is considered to be unquestionably true at the point of retrieval; and (d) whose total body of information has been 'consciously endorsed at some point in the past' (Clark and Chalmers 1998: 19). This limited class of artefacts, Clark and Chalmers seem to imply, constitutes a set of exterior cognitive modules, in that they are 'informationally encapsulated' to the point of having the capacity to engender conceptual outputs (i.e. 'external beliefs') whose truth-value is taken for granted by their users.

The activity of thinking through things, on this interpretation, in certain cases amounts to the artefacts themselves enacting a certain intuitive theory of the world within the agents engaging with them, and these 'external beliefs' cannot exist disembedded from the total cognitive fact constituted by the integrated platform of artefact(s) and user(s) at hand. It therefore *is* true that 'the external factors which Clark and Chalmers take to partially constitute the mind are not part of the self in the core philosophical sense of "self" (Gertler 2001). However, as the argument here becomes quite technical (involving the wider philosophical debate between internalists and externalists), it is fortunate that our main concern as anthropologists must involve, not the 'core philosophical' sense, but rather different *ethnographic senses of the self*. Indeed, as we are about to see, one anthropological theory of the person in particular not only resonates well with the active externalist approach, but actually suggests ways in which it might be significantly refined.

Cognitive scaffolds and distributed persons

Do humans also employ artefacts to augment their manner of thinking such complex phenomena as social and religious forms? I will try to establish that this is so by bridging the above critique of representational internalism with recent developments in the anthropology of artefacts. Material culture, Day (2004) suggests, plays a more fundamental role in religious thinking than has hitherto been granted in cognitivist approaches to religion. With explicit reference to Boyer (1994), Day writes:

> If it is true that we have *our kinds of gods* because we have *our kinds of mind*, then it may also be the case that religious cognition is computationally impossible without the external cognitive scaffolding that supports it. [. . .] So while it is correct to insist that these cognitive artefacts have been sculpted by the features and constraints of the mind's design, is it possible that we are missing something crucial when we don't concurrently observe how this kind of scaffolding allows us to think things that we could not otherwise contemplate?
>
> (Day 2004: 113–14, original emphases)

To be fair, Boyer does recognise that religious thinking is structured by other mechanisms than those hardwired by evolution into the make-up of the human mind-brain (1994: 20; see also Whitehouse 2001: 207–9). Still, Boyer grants primary explanatory power to evolved human cognitive dispositions, which, he claims, impose 'necessary rather than contingent' (1994: 20) constraints upon the causal processes through which religious ideas are formed and transmitted (see also Boyer 2001: 79–81). As Day notes (2004: 109–10), there is something curiously non-Darwinian about the evolutionary psychologists' insistence on situating the adaptive and selective processes, which – allegedly – developed into the mind of homo sapiens, entirely within the *longue durée* of our Pleistocene ancestors (see also Ingold 2001). The '*short durée*' demarcated, for instance, by the millennia-long time span running from the emergence of Northern and Inner Asia's 'shamanic complex' until today (see Samuel 1993) is left outside the cognitive evolutionary loop, presumably on the unsubstantiated evolutionary psychological assumption that this period represented an unchanging 'standard epigenic environment' (Boyer 2001: 81; for a recent critique of this assumption, see Sterelny 2003). In my view, this overly conservative perspective on human evolution ignores not only the global cognitive impact of the so-called creative explosion of the Upper Palaeolithic (Mithen 1998), but also the more local 'ontological revolution' which, as is implied below, was kick-started by the introduction of shamanic cognitive technologies within the animistic cultures of Northern and Inner Asia.

This, of course, is where the anthropological idea of 'the distributed person' takes centre stage.[3] Crucial here is the stipulation that, in Melanesia as well as elsewhere (including, as we shall see, Northern Asia), persons and things can be analytically collapsed into mutually analogous, or could we say 'functionally isomorphic', objectifications of social relations (see e.g. Strathern 1988; 1999). Strathern's own favourite example involves ceremonial gift exchange in the Papua New Guinea Highlands. At these spectacles, she argues, certain otherwise implicit aspects of peoples' social life are revealed to them (and to ethnographers) in the form of a visualisation of certain social relationships at the expense of others. Just as in the case of the 'extended beliefs' discussed above, the particular material configuration (and, more generally, the entire mode of display) of these gift prestations is not arbitrary with respect to the kind of social knowledge revealed; hence, 'a clan of men and women only appears as a "clan" [. . .] if the contours, the shapes, are right' (1999: 14). By ceremonially exchanging gifts with one another, then, two clan elders at the same time will exchange each other's perspectives *as* male clan leaders (rather than, say, as cassowary hunters). In that sense, these and other Melanesian gift prestations act to distribute persons across a wider spatio-temporal terrain, for each prestation is perceived (in Gell's terms) as a material 'index from which one can "abduct" the magnitude of the donor's social agency. This basic argument can be extended to a wide range of non-Western artefacts conventionally labelled as "primitive art" (Gell 1998). Rather than being evaluated simply according to their degree of beauty (whatever that might be), the perceived quality of these objects is a function of their capacity to bring about certain beliefs and actions within a given social field (like, say, induce in a recipient the propensity to return a gift).

Material culture, then, under certain circumstances, seems to work a bit like a calculator of social relations. Just as certain purely abstract computations (such as number crunching) are difficult – if not impossible – to carry out without the aid of cognitive technologies, the thinking of certain altogether more messy social relationships also is dependent upon the strategic use of different artefacts by virtue of which the conceptualisation of this social knowledge is rendered into an 'on-line' cognitive task. There certainly is ample ethnographic evidence to support the proposition that material culture allows people 'to think things that [they] could not otherwise contemplate' (Day 2004). This, after all, is exactly what anthropologists are so often told when probing into why access to a given artefact in a given society is considered taboo to, say, the unmarried women (who, it so often seems, are not supposed to think certain things).

Indeed, an important analytical convergence exists between the anthropological study of social reproduction (e.g. Bloch 1992; Godelier 1986) and the anthropological study of social cognition (e.g. Hutchins 1995; Whitehouse 2000; 2001). In either case, we are interested in the specific forms through which knowledge is acquired, distributed and transmitted between differently situated social persons, and in either case such an analysis can only be carried out by paying meticulous attention to even the smallest details of ritual and everyday life. A conventional anthropological study of micro-politics, then, at the same time may also yield important insights into the uneven distribution of cognitive technologies. Certainly, as Sterelny notes (2004), it is 'a fact that external epistemic artefacts are used in shared and sometimes contested space. Indeed, our most important cognitive tools are the multigenerational products of many minds' (see also Sterelny 2003). Spivey et al. go a step further when they state that 'mind appears to be an emergent property that arises among the interactions of a brain, its body, and the surrounding environment – which, interestingly, often includes other brains and bodies' (2004: 180).

I take these observations – along with their critique of the internalist picture of a monomorphic mind – as a strong vindication of the classical virtues of anthropology and, therefore, as an open invitation for anthropologists to contribute more confidently to the field of cognitive science. As much as I acknowledge the critique of some of cultural anthropology's more unsubstantiated assumptions made possible by recent findings in cognitive psychology (see e.g. Boyer 1994; Sperber 1996; Bloch 1998), it therefore also seems to me that social anthropology, with its long tradition for studying 'contested spaces', has something more upbeat to offer in return. For what if, by accepting the active externalist challenge posed above, we can posit 'human mind' to be something like a modularly co-opted cognitive platform characterised by always being 'tuned and applied to the special domain of external and/or artificial cognitive aids'? (Clark 2003, cited in Sterelny 2004). If this picture were true, and keeping in mind that the access to and use of many such technologies is strongly socially sanctioned, then a psychologically robust but still independent socio-cognitive anthropology of material culture is made possible, whose general object of analysis is the social distribution and effects of external cognitive technologies on a cross-cultural level. Central for such an approach would be, first of all, a detailed ethnographic description of how, when and by whom such technologies are being used, and, subsequently, a culturally sensitive interpretation (there can be no other) of the distinct social and ontological (i.e. intuitive theoretical) effects engendered by the uneven distribution of these cognitive scaffolds.

In fact, a fine example of such an approach already exists. I am thinking of the famous *malanggan* sculptures from the New Irelands, Melanesia, as thoroughly studied by Suzanne Küchler (e.g. 1988; 1992). The *malanggan* sculptures, whose intricate woodcarvings have earned them fame among collectors of 'primitive art' and anthropologists alike, are constructed by commissioned local artists upon the death of prominent clansmen, with the explicit purpose of providing the deceased person with a temporary 'body' or 'skin'. The interesting thing is that a given *malanggan* sculpture is only revealed to the public for a brief period during the subsequent funeral rites. Then it is destroyed, or sold to an ethnographic museum in the West. Based on Küchler's own analyses, Gell (1998: 223–37) discusses the *malanggan* sculptures' mnemonic properties. The sculptures' unique design and mode of display, Gell argues, facilitate the socio-cognitive transmission of memories of particular social relationships (only certain people are allowed to memorise the *malanggan* designs at the funeral, and the possession of these pictorial mnemonic data then correspond to the land-claims, etc., of the deceased person). In that sense, as Gell puts it, the *malanggan* sculpture is 'a kind of body which accumulates, like a charged battery, the potential energy of the deceased dispersed in the life-world' (1988: 225). Less metaphorically put, these sculptures quite evidently form a necessary material basis for the formation of certain cultural concepts (socially sanctioned memories of images), whose subsequent re-externalisation (into new *malanggan* sculptures) is capable of engendering still further social effects.

I shall return to the malanggan case in my own ethnographic analysis below. Here I want to emphasise how it corroborates the socio-cognitive approach sketched above. We might say that these sculptures offer New Irelanders access to a particular kind of social ontology (the totality of relations and objects through which a deceased person was 'distributed' in the course of his life), and this is a kind of intuitive knowledge which people are unable to contemplate through any other means of conceptual activity, whether this thinking is occurring through other things or not. Unlike some of its Euro-Western analogues, the *malanggan* 'patent' (Strathern 2001) is known to be transmitted (acquired, recollected, communicated) *only* by virtue of its continuous exteriorisation into new sculptures, just as its successful completion relies upon it being 'the multi-generational product of many minds' (Sterelny 2004), given the near-symbiotic relationship between the design-holder and the wood-carver in the course of its production (see Küchler 1988). A *malanggan* sculpture, then, can be described as a cognitive technology, which, by virtue of its intricate design and circumscribed mode of access, offers a poignant example of the kind of things through which peoples' 'on-line' thinking about complex socio-cultural phenomena (such as the constant permutation of land claims) is made possible.

Introducing Darhad shamanism

The Darhads, who presently number around 18,000, are a Mongolian-speaking group of pastoralists, hunters and village dwellers, who inhabit the remote northwestern corner of Mongolia's Hövsgöl Province. Unlike in most other areas of Mongolia, the Buddhist church never managed to eradicate the Darhads' shamanist religion (see Zhamtsarano 1979; Sandschejew 1930). Rather, shamanism and Buddhism continued to exist side-by-side in an often conflictual relationship; giving rise to the culturally pertinent notion that Darhad persons are made up of a 'black side' (*har tal*) and 'yellow side' (*shar tal*) respectively (Pedersen forthcoming). Nor did Darhad shamanism suffer a fatal blow during the seventy years of state socialism. It still plays a crucial role in Darhad social life, and a range of non-Buddhist religious specialists today practise across the region, though the actual shaman population is largely confined to one of its three districts. Instead, one encounters a plethora of quasi-shamanic practitioners, such as black-smiths (*darhan*), midwives (*eh barigch*), 'bone-setters' (*bariach*) and diviners (*meregch*), all of whom, like the shaman (*böö*) proper, are held to be imbued with an extraordinary power/ability (*hüch chadal*), typically derived from a line of either male or female ancestors (see also Hamayon 1990; Humphrey 1996).

Full-blown shamanising (*böö böölöh*) is not the only activity of Darhad shamans. They also engage in more low-key activities like divination séances for individual clients, much like the diviners and other practitioners mentioned above who are not considered 'genuine shamans' (*chinhene böö*). Importantly, while these activities may involve an element of trance (*hii uhaantai*), and while they may also involve the use of various sacred para-phernalia (such as the Jew's harp, or *hel huur*), they do not involve the religious practitioner wearing any special outfit. Indeed, possession of a shamanic costume (*böö huvtsas*, also known as *huyag*, or armour) is a main marker of difference between the genuine and not-so-genuine shamans. The costume is not only what enables the shaman to fully master the spirits (see below); it is also physical evidence of the shaman's acceptance by the community. Indeed, the consecration of new shamans used to be a highly communal affair, both in the sense that it was considered a major event in the clan's (*omog, yas*) social reproduction, and in that the cost of the initiation ritual – as well as the new shamanic costume – was incurred collectively by the clan members (see e.g. Sandschejew 1930: 33, 56–7; Badamhatan 1986: 185–6).

Today, the Darhad clan system has broken down for all significant socio-logical purposes, and serves primarily as an elite mark of indigenousness among the minority of Darhads who still subscribe to this identity (such as the shamans). For the same reason, most shamans have had their shamanic paraphernalia provided for them by atomised, bilateral kin groups, and they now mainly serve ritual communities composed of local inhabitants. Possibly, the fact that contemporary Darhad shamanism is no longer linked to the reproduction of patrilineal groupings explains why a majority of shamans are women (cf. Hamayon 1984); in any case, gender does not play a significant role in peoples' evaluation of shamans, whether in terms of what particular abilities they have, or how powerful they are.

Spirit bundles and the knots of knots

Shamans' yurts or houses are dominated by the altar in the north section (*hoimor*), which is also where the different shamanic paraphernalia are kept. Among the Darhad shamans I have visited, the most common situation is that these sacred artefacts are kept out of sight, only to be produced from drawers and cupboards immediately before ceremonies commence. This is, for instance, the case for the shamanic spirit 'vessel' (*ongon*), which, during ceremonies, is suspended on the wall in the yurt's northwest section (*baruun hoimor*).[4] I shall now consider this artefact in some detail, as this will serve as a good starting point for considering the role of material culture in Darhad religious cognition.

The spirit vessels possessed by shamans are similar to those kept in other Darhad households; only they are bigger and of (even) more intricate design.[5] A typical spirit vessel consists of multicoloured cotton pieces (*tsuudir*), ceremonial silk scarves (*hadag*), leather strings, odd metal pieces, as well as fur, teeth, bones, claws and beaks from different wild animals; all pieced together to form a complex bundle of heterogeneous substances (indeed, it is hard to find a better description). Sometimes, spirit vessels are kept inside the home (*geriin ongon*), at other times outside on the steppe or in the forest (*heeriin ongon*). All vessels should ideally be designed or at least consecrated by shamans, and they may be commissioned both by households and by individuals (in either case, they will eventually be passed down through either male or female lines).

Such a vessel, a hunter explained to me, is the 'most precious thing' (*hamgiin hairhan yum*) a person has. For it is nothing less than a 'container of souls' (*sünsnii sav*), which is always pulling (*tatah*) you towards where it is. If you lose contact (*holboo*) with it, you will die. In fact, to him and other hunters, the vessels constitute indispensable tools, for hunters will feed these objects with fat and milk before going hunting, just as, more generally, households will add new elements (e.g. silk scarves) to their vessels when significant events occur, like, say, when someone falls ill, or when a hunter has killed a big beast, such as a bear (see also Badamhatan 1986: 88, 186; Sandschejew 1930: 48).

Like many spirit vessels, the shamanic costume – comprising, essentially, boots (*böö gutal*), gown (*böö deel*), headgear (*böö malgai*), drum (*hengeregl hets*) and drumstick (*tsohiurlorov*) – is usually locked away in drawers beneath the altar, only to be taken out during the final hours before a ceremony (for more detailed descriptions, see Badamhatan 1986: 158–69; Dioszegi 1963: 57–69; Pürev 1999: 176–267). Essentially, the shaman's donning of the costume is believed to place him or her in a 'world-conquering time-machine' (Humphrey 1996: 202). The costume is believed to enable the shaman to travel to the spirits, and, conversely, the spirits to travel to the shaman (the direction of this movement is entirely unclear), a journey that is often imagined as riding (*unah*) a horse or a deer. The different parts of the costume play distinct roles in this respect: the drum is conceived as the mount, the drumstick as the whip, and so forth (see Pürev 1999; Dulam and Even 1994; Dioszegi 1961).

At the same time, the gown (and to some extent the drum) is understood to constitute an entire cosmos in its own right. It comprises materialities and textures which invoke a multitude of spatial and temporal dimensions, including the *taiga* and its different animate beings, the ninety-nine shamanic 'skies' (*tenger*), and – most importantly for the present analysis – all the past performances of the shaman (see also Badamhatan 1986: 158–71). This temporal dimension is instantiated by means of knots tied into several strip-rolled cotton strings (*manjig*) attached to the rear side of the gown. Each knot represents a particular curing event as clients (or their relatives) will tie new ceremonial scarves and streamers (*mog(oi)*, lit. 'snakes') onto of the *manjig* during ceremonies. The complex logic behind the different knots cannot be accounted for here (see Pürev 1993; 1999: 176–89), but the significant point for our purposes is that the performing shaman is perceived as the 'knot of knots' (Humphrey 1996: 270), that is to say, appears to the audience as a visualisation of the totality of events (i.e. misfortunes) which have prompted clients to visit the shaman (i.e. to tie knots) in the course of his or her career. Let me now substantiate this observation by taking a closer look at what takes place during a shamanic ceremony.

A shamanic ceremony

During a ceremony's introductory phase, the shaman sings a variety of praises (*magtaal*), prayers (*daatgal, zalbiral*), and invocations (*duudlaga, tamlaga*), and also makes milk and vodka libations towards the altar, the spirit vessel, the fire, and in the directions of the ninety-nine skies. Importantly, the shaman is not considered to be entirely 'without consciousness' (*uhaangüi*) at this point. At most, the shaman's consciousness 'deteriorates' (*muudah*), meaning that it becomes increasingly unclear and hazy. This idea of gradual mental dissolution is also reflected in the donning of the costume. The shaman begins by purifying the shamanic boots over the smoke of burning juniper (*arts*), then addresses some silent prayers to the boots, after which the assistant puts them on the shaman.[6] After a while, the gown is subject to a similar treatment, but this time the assistant also performs the purification, for the shaman's consciousness apparently has now 'deteriorated' further. Finally, the headgear is put on, and the shaman is now ready to become possessed by his or her spirits. The shaman now makes three violent jumps, picks up the drum, and is offered a sip of vodka by the assistant, after which the actual shamanising begins.

The middle phase is when shamans make invocations for and are possessed by their protector spirits (see below). The moment of possession is marked by the shaman beginning to drum faster and making vomiting (*böölöh* – 'to shamanise' – also means 'to vomit') and animal-like sounds. Then follow the 'words uttered' (*heldeg üg*) by the spirit – also known as 'what is sung by it' (*duudag n'*). These and other terms cover the plethora of requests, 'spirit-autobiographies', exclamations, verdicts, etc. which make up the actual message from the spirit to the audience (cf. Even 1988–9: 366–7). Then, as the curing session is over (each spirit calls only one person), the spirit 'departs' (*garah*), an event typically marked by the shaman drumming one single, loud, beat.

The end phase is marked by the shaman violently throwing the drumstick. The assistant must now rush to undress the shaman (headgear first, followed by the gown, and finally the boots), for it is considered extremely dangerous to wear the costume without continuing drumming. Then, as the shaman slowly becomes herself, she starts making prayers, offerings and libations similar to those of the introductory phase. Eventually, the shaman sits down, lights a cigarette, and is offered tea and snacks. Relatives distribute the remaining offerings between the audience, and fresh tea is served. At sunrise, the gathering disperses.

The carefulness with which the assistant helps the shaman in donning and undressing the costume makes it clear that the use of this artefact is considered to put an enormous stress on both mind and body. It is true that the 'armour' is believed to protect the shaman by 'absorbing' (*shingeh*) the souls of both people and spirits into its many 'layers' (*salbagar*), so they do not 'pierce' (*tsoolnoh*) into the shaman herself. However, wearing the costume also presents a real danger of getting lost in the occult world of the spirits, as is believed to happen when a shaman ceases drumming, for example. I now suggest that this very concept of an unfathomable realm of the unknown is enacted by the distinct characteristics of the shamanic costume. Unlike an ordinary Mongolian gown (*deel*), which is believed to contain its wearer within a protective enclosure (Lacaze 2000), the shamanic gown – which is not worn with the otherwise ubiquitous sash and whose baggy exterior is covered with tentacle-like strings and flaps – thus seems to be perceived as *hyper surface*, which, far from maintaining the boundaries of the wearer's person, has the effect of opening her up towards the cosmos. Keeping in mind the multitude of knots on the shamanic gown, consider Küchler's description of the distinct virtuality engendered by the knot's unique topological properties:

> As virtual space, the knot-spanning surface acts synthetically in bringing together, like the mathematical formula or the architectural plan, experiences from a number of domains; rather than just articulating already existing knowledge, the knot as an artefact is thus capable of creating something 'new' – a momentary integration of distinct domains of experience.
>
> (2001: 68)

It seems to me that this description very precisely captures the necessary material conditions of the occult journey that the Darhad shaman undergoes, or is said to undergo, in donning the gown. Like the variety of nonhuman souls called upon at the beginning of the possession ceremony, the shaman's own soul is attracted to this dazzling labyrinth of layers upon layers, and knots upon knots, and just like these other souls cannot avoid becoming 'absorbed' into this virtual totality of interconnections and heterogeneous substances, the shaman's own consciousness is understood gradually to 'deteriorate' into increasingly atomised fragments, not unlike an exploding haze of gas (tellingly, the term for 'trance' – *hii uhaantai* – literally means 'gassy' or 'airy' mind). Thus understood, it is probably no coincidence that the direction of the journey between spirits and shaman has been described as fundamentally ambiguous in the literature on Mongolian shamanism (see Humphrey 1996: 199–26). Rather than the shaman travelling to a transcendental realm inhabited by spirits, or conversely the spirits travelling to an ordinary realm inhabited by people, what is perceived to happen during the Darhad shamanic possession ritual is that the world of humans and the (other) world of spirits momentarily are collapsed onto the immanent hyper-surface of the shamanic costume by virtue of this artefact enacting a certain distinct knotted virtuality.

Talismans of thought (1)

With these observations in mind, we may return to our more general question as to how thought occurs through artefacts. Clearly, each of the two talismans of thought discussed above – the spirit vessel and the shamanic costume – augments and distributes peoples' conceptualisation of their social life in significant ways. In either case, we are faced with a talisman, which is deliberately constructed to draw visual attention. Following Gell (1999), both artefacts appear to share – by virtue of their bundles and knots – the formal requirements of an aesthetic trap within which the viewer's perception (just as in the case of certain more conventional art objects) becomes entrapped by being confronted with a sort of cognitive maze in which one's visual faculty will, so to speak, lose its way. Somewhat paradoxically, there is no doubt that the spectators of these objects nonetheless feel compelled to remember their design quite carefully, if only because the consequences of doing otherwise could turn out to be very dangerous indeed. The wife of a prominent bear hunter, say, must remember exactly which (unique) element of the household's hunting vessel refers to her husband's current hunt, for she will need to know this in order to lure his soul back if he encounters trouble on the road (cf. Chaussonnet 1988). Likewise, the households belonging to a given shaman's ritual community have an obvious interest in memorising the complex distribution of knots upon her gown's *manjig*, for the possession of this indigenous 'patent' equips people with an imagistic knowledge of the total distribution of misfortune amongst the shaman's clientele (a useful thing in a context where sorcery accusations are abundant, cf. Lacaze 1996). Finally, in both cases we are also faced with highly tabooed artefacts, whose degree and mode of accessibility is sanctioned according to social and religious hierarchies. While shamans (and hunters) are more or less free to access these objects according to their own will, many ordinary people (and particularly children) are only allowed to see these artefacts under particular circumstances prescribed by others. In all these senses, the Darhad shamanic paraphernalia constitute powerful socio-cognitive technologies, which enable certain people to remember and know certain things to a higher degree than others.

These conclusions, however, do not fully account for what these artefacts 'allow people to think that they could not otherwise contemplate' (paraphrasing Day in Day 2004). Or, more precisely, we have not so far properly considered what role these artefacts might play in the wider sense of how the Darhads conceive of themselves as persons inhabiting a local universe dominated by shamanic forces and entities. As implied in my earlier discussion of the active externalist approach, the implications of this paradigm do not stop with the recognition that humans enhance their capacity to think by surrounding themselves with various kinds of cognitive scaffolding. Along with this essentially epistemological question of how people come *to think* through things, I now suggest, a no less profound ontological question is automatically posed as to how people come *to be* through these very things. Do not forget that this precisely is what so many (non-anthropologists) consider untenable in Clark's theory: it opens up for an anthropology which fundamentally destabilises 'the core philosophical sense of "self"' (cf. Gertler 2001).

In what remains of this chapter, my aim is to discuss the two above artefacts with respect to the 'ontographic' (Holbraad 2003) question just raised. I want to show that, by importing certain theoretical ideas from Melanesian and Amazonian anthropology, it becomes possible to explain how a particular

Darhad sense of the self is enacted through these shamanic things. First, however, we need to consider certain general characteristics of the Darhad spirit world, in particular the fundamentally labile and heterogeneous state in which the shamanic spirits are believed to exist.

The fluid world of ongod

Darhad popular lore is awash with narratives about *ongod*, most of which have the same basic plot. Once upon a time, a tragic event took place (usually involving one or more persons with shamanic ancestry), and this event then caused the creation of a distinct *ongon*. Since then, certain peoples' lives have in decisive ways unfolded in accordance with the subsequent 'path' (see below) undertaken by this shamanic spirit, notably in the case of those descendents who have themselves inherited the shamanic ability (*udha*), and who may therefore have become full-blown shamans themselves. However, in addition to these primordial shamanic spirit scenarios, an ever increasing number of *ongod* come into being as shamans pass away, for the soul (*süns*) of each deceased shaman is understood to turn into a discrete *ongon* in its own right, and each such *ongon süns* will then (three years after the shaman's burial) also begin to interfere in peoples' lives.

Each *ongon* should be conceived of as a complex amalgamation of events, social relationships and material substances which continuously absorbs ever more events, social relationships and material substances in accordance with the particular spatio-temporal trajectory defined by the original event from which the spirit was created. Even reaches the same conclusion in her detailed study of Darhad shamanist invocations (1988–9). The 'multiplicity' of a given shamanic spirit, she observes, 'rests upon the adjunction of ancestral shamanic *ongon's* [consisting of] auxiliary spirits, [i.e.] the different forms they can adopt, which in shamanic terminology is often known under the name of "servants" or "metamorphoses" (1988–9: 115; my translation).

Even tells us two important things here. First, she draws attention to the general distinction between spirit protectors and spirit helpers in Darhad shamanism. A spirit protector is a distinct spirit mastered by one or more shamans. Each spirit protector is 'absorbed' (*shingeh*) into the burial place (*ongony asar*) of the original, now deceased shaman to which it corresponds, has its own material manifestations on the shaman's paraphernalia (see note 4 below), and is the subject of the shaman's possessions. A shaman will master a certain number of such protectors, typically between five and fifteen (see also Badamhatan 1986: 169–72). These protectors are either 'clan spirits' (*yazguuryn ongod*), *ongod* from other clans acquired in a variety of ways (typically from shaman teachers), and then there are *ongod* which do not correspond to any specific line. The spirit helpers, on the other hand, are the different metamorphoses (*huvilgaan*) a given *ongon* may take. Typically, these take the form of wild animals whose specific capacities the spirits appropriate when travelling, but they can also take the form of non-zoomor-phic phenomena, such as rainbows (see, for example, Dulam 1992: 76). In fact, protector spirit helpers can take the form of virtually any helper (including phenomena as ephemeral as the flow of gossip), as long as these forms engender the spirits to cause certain effects.

Second, and following directly from this, Even tells us that a given *ongon* must be conceived of as an 'adjunction' of multiple forms. This is crucial for our present purposes, because it enables us to posit an isomorphism between the shamanic spirits' complex ontology and their equally heterogeneous material objectifications. Like the Melanesian *malanggan* sculptures, we may thus think of each *ongon* as a sort of thunderstorm inasmuch as it consists of 'many physical indexes [. . .] but [nevertheless] amount[s] to a single temporal entity, like a persistent thunderstorm which is made up of many, quasi-instantaneous flashes' (Gell 1998: 236). The *ongod* traverse through time and space according to the particular vectoring of forces which define their occult movements. In doing so, the *ongod* come to 'flash' in an ever increasing multiplicity of forms, or spirit metamorphoses, each of which are incorporated into their multiple constitution as discrete spirit protectors. A given *ongon*, then, is an inherently polymorphous and labile entity, for it is irreducible to any singular form, and is always moving along the inchoate path defined by its propensity to transmute from one form to another.

Talismans of thought (2)

How, one might now ask, would one go about making a 'map' of a given *ongon* thunderstorm distributed across time and space? I suggest that the Darhad spirit vessels are formally comparable to the *malanggan* sculptures, for each is clearly seen as 'a kind of body which accumulates, like a charged battery, the potential energy of the deceased [shaman] dispersed in the life-world' (Gell 1998). Certainly, their intriguing design points to this capacity. Unlike the stones used to build the sacred cairns (*ovoo*) erected on mountain tops by Mongolians to ensure the spiritual blessing and reproduction of pastoral communities (see e.g. Humphrey 1995; Sneath 2000), the disparate elements of a given Darhad spirit vessel are all distinguishable from one another (and therefore able to be memorised individually), just as each newly added substance corresponds to events in peoples' lives which are perceived as unique (like, say, a successful bear hunt).

The challenge of shamanist iconography, therefore, is to depict something inherently non-depictable, namely the totality aggregated by the movements of a given *ongon* thunderstorm across time. The 'representational' problem, insofar as it can really be described as such, consists in the fact that the ontological status of the Darhad shamanic spirits is not transcendental in the Platonic sense, where divine entities are held to exist in a supra-stable form (as atemporal ideas) of which humans can have access only to 'shadows' which are less stable. Rather, it is exactly the other way around: the shamanic spirits are perceived to be labile *an sich*, and the problem about their material instantiations is that these inevitably will be *too stable*, too 'ideal'. Obviously, this occult movement cannot therefore itself be depicted, but, I suggest, it is so to speak rendered *negatively visible*, or could we say 'virtually present', in that people, as described above, will mark each spirit intervention on their lives by adding a new element to their shamanic bundles.[7] The extremely heterodox constitution of the Darhad spirit vessels, then, can be said to depict the visible shadow cast by the *ongod's* invisible movement from one metamorphosis to another. In that sense, these artefacts constitute a sort of objectified movement, for the ongoing addition of new elements serves to itinerate each and every 'flash' of the *ongod* thunderstorms, as manifested in particular instances of human misfortune and luck.

Even more so than the spirit vessel, the Darhad shamanic costume may be fruitfully compared to a *malanggan* sculpture. Apart from the fact that both artefacts reflect an indigenous attempt to objectify movement itself, the analogy now also exists on a more sociological level, as both artefacts are only displayed on very particular occasions, and then only for a brief period of time. It is true that, unlike the *malanggan* sculptures, the Darhad shamanic costumes are not physically destroyed after having first been displayed at shamans' initiation rituals. However, each costume is socially destroyed following its owner's death, at which point it is placed on a spirit platform (*ongony asar*) constructed at the shaman's burial place (which only shamans are allowed visit) – or, indeed, is sold to an ethnographic museum, just like many *malanggan* sculptures are.

To sum up, the kind of knowledge enacted by the two shamanic artefacts must, just like that revealed through the *malanggan* sculptures, be a deeply esoteric one, for people's tabooed access to these talismans of thought renders something (negatively) visible which people cannot normally 'see', namely the invisible flow of shamanic forces. But the potential scope of our analysis is not covered by this epistemological observation. I now want to show that these shamanic artefacts are perceived not only to enact the labile ontology of the Darhad shamanic spirit world, but also to bring about a similarly fluid transformation of the Darhad person. Or, put differently, apart from enabling people *to think* their shamanic spirits in a certain esoteric way, the two artefacts in question also make people (and, in particular, shamans) come *to be* in a certain extraordinary way.

The shaman's two bodies

In order to bring the above point home, it is necessary to briefly consider Viveiros de Castro's 'perspectivist' theory of Amerindian social life (1998a; 1998b). Of particular relevance is his notion of 'multi-naturalism', that is, the widespread Amerindian conception that the world is divided into a multiplicity of ontologically discrete bodies (notably those of humans and game animals), which all share the same invisible intentionality, namely, the capacity to have a (body-specific) perspective. It follows that it requires another kind of body to perceive the world in another way, and this is exactly what many Amerindian shamans are held to have. This intriguing notion, which also appears among many of North Asia's indigenous peoples (Pedersen 2001; Willerslev 2004), has important ramifications for our understanding of the occult agency of Darhad shamanic artefacts.

Consider, for example, the case of the 'hunting/wild animal vessels' (*angiin ongod*), which, as earlier described, are used by hunters to ensure successful hunts. Apart from rendering the mysterious trajectories of the spirits virtually present, these artefacts are also imbued with the capacity to momentarily transform the bodily appearance of the hunter's person. As one hunter told me, this is 'the deepest of shamanic secrets' (*böögiin shashny hamgiin nuuts*), because it is the one with the most 'dangerous' (*ayultai*) implications for his own profession. 'Let us say', he went on,

> that I want to be a good wolf hunter. Then I must make a wolf *ongon*. If I make an *ongon* looking like a wolf out of sheep wool, then the wolf will think (*bodoh*) that *I am* a wolf. The point is that I will become like a wolf (*chon shig bolj baina*). A person who thus nearly has become a wolf (*barag chon bolchihson*) will not be known (*medehgüi*) as a human (*hün*) by the wolf. So I can kill him easily. This is what is called a hunting *ongon*. They all have the same purpose.

The explicit purpose of these artefacts, then, is to enable hunters to take upon the appearance (and, by implication, the perspective) of nonhuman entities. Turning now to the shamanic costume, a shaman from the Tsaatang community (a neighbouring group of reindeer-breeders which maintains close religious links to the Darhads) once proudly exclaimed that he 'has two bodies' (*hoyor biyetei*), one being his ordinary body and the other his shamanic body (Alan Wheeler, personal communication). Given that the Darhad shamanic costume by all accounts is also seen to provide the shaman with an additional – or, more precisely, a *perfected* – body, we may conceive of the costume itself as a sort of extra-corporal scaffold, which, by means of its toolbox of magical gimmicks (bundles, layers, 'snakes'), enables the shaman to traverse otherwise unsurpassable ontological divides. However, unlike the hunting vessel (for example), the shamanic costume does not just provide its user with *one* other corporal form (say, a wolf one); it rather seems to engage the shaman within a whole series of nonhuman bodies. Remember that, during a ceremony, a Darhad shaman is possessed by not just one, but most of her spirit protectors – each of which can take the shape of just about any kind of spirit helper – just as the shaman's costume (and own spirit vessel) comprises objectifications of all the spirit protectors and helpers, he or she masters. By donning the costume, then, a Darhad shaman is transformed into the *ultimate multinatural entity*, as this hyper-surface is believed to transport the shaman to an immanent space of multiplicities (Deleuze and Guattari 1999), which, unlike the more 'objectified' vessels, is isomorphic with the fluid ontology of the *ongod* themselves.

It is precisely in this sense that the two artefacts in question, and the shamanic gown in particular, can be said to be constitutive of a Darhad sense of the self. Humphrey (1996) has convincingly shown that the fluid personhood of the Daur Mongolian shaman (*yadgan*) was perceived to be constituted in a qualitatively different manner than the stable personhood of the 'old man' (*utaachi*). A similar observation can be made about Darhad social life; my point is that the shamanic gown plays a crucial role in keeping both this and other sociological divisions in place. For, as we shall now see, not only is the Darhad shamanic costume fully completed only by being (properly) worn, but the shaman's own person is also only fully completed by being able to wear it.

Keeping in mind the earlier described knotting practice that takes place during shamanic ceremonies, we may thus conceive of the Darhad shaman (in his or her costume) as an eversion of a prominent elder man (in fact, of all ordinary persons), in the sense that the visible surface of the performing shaman seems to correspond to what is perceived as the invisible 'inside' of an ordinary person. Certainly, the fact that the moment of possession is marked by the shaman making vomiting (*böölöh*) sounds seems to convey the idea of a sort of figure-ground reversal occurring in the composition of his or her person.[8] That is, the performing shaman can be said to personify an ordinary Darhad person turned inside out, for by so to speak wearing peoples' misfortunes (i.e. knots) on his or her shamanic skin, the shaman is momentarily making visible what normally cannot be told from a person's appearance, namely the hidden propensity for greediness, envy and violence, which constitutes what the Darhads describe as their 'black side' (*har tal*) (see also Pedersen forthcoming). The shamanic ceremony, on this interpretation, separates the ritual community into the two interdependent (and reversible) sociological kinds of perpetrators and receivers of misfortune. While the latter will necessarily be present at the ceremony (as the clients who are being cured), the former might not, but their 'black' agency is nonetheless made visible by the new knots which are fastened onto the performing shaman's costume. In that sense, this artefact serves to lock the clients into a sort of double perspective not unlike that afforded by the Maussian gift, for both can be described as material configurations, which, by exteriorising the direction in which social relationships flow, forces 'each person [to see] him or herself from the viewpoint of the other' (Strathern 1999: 254).

What makes a Darhad shaman a 'genuine' (*jinhene*) shaman, therefore, is her capacity to personify as many disparate relations as possible, both in the 'exterior' sense that the shaman alone has access to multiple bodily perspectives within a multinaturally constituted world, and in the 'interior' sense that the shaman alone is capable of making peoples' 'black' insides visible to themselves and others. As in the Cuna shamanic ceremonies studied by Severi, 'a systematic relationship [is thus] established between two negatively defined dimensions of the universe, an invisible landscape within the body and an external, though inaccessible, world' (1993: 176). My specific point is that shamanic costume is crucial for this doubly transformative constitution of the shaman's person. This is not only because, sociologically, it is the acquisition of the costume that marks a shaman's approval as a shaman, but also that the costume, ontologically, is what envelops the shaman's occult journey within an extra-ordinary sequence in time and space. For, if the shaman (in wearing her costume) is an eversion of an ordinary person, then this costume also is a sort of ontological tool by which she is rendered (relatively) ordinary when *not* wearing it. The costume, on this interpretation, simultaneously invites and exorcises spiritual attention, for, if the shaman is cast into the fluid world of the *ongod* by donning the costume, then she is also simultaneously capable of arresting this movement by taking it off. Seen from the 'labile point of view' of the spirits, then, the costume is imbued with an occult agency, not only for setting magical things in train, but also for bringing them to a halt, since the shaman's undressing of the costume makes her loop out of the orbit of the spirits' occult movement, i.e. renders the shaman still, just like an ordinary person ought to be.

Darhad shamans, in that sense, are both perceived to be ontologically stable (as ordinary humans are supposed to be) and ontologically fluid (like spirits). And, as I have argued, it is precisely the costume (and, with that, the recognition of the shamanic office) that makes all the difference in this respect, for this artefact constitutes the material detachment, or could we say 'intraface', which divides the shaman's person into a complete double entity, at once human and nonhuman. On the above background, it seems to me that the Darhad case represents a third, intermediate position on the comparative axis set up by Strathern in her discussion of the differences between Amazonian and Melanesian perspectivism (1999: 252–3). For the 'perspectival traffic' taking place in Darhad shamanism simultaneously seems to hinge on the shaman's ability to transgress the human/nonhuman divide (as in the Amazon), and her ability to personify multiple sociological positions *within* an interhuman ontological divide (like certain persons do in Melanesia).

Conclusion

The two kinds of shamanic artefacts discussed above, I now hope to have established, not only constitute distinct cognitive technologies, with the different epistemological implications arising from adapting an active externalist understanding of human cognition. They also play the role of indispensable ontological tools in that they, following Viveiros de Castro, are perceived to provide extra-bodily material forms by means of which nonhuman perspectives can be entertained, and, consequently, the appearances of humans from the point of view of humans as well as nonhumans can be altered.

To put this conclusion into perspective, it is worthwhile to consider Viveiros de Castro's (1998b) distinction between 'seeing' (as the ontological state defined by entertaining a species-specific perspective in the world) and 'knowing' (as the epistemological state of reflecting upon the world). Clearly, the latter form of 'knowing' refers only to the orthodox representational theory of mind, which this chapter explicitly has sought to challenge. Yet, as we have seen in both this and various other chapters of the present volume, there surely exist other (and much less representational) forms of knowing as well, namely those eruptions of knowledge which, in Strathern's apt phrasing, 'consis[t] in "seeing" relations' (1999: 260, emphasis added). Evidently, the deeply alarming and yet strangely alluring prospect of 'seeing' social relations in the Darhad shamanic artefacts described above cannot be reduced to a question of forming mental representations in the standard internalist sense. Much more, this relational knowledge, or relational knowing, seems to take the form of what Clark and Chalmers coined *external beliefs* – that is, a sort of intuitive 'on-line truth', which is enacted (as opposed to constructed) by probing ever deeper into the materiality of these talismans of thought.

What future studies would have to address in further detail, I believe, is the (unique?) human capacity *to imagine things from the point of view of other things*, as certain Melanesians do when they 'see' themselves and others from within the 'theoretical body' of a clan, or as certain Amerindians do when they 'see' themselves and others from the nonhuman perspective of, say, a jaguar. Ideally, this is not only an anthropological project, for, if the cognitive scientists take seriously the significant ethnographic challenges posed from adapting the active externalist model, they might also take part in the cross-cultural study of how things are appropriated in extra-human imaginative projects. For this is precisely the point I have been trying to make, namely that certain Darhad shamanist knowledge simply cannot be formed (let alone be transmitted) without the cognitive process in question being actively embedded within certain artefacts. Crucially, this should be understood both in the epistemological sense that the nature of this materially constituted knowledge is contingent upon the particular kind of body (human, shaman, animal, victim, perpetrator) which the thinking agent is imagining to have, and in the ontological sense that this agent is him- or herself constituted (as a specific kind of entity) as the perspectivist implication of having been rendered into a particular kind of subject from perceiving this knowledge. Humans, then, are not only thinking through things. They also come to be through them.

Notes

1 Fieldwork was carried out in the Darhad districts of Ulaan Uul and Tsagaan Nuur from July 1998 to September 1999, and during the summer of 2000. I thank the Danish Research Academy, King's College, Cambridge, and the William Wyse Foundation for their financial support. A special thanks to Martin Holbraad for many late-night discussions about religious ontologies. I am very also grateful to D. Bumochir, Lars Højer, Caroline Humphrey, Marilyn Strathern and Alan Wheeler for their comments on earlier versions of this manuscript.

2 Inspired by Fodor's cognitive theory of language (1983), the massive modularity thesis postulates that the human mind comes pre-equipped with a number of quasi-autonomous, special-purpose computational mechanisms, or 'modules'. However, as both Mithen (1996: 33–60) and Sterelny (2003: 177–210) note, no consensus exists as to how 'informationally encapsulated' (Fodor 1983) the different modules might be, let alone whether higher-order conceptual processes are also subject to domain-specific differentiation. Some cognitive scientists, especially those adopting a neo-Darwinian evolutionary stance, hold that practically all activities of the human mind, whether perceptual or conceptual, are based on autonomous, innately specified dispositions/modules, which 'organise information in a certain manner and [. . .] perform computations of a certain form' (Sperber 1996: 136; see also Cosmides and Tooby 1994). Others, such as Fodor himself (2000), argue against this thoroughly modular picture of the human mind, and opt instead for various models of 'hybrid mental architectures', which seek to balance 'the intelligent automaticity of much human cognition with our flexible and open-ended capacities' (Sterelny 2003: 189).

3 In the following discussion, I refer to a number of cognate terms associated with Melanesian anthropology (Gell's 'distributed person', Wagner's 'fractal person' and Strathern's 'dividual') as if they constituted a single concept.

4 The word for shamanic spirits – ongon, pl. ongod – is probably etymologically related to the word ongots ('vessel, receptacle, boat') (Humphrey 1998: 427; Even 1988–9: 387). Crucially, it is used to denote both the shamanic spirits themselves and their material instantiations.

5 Shamans' vessels may also comprise anthropomorphic or zoomorphic figures suspended on a string of cloth (Badamhatan 1986: 169–71; Dioszegi 1963). However, I shall here concentrate on the more bundle-like vessels, for these seem to be the dominant form found in the Darhad region today.

6 Two close relatives of the shaman play important auxiliary roles before and during ceremonies: the shaman's 'assistant' (tüshee), who, among other things, is responsible for aiding the shaman in dressing the costume, and the 'interpreter' (helmerch), who communicates messages between the spirits and the audience.

7 I borrow the notion of virtual presence from Noë's phenomenology of perceptual experience (Noë forthcoming). Discussing the mundane activity of seeing, say, a tomato, Noë observes that

> we experience the presence of the occluded bits even as we experience, plainly, their absence. They are present as absent. Psychologists call this phenomenon amodal perception: perception, as it were, but not in any modality. This is not quite adequate as a characterization, however. The

paradoxical quality is sharper. The phenomenon would better be characterized as amodal visual perception, as a kind of seeing without seeing.

(Noë forthcoming)

My contention is that this 'paradoxical quality' of everyday visual experience also applies to the perception of what are considered to be magical objects. In fact, there is reason to believe that this amodal phenomenology is especially characteristic for the visual experience of religious artefacts, given that many such objects are explicitly designed to perform the role of technologies of the imagination; that is, of cognitive technologies particularly capable of enacting conceptualisations of virtual worlds.

8 I am grateful to Lars Højer for having directed my attention to this interpretation.

References

Badamhatan, S. (1986) 'Les chamanistes du Bouddha vivant', *Études Mongoles . . . et sibériennes*, 17.

Bloch, M. (1998) *How We Think They Think: Anthropological Approaches to Cognition, Memory, and Literacy*, Oxford: Westview Press.

——(1992) *Prey into Hunter: the Politics of Religious Experience*, Cambridge: Cambridge University Press.

Boyer, P. (2001) 'Cultural inheritance tracks and cognitive predispositions: the example of religious concepts', in Whitehouse, H. (ed.) *The Debated Mind: Evolutionary Psychology versus Ethnography*, Oxford: Berg.

——(1994) *The Naturalness of Religious Ideas: a Cognitive Theory of Religion*, Berkeley: University of California Press.

Chaussonnet, V. (1988) 'Needles and animals: women's magic', in Fitzhugh, W. and Crowell, A. (eds) *Crossroads of Continents: cultures of Siberia and Alaska*, New York: Smithsonian Institution Press.

Chrisley, R. and Ziemke, T. (2002) 'Embodiment', in *Encyclopedia of Cognitive Science*, London: Macmillan.

Clark, A. (2003) *Natural Born Cyborgs*, Oxford: Oxford University Press.

——(1997) *Being There*, Cambridge MA: MIT Press.

Clark, A. and Chalmers, D. J. (1998) 'The extended mind', *Analysis*, 58: 10–23.

Cosmides, L. and Tooby, J. (1994) 'Origins of domain specificity: the evolution of functional organization', in L. A. Hirschfeld and S. A. Gelman (eds) *Mapping the Mind: Domain Specificity in Cognition and Culture*, Cambridge: Cambridge University Press.

Day, M. (2004) 'Religion, off-line cognition and the extended mind', *Journal of Cognition and Culture*, 4(1): 101–21.

Deleuze, G. and Guattari, F. (1999) *A Thousand Plateaus: Capitalism and Schizophrenia*, London: Athlone Press.

Dennett, D. C. (2000) 'Making tools for thinking', in Sperber, D. (ed.) *Metarepresentation: a Multidisciplinary Perspective*, Oxford: Oxford University Press.

Dioszegi, V. (1963) 'Ethnogenic aspects of Darkhat shamanism', *Acta Orientalia Hungaria*, 16: 55–81.

——(1961) 'Problems of Mongolian shamanism', *Acta Ethnographica*, 10(1–2): 195–206.

Dulam, S. (1992) *Darhad Böögiin Ulamjlal*, Ulaanbaatar: MUIS-iin Hevlel.

Dulam, S. and Even, M-D. (1994) 'Animalité et humanité dans le chamanisme des Darkhates de Mongolie', *Études Mongoles . . . et sibériennes*, 25: 131–44.

163

Even, M-D. (1988–9) 'Chants de chamanes de Mongols', *Études Mongoles . . . et sibériennes*, 19–20.

Fodor, J. (2000) *The Mind Doesn't Work That Way: the Scope and Limits of Computational Psychology*, Cambridge MA: MIT Press.

——(1983) *The Modularity of Mind: an Essay on Faculty Psychology*, Cambridge MA: MIT Press.

Gell, A. (1999) 'Vogel's net: traps as artworks and artworks as traps', in *The Art of Anthropology: Essays and Diagrams*, London: Athlone Press.

——(1998) *Art and Agency: an Anthropological Theory*, Oxford: Clarendon Press.

Gertler, B. (2001) 'The narrow mind', presentation at the National Endowment for the Humanities Summer Institute on Consciousness and Intentionality, http://humanities.ucsc.edu/NEH/gertler.htm.

Gibson, J. J. (1979) *The Ecological Approach to Visual Perception*, Boston MA: Houghton Mifflin.

Godelier, M. (1986) *The Making of Great Men: Male Domination and Power among the New Guinea Baruya*, Cambridge: Cambridge University Press.

Hamayon, R. (1990) *La chasse à l'âme: esquisse d'une théorie du chamanisme sibérien*, Nanterre: Société d'ethnologie.

——(1984) 'Is there a typically female exercise of shamanism in patrilinear societies such as the Buriat?', in Hoppal, M. (ed.) *Shamanism in Eurasia*, part 2, Göttingen: Editions Herodot.

Holbraad, M. S. (2003) 'Estimando a necessidade: os oráculos de ifá e a verdade em Havana', *Mana*, 9(2): 33–77.

Humphrey, C. (1998) *Marx Went Away – but Karl Stayed Behind*, Ann Arbor MI: University of Michigan Press.

——(1996) *Shamans and Elders: Experience, Knowledge, and Power among the Daur Mongols*, Oxford: Clarendon Press.

——(1995) 'Chiefly and shamanist landscapes in Mongolia', in Hirsch, E. and O'Hanlon, M. (eds) *The Anthropology of Landscape: Perspectives in Place and Space*, Oxford: Clarendon Press.

Hutchins, E. (1995) *Cognition in the Wild*, Cambridge MA: MIT Press.

Ingold, T. (2001) 'From the transmission of representations to the education of attention', in Whitehouse, H. (ed.) *The Debated Mind: Evolutionary Psychology versus Ethnography*, Oxford: Berg.

Küchler, S. (2001) 'Why knot? Towards a theory of art and mathematics', in Pinney, C. and Thomas, N. (eds) *Beyond Aesthetics: Art and the Technologies of Enchantment*, Oxford: Berg.

——(1992) 'Making skins: malanggan and the idiom of kinship in Northern New Ireland', in Coote, J. and Shelton, A. (eds) *Anthropology, Art and Aesthetics*, Oxford: Clarendon Press.

——(1988) 'Malanggan: objects, sacrifice, and the production of memory', *American Ethnologist*, 15(4): 625–37.

Lacaze, G. (2000) 'Représentations et techniques du corps chez les peuples mongols', unpublished Ph.D. thesis, Université de Paris-X.

——(1996) 'Thoughts about the effectiveness of the shamanism speech: preliminary data to the study of today's uses of maledictions by the Darxad of the Xovsgol', in *Tsentral'no-azyatskii Shamaanizm*, Ulan-Ude: Russian Academy of Sciences.

Layton, R. (2003) 'Art and agency: a reassessment', *Journal of the Royal Anthropological Institute*, 9: 447–64.

Mithen, S. (1998) 'A creative explosion?', in Mithen, S. (ed.) *Creativity in Human Evolution and Prehistory*, London: Routledge.

——(1996) *The Prehistory of the Mind: a Search for the Origins of Art, Religion and Science*, London: Thames and Hudson.

Noë, A. (forthcoming) 'Experience without the head', to appear in Gendler, T. S. and Hawthorne, J. (eds) *Perceptual Experience*, Oxford: Oxford University Press.

Pedersen, M. A. (forthcoming) 'Tame from within: landscapes of the religious imagination among the Darhads of Northern Mongolia', to appear in Bulag, U. and Dienberger, H. (eds) *The Tibetan-Mongolian Interface*, Leiden: Brill.

——(2001) 'Totemism, animism and North Asian indigenous ontologies', *Journal of the Royal Anthropological Institute*, 7(3): 411–27.

Pinney, C. and Thomas, N. (2001) *Beyond Aesthetics: Art and the Technologies of Enchantment*, Oxford: Berg.

Pürev, O. (1999) *Mongol Böögiin Shashin*, Ulaanbaatar: Mongolian Academy of Science.

——(1993) 'The problem of knots of Mongolian shamans' garment', in Zhang, J. (ed.) *International Symposium of Mongolian Culture*, Taipei.

Samuel, G. (1993) *Civilized Shamans: Buddhism in Tibetan Societies*, Washington DC: Smithsonian Institution Press.

Sandschejew, G. D. (1930) *Darkhaty*, Leningrad: Akademie Nauk SSSR.

Severi, C. (1993) 'Talking about souls: the use of a complex category in Cuna ritual language', in Boyer, P. (ed.) *Cognitive Aspects of Religious Symbolism*, Cambridge: Cambridge University Press.

Sneath, D. (2000) *Changing Inner Mongolia: Pastoral Mongolian Society and the Chinese State*, Oxford: Oxford University Press.

Sperber, D. (1996) *Explaining Culture: a Naturalistic Approach*, Oxford: Blackwell.

Spivey, M. J, Richardson, D. C. and Fitneva, S. A. (2004) 'Thinking outside the brain: spatial indices to visual and linguistic information', in Henderson, J. and Ferreira, F. (eds) *Interfacing Language, Vision, and Action*, San Diego: Academic Press.

Sterelny, K. (2004) 'Externalism, epistemic artefacts and the extended mind', in Schantz, R. (ed.) *The Externalist Challenge*, Berlin: Walter de Gruyter.

——(2003) *Thought in a Hostile World: the Evolution of Human Cognition*, Oxford: Blackwell.

Strathern, M. (2001) 'The patent and the Malanggan', *Theory, Culture and Society*, 18(4): 1–26.

——(1999) *Property, Substance and Effect: Anthropological Essays and Persons and Things*, London: Athlone Press.

——(1988) *The Gender of the Gift: Problems with Women and Problems with Society in Melanesia*, Berkeley: University of California Press..

Sutton, J. (2002) 'Representation, reduction, and interdisciplinary in the sciences of memory', in Clapin, H., Staines, P. and Slezak, P. (eds) *Representation in Mind: New Approaches to Mental Representation*, Amsterdam: Elsevier.

Von Uexküll, J. (1921) *Umwelt und Innenwelt der Tiere*, Berlin: Julius Springer.

Viveiros de Castro, E. (1998a) 'Cosmological deixis and Amerindian perspectivism', *Journal of the Royal Anthropological Institute*, 4(3): 469–88.

——(1998b) 'Cosmological perspectivism in Amazonia and elsewhere', general lectures, Department of Social Anthropology, University of Cambridge.

Wagner, R. (1991) 'The fractal person', in Godelier, M. and Strathern, M. (eds) *Big Men and Great Men: Personifications of Power in Melanesia*, Cambridge: Cambridge University Press.

Whitehouse, H. (2001) 'Conclusion: towards a reconciliation', in Whitehouse, H. (ed.) *The Debated Mind: Evolutionary Psychology versus Ethnography*, Oxford: Berg.

——(2000) *Arguments and Icons: Divergent Modes of Religiosity*, Oxford: Oxford University Press.

Willerslev, R. (2004) 'Not animal, not not-animal: hunting, imitation and empathetic knowledge among the Siberian Yukaghirs', *Journal of the Royal Anthropological Institute*, 10(3): 629–52.

Zhamtsarano, Ts. (1979) 'Ethnography and geography of the Darkhat and other Mongolian minorities', The Mongolia Society, Special Papers, 8.

8

DIFFERENTIATION AND ENCOMPASSMENT

A critique of Alfred Gell's theory of the abduction of creativity

James Leach

The place of objects in anthropological investigation has, all too often, been secondary to the cultural and social. Objects are fitted into cultural contexts, while 'things' often are discussed only as the necessary material backdrop to the workings of society. Culture can be read from objects through symbolic analysis, sense is made of their form and use by reference to prior cultural systems of meaning (Strathern 1990). It is as if the category of the material, the inanimate, was a pre-analytic given, one of the basic building blocks upon which a social or cultural theory of meaning could (unreflexively) be built. That is, because the material and the object world exist in particular relation to the person of the analyst, and this relation is so thoroughly naturalised as to appear given by the human condition, much anthropological theory has relied upon 'things' material stability of form and substance, opposing objects to the persons who act, create and utilise them. 'Things' then populate our descriptions of others' worlds with our own distinctions between mind (spirit) and matter, subjects and objects, agents and patients. One might say that we are already used to 'thinking through things'. There seems work to do in becoming conscious of the effects these 'thinkings' have on the outcome of our endeavours.

This volume has the aim of making some of the consequences of this naturalisation apparent. We also positively suggest where we might take an analysis of the social world which does not define it as separate from (albeit connected to) the world of objects and things. I take this challenge here in the following terms: The way that people are connected to what they produce, and the terms of their claims upon those productions (Hirsch and Strathern 2004) reveal assumptions about the nature of the person which are already embedded in particular schemes for object production. One can ask certain questions following from this. What is it that the person does in order to be recognisable as a person? How does this relate to 'things'? What effect do their intentions and actions have? An old model of civilisation posited that the effects people have are on the environment that surrounds them; on things. It is the progressive specialisation and development of these effects that marks the vital stages of human history. Through the modification of the external, object world, persons come to realise themselves as civilised beings of the kind who rightfully control the world, and are connected to it through ownership of various kinds (see Pocock 1992).

In this chapter, I examine the correlations between a recent and powerful theory of objects that professes to move beyond previous understandings, and contemporary object production (of a very particular kind). The correlations tell us something about the analyst's embeddedness in the same series of assumptions about things as those involved in this object production. Creativity is the focus of my analysis as it is in the mechanisms for the recognition of creativity that the process of making things and persons in the form they appear can be seen.

I begin with a very contemporary interest in the boundaries of knowledge practices, and the (creative) potential to cross them through novel object production. It is the notion of the agency of these objects, and thus how they relate to persons, that points me initially to Alfred Gell's theories of abduction, agency and the mind. And that puts us squarely in the territory of thinking through how persons and things are potentially equivalent in their effects.[1]

Analysts and practitioners

Interdisciplinary initiatives abound, and inside academia as well as beyond it we hear of the importance of working across boundaries and making new connections.[2] This chapter addresses some of the issues that these imperatives precipitate. My focus is on an initiative that sought to bring visual artists into collaboration with research scientists. The scheme's originators intended that outcomes would include artworks and/or technological artefacts that *reflected their collaborative origin*. Bringing vision and expertise from different domains into the production of novel and possibly valuable objects, participants understood the potential for an interdisciplinary, and 'inter-cultural' exchange between kinds of knowledge and skill.[3] This was to result in object production. These objects were to have novel and interesting effects (see note 16 below), to act as 'agents' (to use Alfred Gell's term) of a particular kind. Moreover, facilitators were interested in the processes, networks, and 'social' outcomes as forms of 'object' production (Leach 2005). In other words, the distinction between persons, processes, and objects seemed blurred, just as in Alfred Gell's theory of the object-nexus (Gell 1998). Social scientists were included as expert 'evaluators' of the scheme as it was thought that capturing the social dynamic might be equivalent to capturing new forms of creativity, making the lessons learned available for others to utilise.[4] Is such evaluation the evaluation of *agency* in Gell's terms? That is, of the extension of persons through the object nexus?

What would such an approach to this collaboration reveal, and what would it obscure?

This chapter was written specifically attempting to use Gell's theories, developed in a number of writings and brought together in *Art and Agency* (1998) to think about art-science collaborations. It has ended up as a kind of exploratory critique of Gell. My impulse to produce a critique comes from the very promise of Gell's work. *Art and Agency* suggests the kind of theory I myself have been trying to advance (see Leach 2002).[5] However, as many have recognised, *Art and Agency* contains different strands, some of which seem contradictory (Layton 2003: 458).[6] In this chapter I will focus on how the intellect and causation are problematic in Gell's argument. It is worth doing so, I believe, as these aspects lie at the heart of what is innovative in the book. In one reading, one can understand Gell as describing how objects and people enter into networks of relationships in which they are not differentiated on the basis of their ability to cause other persons to act.[7] The idea of the 'causal nexus' in Gell mitigates against the necessity of viewing the individual as the only agentive component in generative social processes.[8]

However, Gell's project to overcome conventional subject/object distinctions is undermined when thing-to-thing and thing-to-person relations are modelled as if any object with agency must demonstrate an intellect, and a will, which derive directly from a human actor. If there were no mind to animate the causal nexus, there would be no art work and no agent, in spite of his attempt to level to playing field between persons and objects in our theorising. A particular conception of the mind, as the source of creativity, and moreover, the individual mind contained within a single person, lies behind this. I do not look to Melanesia,[9] where one might expect to find the notion of the individual author destabilised, but rather to artistic and scientific collaboration in the UK to reveal this aspect of Gell's thinking.

My approach to Gell stems from the kinds of issues that interdisciplinary collaborations pose to practitioners (specifically the sci-art collaborations I have been participating in).[10] The link I make is that these issues arise because of similar conceptual relations (which I go on to elaborate) to those implied in Gell's theory itself. So whereas we might say sci-art collaborators are genuinely struggling (because of the interdisciplinary intent) with the consequences of a (deeply embedded) way of imagining persons and knowledge, Gell's theory in *Art and Agency* is limited because it does not move beyond a similar conception of the artist/author. To state this plainly, I believe that Gell's approach to creativity shares fundamental assumptions with the ethnographic subjects I discuss.

Creativity is not an explicit focus of Gell's in *Art and Agency*. However, I seek here to uncover the implicit theory of creativity embedded in his use of the notion of 'abduction'. Gell's analytic position on the agency of objects, and the extension of persons through the abduction of their agency from those objects, is structured by assumptions about persons embedded in the language of cognitive science which Gell enthusiastically adopts. Paradoxically, Gell's theory was directly inspired by Marilyn Strathern's writings on the partible nature of persons in Melanesia. She has famously outlined how objects substitute or stand in for persons in ritual and exchange contexts (Strathern 1988; and see Gell 1999). However, in Gell, the possibility of describing the reality of multiple relational referents for both objects and persons is obscured by the way creativity itself is envisaged.[11]

I focus upon what I call the 'differentiated' nature of those persons who collaborate in sci-art, and how this initial difference is understood as a source of creative potential. The differentiation of persons, and of kinds of knowledge, is seen as a pre-requisite for the development of collaborative outcomes, and for the power and success of these outcomes. My argument then utilises transformations between states of individuation (through differentiation), and states of encompassment, where many people's collaborative endeavour is made to appear as the outcome of a single mind's internal labouring.

The New Technology Arts Fellowships

A pilot scheme in interdisciplinary collaboration was begun in Cambridge, UK, in January 2002. I was asked to participate as a social scientific observer, and to write an evaluation of the project, which was called the New Technology Arts Fellowships (NTAF).[12] NTAF was a partnership between the Arts Council of England, Crucible, which is an interdisciplinary network of researchers in Cambridge University, Kettle's Yard (the contemporary art gallery of the University of Cambridge) and The Junction CDC (an arts and music venue in the city). NTAF intended to move collaborations between scientists and artists on from a recent vogue, which is to have artists utilise images from science to make interesting or arresting visual presentations.[13] Those behind NTAF stated that artists utilising imaging techniques within science to make art is little more than a marketing exercise for science, highlighting the potential to make science accessible to a wider public though the presentational skills of artists.[14] In NTAF, artists and scientists/technologists were encouraged to collaborate on the same projects, bringing vision and expertise from different domains into the production of objects. There was a research element, in other words, an exploration of new technologies in a novel way. And there was an explicit aim of fostering creativity too, of adding to science, and to art, through new combinations of the knowledge and vision in each. Thus the focus was on embryonic technologies, looking to influence their development.

The scheme, which began in January 2002, involved the recruitment of three artists who came to Cambridge as visiting fellows. This was for what was called 'Phase 1'. Phase 1 was the period of establishing collaborative working relationships between these artists and scientific collaborators.[15]

Phase 1 fellowships lasted for six months, in which the artist-fellows were asked to reside for thirty days each in Cambridge. During this time they were introduced, depending on their stated interests, to scientists and technology researchers whose work appeared to offer the promise of collaboration. Phase 1 ended with an 'Exposition of work in progress' at Kettle's Yard – a gallery display of the collaborative work. I come back to the gallery display later in the chapter.

The idea of NTAF was to foster new creative partnerships. Its aim was 'to create new models of interdisciplinary collaboration'.[16] The web-based publicity continues: 'the scheme aims to bring together creative individuals from different fields and nurture synergy between them'. There is an explicit focus on creativity, which is to be made present by bringing together different knowledge bases, and different approaches to knowledge and object production. While it was left ambiguous as to where the actual outcome was to be located, it was also made explicit that the scheme was intended 'to produce innovative outputs in arts and technology'. The publicity material goes on: 'The range of possible outcomes looked for from the scheme include new art works, academic papers in a range of disciplines, product development, patent registration, and financing for commercial exploitation.'

Here then is a conscious attempt to have input from various sources. One of the questions this project seemed to address, in its consciously open-ended and process-centred focus, was how commensurate highly specialised and intricate forms of knowledge are. Acknowledging a complex world, and a complex differentiated knowledge about it, 'knowledge' is made into an over-arching category that then encompasses difference and specialisation. It is on this basis that such a collaboration could be envisaged. Beneath the difference, there is a commonality. Art and science are both 'knowledge practices'.

What was the effect that these collaborations were to have? In the end they looked to the production of new kinds of object. And it would be in the effect these objects could have (as art works, as technology), that the scheme would achieve its long list of aims.[17] In fact, such an object-outcome seems absolutely ripe for Gell's descriptive and analytic apparatus.

Gell's theory of the abduction of agency

In *Art and Agency*, Gell discusses how art objects are a 'nexus' of social relations, how they have effects, how they embody intentions, carry agency and produce results in the field of social relations in which they are embedded. He distinguishes between the 'causal milieu' (that is, things that happen because of well known physical laws), and those things which are apparent against the causal milieu (the happenings which point to agents) and which have their significant effect in and on social relations and persons.

Gell begins with the observation that an anthropological theory of art cannot be concerned with aesthetics. It is social relations that anthropologists study, and any discussion of art must locate the art work within the social relations which produce it, and in which it has its effect. He borrows from the language of cognitive science to outline how it is that objects can have effects upon persons, and thus be seen as agents in their own right. It is the idea that objects *index* their producer's agency that I am most interested in. Objects are not representations, not vehicles for symbols, in this theory. Idols, for example, do not provide the focus for beliefs because they externally embody a representation, a symbol, which is linked (in the mind) to other symbols, embedded in other representations (see Boyer 1994). Idols, to the extent they are significant, operate in social relations. It is here, not as vehicles for representational meaning, that they have their effect. Gell then defines his interest as 'social relations in the vicinity of objects mediating social agency' (1998: 7). He calls the objects he discusses (the idol, for example) 'indexes'. Indexes are material objects that permit a particular cognitive operation which Gell defines as 'the abduction of agency'.

An index is a sign from which a causal inference can be drawn. Gell gives the examples of a smile that betokens friendliness, or smoke which betokens fire. The cognitive operation here is not the same as that which is utilised when I say 'two plus two equals four', or when I say that a dog is an animal. Indexes are not part of a calculus, a tautology in which one thing leads inevitably to the next. Nor is the abduction of agency a process of deduction. Smoke is an index of fire even though we know smoke does not have to mean fire. Thus we need another term for the inferences we bring to bear on indices. This term is abduction. Abduction is a synthetic inference based on a combination of a causal inference and representational inference. Or in Boyer's language, 'a variety of non-demonstrative inference, based on the logical fallacy of affirming the antecedent from the consequent' (1994: 14).[18] Boyer makes a distinction between true premise (fire produces smoke) and not true inference (that particular smoke is produced by a fire). He uses this to show how, with true premises, people can arrive at irrational (untrue) conclusions. Gell takes this language (abduction) and utilises it as a metaphor. He tells us how it is possible that inference in the mode of abduction is made true. He describes forms of thought which could not stand up to much philosophical scrutiny, 'but which are none the less socially and cognitively practicable' (1998: 17).[19]

What of a picture of a person smiling? The viewer attributes 'friendliness' to the person in picture. This is abduction. And Gell tells us that through the object (the picture) we have access to another person's mind. We see the person in the picture as well disposed. The inferential schemes (abduction) we use to look at objects are very like the ones we bring to bear on social others for Gell. Smoke is a 'natural sign'. It is the outcome of a physical, causal process. However, if we took smoke to indicate someone having set fire to something (a bonfire in a garden, or a swidden burning, are Gell's examples) then smoke itself becomes *an artefactual index*. It is an artefact that has become the index of another's person's agency. Gell writes of a flint tool as just such an artefactual index. We can abduct, from the object, the intention of the maker; that was, to make a tool, to open shell fish, to eat, and so forth. In many cases, the abduction of such agency makes the person who is in the vicinity of the object respond. Objects become an index of another's agency which causes the viewer to act in turn. They thus become social agents in themselves.

What, though, is agency? Gell says it is what distinguishes physical happenings – things that physical laws can explain – from 'actions'. 'Actions' imply intention. And intention implies a mind. Gell tells us that anything that is seen to act intentionally (animals, objects) in some residual sense is thought to have a mind, and as human minds are the only ones we know, these are ones that get imputed to things. Gell has a wonderful passage about 'vehicular animism', 'a widespread belief in our society' (1998: 17).

Cars, Gell points out, have ethnicities, and personalities. But more, it is very hard for an owner not to see their car as a body part, a prosthesis. We all know cars are not agents or body parts, but a means of transport. Yet, think of the travelling sales representative, Gell says. He presents a neat and tidy appearance, smart suit and brushed hair, as an index of business competence. One abducts from his appearance that he is a sensible, reliable and trustworthy person. His car falls squarely into the overall impression. Big BMWs mean (German) bankers, Ford Mondeos mean sales reps. The car then, like shining teeth, is a part of his person. This works in reverse. An attack on one's car is an attack on one's person. It is usual to feel outrage, to take it as a personal blow. And this goes even further. When one's car breaks down far from home on a dark night in the rain, it is seen as an act of treachery. The car is morally and personally culpable. In this case, the car has exhibited agency. It has done something to you. It may be an 'error' to impute agency to a car – but nevertheless it happens. The attribution of agency to objects is basic to Gell's theory.

His concept of agency, then, is relational. For every agent, there is a *patient* who is acted upon. Human agency is exercised in the material world. Material/physical cause and effect is the background against which human agency is visible. Intent is initiated in the minds of actors, and intent is often to affect the state of mind of others. This can be achieved though the mediation of the physical world. Thus for Gell, agents are recognisable because something in the causal milieu surrounding them is changed in a way we must attribute to the actions of a non-physical law, in other words, to another's intention (agency).

Not only can we abduct agency from objects – that is, they embody others' intentions – but the index itself makes possible the intention. Cars and works of art cannot actually act in themselves. But no one ever said they could. Rather they act on and within social relations. It is there that their significant effect is felt. (It might be pointed out here that these objects actually 'act' upon persons, not 'in social relations' other than to the extent that all human experience is grounded in the social – broadly conceived as in this volume. 'Social relations' as a category independent of things is as much a reification as is 'material objects'.[20] But I digress.)

Take land mines. Are they agents? No says Gell, it is those who lay them that are the agents of destruction. But hold on, he says, what is a person who lays a land mine without a mine to lay? He is no longer an agent of destruction. Like the salesman and his car, land mines are part of what makes the soldier the agent that he is. Land mines, then, are how the social agent who is a soldier realises his agency. They are the objective embodiments of his power and capacity to will their use. There is no one-way causation here, but rather a vision of the mutual constitution of persons and things in a relational process, a dispersed creativity. But this vision is fleeting. Alongside it is the argument that objects are how agency manifests itself (is mediated), how social agency is realised.[21] My objection to this is not that I believe objects act independently of social relations, but first, that it is always an individual agency which is mediated (one agent always encompasses any number of others in the effect they have on a patient). Second, that this individual agency is always the imposition of subjectivity onto an inert material world. I go onto elaborate these points below.[22]

Gell says that the kinds of index with which an anthropological theory has to deal are those objects that 'have the capacity to index their "origins" in an act of *manufacture*' (1998: 23, original emphasis). Without wishing to labour the point, this is also what NTAF set out to achieve. That is, produce objects that have the capacity to index their origin in a unique process of collaboration.

Objects and persons

We have seen that Gell writes of how art objects stand for persons and carry their intention or agency into an expanding social milieu. But interestingly, the kinds of objects that Gell analyses are either those produced by an artist in the conventional sense of European art history, or they are ritual, religious, or otherwise 'marked' objects in other cultures.[23] Gell discusses the difficulty that the philosopher/critic Danto has in seeing these ritual or religious objects as 'art', as they have no identifiable maker (1999: 192). A very important point. But he goes on to say in one of the papers foundational to the theory developed in *Art and Agency* ('Vogel's net') that objects such as the Zande hunting net displayed by curator Susan Vogel are used 'either as part of specific rituals [. . .] or at the very least in a highly ritualised manner' (*ibid.*: 197). His point in that argument is to make clear that traps, nets and other 'artefacts' can indeed be seen as art works precisely because one can read from them both the intentions, and indeed the dispositions, of the makers. They stand for those persons in a revealing manner, and were extensions of their person in the world despite the fact that there is no named author. Gell is concerned with the manufacture, and with the brilliance (specialisation) of the artist or craftsman in making objects. The objects objectify the relations and skills of production (1999: 163), and thus capture the attention of the viewer.

NTAF was about combining different kinds of knowledge in a process of object manufacture. But, paradoxically, it is not knowledge in the abstract that was being combined; rather it was people who were brought together by the scheme. We could think of this in the following way: Where does specialist knowledge exist? One might answer in books and journals. But the skills required to read and understand such things are embodied in persons. Hence we have a variety of persons here. Each somehow carries or represents knowledge of a specific kind. Experts carry around understandings that can never be fully translated or represented. And to emphasise this interpersonal aspect, the language used in the project was one of relationship, network, interaction. A question for the participants became that of where the outcome was to be located. What would 'embody' the knowledge that was produced? This is a question about form. And that in turn is dependent on the process of generation (Whitehead 1929).

There were a number of answers offered to this question during a two-day workshop convened to review the progress of the various collaborative partnerships. One answer was that the outcome may be located in individual persons. That is, in their biographical development. Their skills and resources to undertake future work and future collaborations were to be enhanced. Or it was suggested that it may be located in a product. That is, in a technical object or process which is the outcome and presentational form of the collaboration. Hence we have something like a relationally constituted entity. It was also said that the outcome might perhaps appear in networks and 'clusters' of people. The significant thing here is also form. External relations constitute the internal make up of bodies, Gell tells us. Especially where those bodies are bodies of human construction. But we might want to add that ownership makes separations in terms of such metaphors. These kinds of entities, objects, persons, bodies, already have built into them modes of connection, disconnection and therefore ownership.

Differentiation

The designers of NTAF clearly imagine that the value of disciplines is in their specialisation. They imagine disciplines as a cumulative creation of knowledge. There is a biography, not unlike that of the expert, whereby more and more intricate understandings that build upon past knowledge need more and more specialised languages for their representation and communication. The more differentiated and specialised the discipline becomes, the more its knowledge is contained and restricted by its boundaries. Similarly, an artist has a progressive biography.[24]

The impetus for this collaboration was made explicit in these terms. There is an increasing specialisation of disciplines. This reflects an ever increasingly differentiated and specialised knowledge. How is one discipline to talk to another, what is the relevance of one kind of knowledge to another? These are questions which are asked more widely than in NTAF, and they situate NTAF as part of a wider series of interdisciplinary experiments (see Strathern 2003) and moves to make institutional space available for new forms of collaboration.

Great art is seen here as universal art, and thus despite the differences, it is like great science. More depth and detail is equal to potentially more applicability to specific problems. This is also a model of progression, so more specialisation also leads to better technology. And thus there is always an embedding of the knowledge and skills of a discipline within boundaries. It is the entity within this boundary, a kind of corporation or body, which is both potentially more effective, but at the same time, more different from other bodies or disciplines through specialisation. The body progressively develops more potential at the same time that its internal make-up becomes less and less communicable beyond itself. The idea of complexity, lying behind both art and science when they are successful, is one way that participants expressed the idea that there is a common denominator to all their skills.[25]

Progressive specialisation has the result of proliferating entities. Sub-disciplines spring up, new disciplines to understand phenomena that come into view because of previous advances. One has (much like a common idea of history, or a common notion of kinship) more and more diverse and different people. At any scale, one can see multiplication of entities in the world (Strathern 1991: xiv; and see Leach 2003a). Differentiation itself provides the possibility for ever-new forms to emerge, all entities are hybrid, and each new hybrid entity provides a new possibility for combination in novel and differentiated form.

NTAF facilitators in some ways imagined that one might make an intervention which does not just proliferate more entities, but that from this diversity, some kind of integrated whole might be created. Such an entity would reflect the diversity of knowledge in the world by encompassing within its own form different elements. The whole might be recaptured. Objects might be produced which demonstrate a re-embedding of different disciplines and knowledge within a single entity – a single object which might stand in the image of 'Renaissance Man' – encapsulating the vision of art with the knowledge base of science.

The object, made of multiple relational inputs, is another kind of 'person' that stands for the persons who authored it. But despite this being exactly the description of objects that Gell uses ('there is an insensible transition between "works of art" in artefact form and human beings: in terms of the networks of human social agency, they may be regarded as almost entirely equivalent' (1998: 153) it is not the multiple inputs (relations) that make objects equivalent to persons, but the fact that people read agency from them. Note, in the following passage, that it is not the multiple persons involved in the manufacture of objects that allow them to stand for persons, but rather, that the agency of an individual creator can be abducted from them. It is this that allows *their* personhood to be distributed:

> Any one social individual is the sum of their relations (distributed over biographical time and space) with other persons [. . .] Our inner personhood seems to consist of replications of what we are externally [. . .] So bearing this in mind, it may not be so aberrant to suggest that what persons are externally (and collectively) is a kind of enlarged replication of what they are internally [. . .] Especially if [. . .] we consider 'persons' [. . .] to apply to all the objects and/or events in the milieu from which agency or personhood can be abducted.
>
> (1998: 222)

Objects here are part of the external form of a person, as the way the agency of the artist or producer can be read from them in some ways defines the contours of the person themselves in the external social milieu.

But what about objects whose status as 'made objects' (Gell 1999: 163) is similarly constituted by a number of differentiated inputs? Could we not describe the socially produced objects of collaborative endeavour as 'the sum of their relations'? Indeed, it is the promise of objects and outcomes that will be the sum of new kinds of relationship that NTAF holds out. But this equally seems to draw us away from the formulation Gell relies upon, where it is the agency of the producer undifferentiated in the object's appearance, which may be read off from technically virtuous, beautifully made, objects.

The above is not quite an accurate description of course, as Gell does describe objects which are the outcome of 'a sequence of actions performed by another agent (artist) or multitude of agents, in the instance of collective works of art such as cathedrals' (1998: 67). But note how the collectivity is undifferentiated in the agency that can be read from the object. In fact, Gell has an encompassing 'person' who can be read, in the instance of objects produced by one person or set of persons, for another: the 'recipient' (1998: 24).[26]

In NTAF, it was the differentiation between the persons who have input, their embodiment of different kinds of knowledge and approach, which was vital. Otherwise there would be no need for collaboration. Thus we have a problem apparent, not unrelated to a problem participants found themselves facing, of how the creation is connected to particular persons, how one person's agency is to be 'read from' the object when it contains many inputs. More pertinently, as I come onto below, the question for participants was how one person's input is to be made distinct in order that they can be recognised as a creative person. There is no sense ever in Gell that who originated the index may be at issue.

Exposition

In the gallery setting, problems were apparent in the way skilled work and agency could be read from the art objects. It was a cause of discord and disruption. In the case of one technical collaborator, the fact that his contribution to an image (which was used on the publicity material) was never acknowledged, was a source of complaint. He threatened to withdraw his help from the collaboration. Further, the fact that the institution he worked for within the university was not credited either was used as material back-up for the threat.[27] The collaboration would not only lose his skilled input, but also the resources of his institution that had been relied upon up until this point. It must be said that the artist in question, despite producing two technically sophisticated demonstrations of his ideas, did not acknowledge his scientific collaborator's input either. Both technician and scientist were subsumed in the overall appearance of the work as the outcome of the artist's vision and effort.

In the gallery exhibition, artists gave talks about their collaborations, and answered questions from the audience on the theme of science in art and art in science. One of the facilitators later told me at this point that he had been angered and upset that his part in the process was hidden by one artist. The narrative the artist told was one of miraculous coincidence. Their needs and interests were exactly matched by a scientific collaborator whom they had come across early on in research visits to Cambridge. The implication was that it was part of their skill to locate and co-opt this scientist's work, an aspect of the artistic practice demonstrated by the installation. The facilitator who had established this artist's meetings with scientists, and who was, in fact, the research supervisor of the scientist in question, was angered that they had been painted out of the picture of creativity being generated.

Cleverness

Why should this (very familiar) kind of conflict occur? Well, there is an answer in Gell, albeit not consciously to the same question. 'The person is understood as the sum total of the indexes which testify, in life and subsequently, to the biographical existence of this or that individual' (1998: 222–3). Authorship and recognition are vital for the self-perception of persons. Indeed productive work externalising the internal capacities of individuals is, one could argue, foundational of a kind of personhood. Gell here describes uncannily accurately a particular construction of the person, defined through what they possess, as aspects of what they create externally reflecting inner qualities, *as if* this was a universal definition of personhood.

And at the back of this conception of the person is a bias in Gell towards the mind and cleverness as the source of innovative value creation. Throughout Gell's project of developing an anthropological approach to art, the theme of technical virtuosity stands clearly forth. From his childhood rapture with a matchstick model of Salisbury cathedral (MacFarlane 2003: 125) to his interest in Duchamp, or his explanation of how Trobriand canoe prows work to bedazzle their viewers, it is in the *technique* that Gell locates the source of wonder. He tells us (in distinguishing art objects from other objects) that 'art objects are the only objects around which are *beautifully made*, or *made beautiful*'. It is 'their characteristics as *made* objects, as products of techniques' (1999: 163), which makes them interesting.

This focus on technical virtuosity is developed in *Art and Agency* through the theory of abduction, and of the way art objects achieve their value. In 'Vogel's net', Gell refers to Simmel. Modifying Simmel's theory of value, Gell describes how it is the resistance to comprehension, rather than merely to crude possession, that makes art works valuable. 'Simmel's theory, as it stands, implies that it is the difficulty of access to an object which makes it valuable' (1999: 168). 'The value of a work of art, as Simmel suggests, is a function of the way in which it resists us.' Gell goes on, 'The resistance which they offer, and which creates and sustains this desire, is to being possessed in an intellectual rather than a material sense [. . .which] since it transcends my understanding, I am forced to construe as magical' (169). It is the attention given to the making of objects which marks their significance as works of art (1998: 68). Technique is an attribute of an agent. Gell's argument is ultimately premised on a kind of individualism that is exemplified by the embodiment of specialisation within disciplines or within experts.

Similarly, Gell focuses on the intellectual prowess of successful Kula traders in the Trobriand Islands. Success is achieved, 'only through knowledge, intelligence, and calculation. For success to accrue, the Kula operator must possess a superior capacity to engage in strategic action, which necessitates a comprehensive *internal model* of the external field within which Kula valuables move about' (1998: 231, original emphasis, reference removed). It is clear, then, that whether we are speaking of Duchamp, of Vermeer, or of Kula traders, creativity, which is read as agency and power, lies within the person, and within their mind, or genius. 'Duchamp is, (or was) an individual mind, one particular person exercising one particular agency' (1998: 250). This has consequences for the way people are connected to objects, and to one another.

Power and claims

When Gell writes of agency, he is explicitly discussing power. Power to influence the minds and actions of others. The question that arises in the context of NTAF collaborations is how it is that objects come to be seen as the extension of *particular* persons. In other words, it is the location of the *source* of power to effect the social milieu which interests me here. How is it that an art work, or indeed a piece of technology, becomes exclusively associated with one artist or technologist or 'recipient'? And here we are into the realm of claims and ownership, most apparent in the proceedings of NTAF at the point in which the collaboration was shown to have an outcome. In other words, the moment the objects produced were to have their effect. I turn to Strathern here for help in formulating the way in which persons in the particular mode she characterises as Western make their claims. She writes,

> Whether people perceive power as a piece of property, estate, a personal attribute, an ability, or as an effect revealed in the reactions of others, power also has the status of a proposition. Propositions evoke their context, and in being context dependent are inherently contestable. An extreme example is a proposition framed as a claim, for a claim derives its character from the adversary context of counterclaim.
>
> (Strathern 1988: 119)

The status of the artist in the gallery exposition is already a kind of claim, a claim over the creation of the object on display. 'Claims', Strathern tells us, are 'seen as the outcomes of particular moments of revelation' (*ibid.*).

How then do such claims work in practice? The issue of where the outcome of the collaboration is to be located is one thing that I have now discussed at length. There is also the linked issue of where the outcome will be revealed or presented. Now in the gallery setting, it seems obvious that it will be the artist who stands forth. The institution is set up for the display of works which are attributed to artist-creators. There was an explicit discussion during NTAF in which the kinds of arena or sphere in which outcomes would be located was opened up. Thus it was said that a scientist who, having been pushed in his work into new discoveries and directions because of the vision or demands of the artist-collaborator, would present these findings in scholarly publications, journal articles, or papers at conferences. In other words, there is also a place in which scientists can demonstrate their work, and see themselves extended through the circulation of its outcomes.[28]

Claims and counter-claims arise when one person, one party to the collaboration is eclipsed or encompassed by another in a particular context. But this oscillation between collaborative endeavour, and re-immersion in the context of one's specialisation is a necessary part of a collaboration explicitly premised on the combination of difference. Differentiation is as necessary to the process as is the combination (encompassment) of differentiated elements in a coherent output. Where the problems arise is in the way these processes of differentiation are obscured as *already existing* differences between persons. In other words, one person, because of their status as 'scientist' encompasses the scientific development, as if the fact that they are a scientist is not being produced at one and the same time as the development of their knowledge through collaboration with an artist. Instead of 'synergy', successful outcomes – those that have a register for their effect – are always either art works, or scientific discoveries. In any moment of presentation, one person and their specialisation is fore-grounded, it seems at the expense of others. This appears then as a moment of encompassment. The work of the technologist is encompassed by the artist, or the contribution of the facilitator is claimed as part of the creative process (genius, fortune) of the artist themselves. The mechanism of this encompassment is central to my argument here.

Strathern discusses how Western anthropologists are inclined to interpret initiation rituals in Melanesia not as moments of differentiation, but in fact as moments which confirm the intrinsic, or internal, nature of the person being initiated. I make use of this formulation as the process described is directly paralleled in the way that encompassment of others' work by an artist, or a scientist, appears to confirm their *internal specification* as this kind of person, and thus *as embodying within themselves* the kind of creativity which is evidenced by the object produced. Encompassment, then, is both of the work of others and other disciplines in any moment of presentation, *and* of the specialisation of particular kinds of knowledge production within the minds of certain individuals. Strathern writes of interpreting initiations:

> Western formulations of identity of a unitary kind would lead one to expect that men become more male by associating with things definable as exclusively male; an intrinsic attribute (maleness) would be elaborated with extra attributes of the same nature (more maleness). The more removed from female matters, on this Western model, the more permanently male is the identity.
>
> (1988: 123)

Strathern was discussing gender when viewed in the mode of Western possessive individualism. One could reasonably substitute other aspects of 'identity' for gender, however. It seems the case that disciplinary training in science makes one progressively 'more' a scientist. A lifetime's practice of art makes one an artist. The continual elaboration of internalised knowledge and practice in the mode of one or another knowledge form comes to be definitional of the person as if the person belonged in, and to, a particular domain of knowledge, and as if in turn their knowledge of that domain belonged to them. The idiom of ownership, of certain properties being attributed to persons which define their self, is crucial to how and why claims are made and/or disputed. Why else would ideas of authorship, recognition, and projects-as-part of the person's own biographical development be so apparent in these collaborations? And it is because of thinking in this mode that Gell is able to write, 'The person is thus understood as the sum total of the indexes which testify, in life and subsequently, to the biographical existence of this or that individual' (1998: 222–3).

Conclusion

It has become commonplace to hear of the importance of interdisciplinary initiatives, and of the necessity for flexible and creative individuals. One way of achieving the latter is to educate people across disciplines. When there are inter-disciplinary collaborations, the 'hybrid' nature of products results in claims made about the value of certain kinds of input. (Artists bring vision, etc.) One of the many fascinations of such collaborations is how persons themselves are seen to be already differentiated through their disciplinary training. In certain cases, making use of different perspectives, it is hoped, will allow the production of objects which themselves combine different kinds of knowledge, and thus appeal to consumers, audiences and users in multiple ways.[29] Knowledge of multiple kinds is not only built into the object through manufacture; this knowledge reflects the multiple distinctions within society because disciplines are taken as representative of certain kinds of social reality.

NTAF organisers were interested in the intellect itself as a site of powerful combination. The outputs of the intellect must appear in physical form if they are to be realised. Once realised in an object, creativity can no longer be in that object because that lies in the mind (or 'cleverness') of the producer. Agency may inhere or be abducted from that object, and that is the agency of creative or innovative power, but creativity is absent. It cannot be anything more than represented by the object. (And in this, we see the working of assumptions about how material objects can only represent social reality, addressed in *Thinking Through Things* more broadly.) It is this representation that makes for the enchantment which Gell is so focused upon, 'the enchantment which is immanent in all kinds of technical activity' (1999: 163–4).

There are some contradictions apparent once one brings artists into collaboration with scientists. The question is how one maintains the idea of the great and creative individual once the process of collaboration is made explicit as part of the art work itself. Artist encompasses scientists/technologists in a gallery setting. Scientists present their findings in context of journals and scientific conferences. Technologists apply for patents. In all cases they may acknowledge others' input, but in the presentation, they encompass these others. At any time that the object has an effect, it is always displayed as if it were more to do with one person than another. It is the sequence – external world – mental representation – internal modification of representations – imposition of form upon external world – that lies behind this. Encompassment then is initially of others' input in the individual creative mind, and then the extension of this principle through institutional contexts set up to recognise differentiated, individual kinds of knowledge/ product.

What this points to is what I have called appropriative creativity,[30] a current model for how things come into being, and one reliant upon an impermeable subject/object divide. Gell has not conceived of art (or other) objects as products of collaboration in the sense it was used within NTAF, and therefore as standing for different, discernible agents. This blind spot is not only Gell's problem, but is a consequence of wider notions of the person and of creativity exemplified by the whole structure and process of NTAF.

Specialisation, knowledge, and creativity, when seen as internal to persons, can only be attributed to individual minds. When collaborators are in the same sphere of action (co-authors of a paper within a discipline for example) they can be equally represented *as if* they were equally present in the object. But this 'as if' is very important. When the collaborators are from different disciplines, and have different arenas in which to present themselves through their object productions, then it no longer looks like the objects stand for all the people, but rather, that they stand for particular persons. In fact, in the moment of display, the effect of ownership in the mode of Western appropriation can be seen to operate. The mechanism of this operation might be described as creativity-as-intellectual-encompassment.

There are the two sides of Gell, and also the two sides of NTAF. In both cases, both sides appear at the same time. NTAF *needs* concrete realisation in the form of object outputs, but these result in encompassing claims. Gell needs objects for people to abduct agency from, but in his theory, this abduction is always ultimately of the creator of the object, who through technique or skill, is having an effect through the object. The transcendence of the abstracted intellect/will combination finds resonances with a Euro-American tendency to locate reason or knowledge in the individual mind, and thus reproduces the self through its operation on the object world. It is this constitution of personhood through a focus on a particular mode of creativity that Gell relies upon. When all is said and done, we are left with the individual mind and its representations, and with the idea that non-humans can only be agents by proxy: There are real subjects, namely we ourselves, and then there are those second-class citizens of subject-dom (i.e. objects and the like).

Why does this matter? Well, in NTAF it seems that such constructions undermine the aim of collaborative production. In Gell, a specifically *non-representational* theory of art turns out to be about the representation of social agency by objects. For Gell, objects can only have effect as representations of others' minds and agency. This, then, is at heart a representational theory of meaning, and this in turn undermines what I see as the potential for analysing objects that have the effect of agents in systems of generative relations between persons. The individual/multiple is one aspect of getting to this, because of the logical necessity for creativity to be individual if it is seen as something that happens in a restricted physical location (the brain). The implication of the representational theory is that this is the only location for meaning-making, therefore we are always returned in the end to the (individual) subject and the object world beyond them.

My objection, then, is to the theory of the abduction of agency and the notion that we should treat an object as an index of something else. I point out that questions about what an object is an index of may obscure something that is very important about the object in diverse contexts. One way of looking at artists and scientists squabbling over who should be credited is to see them as locked into a model where it is the abduction of agency that is what matters about an object, and where there are conventional clues (labels naming the artist, etc.) which assist that abduction of agency. Once one refuses abduction and says that agency belongs to the art object, or in other words admits that the art object has a life of its own for which the producer(s) can claim at best partial credit or responsibility, then the squabble appears (even more) ridiculous (but then so does the label claiming responsibility). The case study presented here is a demonstration of how, even when one gets people from different disciplines collaborating with a view to producing effective art objects, the model of 'author/artist'-encompassment continues to re-assert itself.

Learning from both Melanesian ideas and practices, and indeed from recent initiatives such as NTAF which look to go beyond the assumed models, we might 'think through things' to new analytic positions, and to recognition of alternative models of creative endeavour. This will require a rather thoroughgoing overhaul of the descriptive language we use (not something I have achieved here), and one which takes account of the ways in which our own practices form the theoretical cast we describe others' worlds within.

Acknowledgements

Discussions with Alice Street, and her input, were foundational to the arguments developed in this chapter. The same could be said of Martin Holbraad, who asked some difficult questions. Thanks are due to my collaborators on NTAF, particularly Alan Blackwell, Lizzie Muller, Eugine Terentjev and Simon Biggs. The paper was initially written for Georgina Born's panel at the ASA Decennial Conference, Manchester, 14–18 July 2003. Eduardo Viveiros de Castro kindly commented upon an early version, as did Gabriella Aspraki. Goldsmiths College Anthropology Department made many useful suggestions. Thanks are also due to Robin Osborne, Souhmya Venkatesan, Harri Englund, Amiria Henare, Ludek Broz, Adam

Reed and Eric Hirsch. Daniel Miller kindly commented in public on the argument. A long list, and I have not always managed to take their comments on board, for which the chapter is the poorer.

Notes

1 I am aware of the parallel endeavours which go broadly under the heading of Actor Network Theory. However, I choose a different trajectory in this chapter.
2 For example, see Smith (2001); Coxon (2001); Council for Science and Technology (2001).
3 The 'two cultures' tradition in academia (Snow 1964).
4 Admittedly, the idea of 'capturing a social dynamic' might not be one all social anthropologists would want to own.
5 In that it hints at the possibility of agency not just being a function of the imposition of individual human subjectivity on an inert material base.
6 I fully recognise that *Art and Agency* was unfinished at the time of Gell's untimely death. This chapter is intended as a genuine engagement with the work, and an attempt to unravel some of the difficulties which the text as it stands seems to present.
7 And indeed, in his discussion of the artist's oeuvre (1998: 231–52), how objects can cause other objects.
8 Hence the similarity some have noted with Actor Network Theory.
9 My previous geographic focus for research into 'creativity' (Leach 2002; 2003a; 2003b). On authorship there, see for example Küchler (2002).
10 http://www.sciart.org/site/
11 I am of course aware of the end of *Art and Agency*, where Gell outlines how Maori meeting houses are also embodiments of the agency of descent groups' and their ancestors' power. I do not believe, however, that this aspect of the work does more than make Maori groups into wholes; the group is an undifferentiated producer. All work to the same goal and with the same intent, thus the object stands as an index of collective agency, if not of reified 'tradition', as Gell is careful to show.
12 NTAF is ongoing, with a second phase of the pilot scheme planned.
13 'adding an artistic dressing to scientific concepts is an effective way of making technically complex material more palatable for wide public consumption' (http://www.wellcome.ac.uk/en/1/sci.html).
14 'The often oblique and ambiguous nature of art and the interpretative demands it places on its audience suggest that it might be an appropriate medium for organisations wishing to communicate science to the public in a non-didactic, thought provoking way' (Wellcome/ACE 2003).
15 A Phase 2 has emerged for some of the collaborators under an AHRB and Arts Council of England joint scheme.
16 http://www.junction.co.uk/ntaf
17 'Aims' of the NTAF, from http://www.junction.co.uk/ntaf –

> To create new models of interdisciplinary collaboration. The scheme aims to bring together creative individuals from different fields and nurture synergy between them. The New Technology Arts fellows will assume a far more equal partnership with technologists than in traditional artistic residencies. New Technology Arts fellows will act as equal collaborators in interdisciplinary research teams.

To place artists at the heart of technology research. The scheme will enable artists to draw on and influence developments within the digital industry. Industrial concerns have often established and defined the categories of interaction in art, limiting them to familiar technological media boundaries such as video, computer and plastic manufacture. Our goal is to establish new direct partnerships between technology researchers and artists, side-stepping the constraints of industrial economics.

To create public engagement with art and technology research. The fellow-ships focus on interactive art – in which the 'circuit' of the artwork is only complete when an audience becomes involved. This places emphasis on audience experience in the development of new work. The scheme is struc-tured to provide opportunities for artists and technologists to work with the 'users' their work during the research period. Ranging from participative workshops to presentations of work in progress, the fellowships create path-ways for public input into the research and development process.

To produce innovative outputs in arts and technology. The range of possible outcomes looked for from the scheme include new art works, academic papers in a range of disciplines, product development, patent registration, and financing for commercial exploitation.

To make an impact on the culture of Cambridge. The scheme aims to demonstrate the effectiveness of engaging artists as equal collaborators in scientific and technological research. The long term goal is to start a new wave of artistic and technological endeavour within Cambridge that brings together arts organisations, the City Council, Cambridge University, surrounding businesses and regional and national funders in support of interdisciplinary research.

To explore new models of ownership in interdisciplinary collaboration. The New Technology Arts fellowship is not seen as 'sponsorship', 'residency' or 'commission', but as an experiment aiming at new modes for integrating and challenging the role of creative arts in a digital society. The scheme is a direct continuation of the possibilities raised by the CODE conference, held in Cambridge, which offered multidisciplinary perspectives on the nature of ownership and reward for creative work.
An anthropological study of the scheme and the approach developed towards collaborative creativity will be carried out.

18 Boyer and other cognitivists are where Gell takes his vocabulary from.
19 There is a risk in this presentation, focusing as it does on the way that agency for Gell is something which begins and ends with human minds, of diminishing the fact that Gell does spend a lot of effort in outlining other forms of agency that people may identify from an object. The care with which he delineates the place of the prototype, and of the audience, as well as the artist-producer, should be mentioned here.
20 With thanks to Daniel Miller. But of course it amounts to much the same thing to speak of objects acting independently of social relations as to speak of rela-tions as an autonomous (and essentially immaterial) sphere of action.
21 Layton (2003: 459–60) has recently pointed out that the examples of objects-agents in *Art and Agency* work in very different ways, a fact that Gell glosses. Layton distinguishes between art objects, in which agency may be attributed to

an author through reading the signs of an inert object, money and treasured objects which effect people through exchange, and land mines which have a mechanical effect independent of the desire to engage them by the victim of their power. These useful refinements may indeed be relevant for an analysis of the various 'objects' produced during NTAF, but I do not pursue this line further in this paper.

22 See note 17 above.

23 Land mines and cars are not subject to analysis in *Art and Agency*. They are used as examples to convince the reader of the 'agency' of objects.

24 As an ethnographer, this explicit tension between kinds of knowledge making and kinds of research practice was central. Many of the interactions highlighted the tendency participants had to fall into familiar channels, with scientists talking about 'real concepts', and artists about a 'mystical' or an 'intuitive' vision. Then there were moments when an encompassing knowledge was imagined. Perhaps mathematics is the grounding of both the pattern and meaning in nature and in art, it was surmised in the context of an interdisciplinary discussion. An oscillation was established between subjective vision, and objective knowledge. One encompasses the other, then there is a reversal. Knowledge appears to act in its own right. Conceptual encompassments and differences are projected onto the world as if the world was those conceptual understandings.

25 At the launch of the Arts Council/AHRB Arts and Science Research Fellowships in London, September 2003, a Cambridge professor of mathematical science (John Barrow) spoke at length about complexity theory promising to make apparent the fundamental links between what both art and science describe.

26 For example, in the case of a great palace, the recipient is the king who ordered it to be constructed. It is his agency which is primarily indexed by the artefact.

27 Anne Roberts, 'New Technology Arts fellowships project documentation: lessons for the future'. Kettle's Yard 2002 (http://www.junction.co.uk/ntaf).

28 I am engaged in a similar process now, it must be said.

29 Aesthetically, functionally, ethically, etc.

30 Leach, in Hirsch and Strathern (2004).

References

Boyer, P. (1994) *The Naturalness of Religious Ideas: a Cognitive Theory of Religion*, Berkeley: University of California Press.

Council for Science and Technology (CST) (2001) 'Imagination and understanding: a report on the arts and humanities in relation to science and technology', UK government/DTI.

Coxon, K. (2001) 'How to have a creative child', *Junior*, 24: 'Creating creativity', June, 34–9.

Gell, A. (1999) *The Art of Anthropology: Essays and Diagrams*, ed. E. Hirsch, London: Athlone Press.

——(1998) *Art and Agency: an Anthropological Theory*, Oxford: Oxford University Press.

Hirsch, E. and Strathern, M. (2004) *Transactions and Creations: Property Debates and the Stimulus of Melanesia*, Oxford and New York: Berghahn Books.

Küchler, S. (2002) *Malanggan: Art, Memory and Sacrifice*, Oxford: Berg.

Layton, R. (2003)'Art and agency: a reassessment', J*ournal of the Royal Anthropological Institute*, 9(3): 447–64.

Leach, J. (2005) 'Being in between: sci-art collaborations in a technological culture', *Social Analysis*, 49(1): 141–60.

——(2004) 'Modes of creativity', in Hirsch, E. and Strathern, M. (eds) *Transactions and Creations: Property Debates and the Stimulus of Melanesia*, Oxford and New York: Berghahn Books.

——(2003a) *Creative Land: Place and procreation on the Rai Coast of Papua New Guinea*, Oxford and New York: Berghahn Books.

——(2003b) 'Owning creativity: cultural property and the efficacy of kastom on the Rai Coast of Papua New Guinea', *Journal of Material Culture*, 8(2): 123–43.

——(2002) 'Drum and voice: aesthetics and social process on the Rai Coast of Papua New Guinea', *Journal of the Royal Anthropological Institute*, 8: 713–34.

MacFarlane, A. (2003) 'Biographical memoirs of fellows, II: Alfred Anthony Francis Gell', *Proceedings of the British Academy*, 120: 123–47.

Pocock, J. (1992) 'Tangata Whenua and enlightenment anthropology', *New Zealand Journal of History*, 26(1): 28–53.

Smith, C. (2001) 'Foreword', *Creative Mapping Document 2001*, UK Government/ Department of Culture, Media and Sport.

Snow, C. P. (1964) *The Two Cultures: and a Second Look*, Cambridge: Cambridge University Press.

Strathern, M. (2003) 'Accountability across disciplines', CBA workshop, 'Languages of Accountability', Girton College, May.

——(1991) *Partial Connections*, ASAO Special Publication 3, Savage MD: Rowman and Littlefield.

——(1990) 'Artefacts of history: events and the interpretation of images', in J. Siikala (ed.) *Culture and History in the Pacific*, Helsinki: Finnish Anthropological Society, 25–44.

——(1988) *The Gender of the Gift*, Berkeley: University of California Press.

Wellcome/ACE (2003) 'Ask the audience: investigating the impact of science and art exhibitions on their audiences', report presented at 'Always in Translation: Conversations in Art and Science' conference, Natural History Museum/Royal College of Art, London, September.

Whitehead, A. N. (1929) *Process and Reality*, New York: Macmillan.

THE POWER OF POWDER

Multiplicity and motion in the divinatory cosmology of Cuban Ifá (or *mana*, again)

Martin Holbraad

As life forces go, *mana* does not animate anthropological debate like it used to. After Lévi-Strauss performed his disappearing-act on the concept, comparing the semantic 'emptiness' of the Polynesian term '*mana*' to that of the French term for 'thing' (and more of this below), few anthropologists have ventured to draw theoretical mileage from it.[1] Of course, if part of the original attraction of *mana*-terms to anthropologists was their peculiarly double universality – their semantic breadth ('*mana* is everywhere', said the native) coupled with their geographical diffusion ('*mana*-terms are everywhere', replied the anthropologist) – it is hardly surprising that these concepts should still feature in diverse ethnographic accounts of indigenous cosmologies (e.g. Empson's and Henare's contributions to this volume).[2] *Mana* is ethnographically unavoidable. That this should be embarrassing, as it seems, to theoretical sensibilities today is also unsurprising. Lévi-Strauss' majestic marriage of universal theory with meticulously documented ethnographic variability has ended with a divorce of sorts. The mantle of universalism has been taken up by cognitive theorists, whose interest in ethnography is limited mainly to illustration, so that *mana* features theoretically only *sub specie*, as an example of wider psychological processes (e.g. Boyer 1986, cf. Severi 2004). On the other hand, the anthropological commitment to ethnography has increasingly been interpreted as a credo for working relativism, so that anthropological theory has tended to disappear down the hatch of ethnographic particularism. So '*mana*' and all the other indigenous terms that early ethnographers glossed as 'life force', 'sacred power' and so forth ('*orenda*', '*wakan*', '*brahman*', etc.), now appear as just bit players in varied stories about how people in different places see and do things differently. And if theory, on this account, is to be sought not in the analyst's unavoidably essentialist supra-cultural imagination, but at most in concrete and historically contingent infra-cultural diffusions (such as modernity, globalisation, or empire), then one can see why the spot for *mana* should be left blind. Impressive though it may have been to earlier generations of anthropologists, still then interested in conceptual rather than political economies, today the universality of *mana* just isn't the right sort. It is, if you like, that of myth rather than history (cf. Gow 2001). So, inasmuch as mythical claims to universality are supposed ineluctably to be trumped, and variably swept over, by the 'real' universality of global history, *mana* can at most feature as a multi-local oddity, out of fashion in an era of *théorie concrète*.

My intention in returning to the debate about *mana* is not, however, to hark back, and particularly not back to the seductive idea that the double universality of *mana* renders it a suitable vehicle for theorising universality for its own sake. In this sense Lévi-Strauss was right to chastise Mauss for elevating a parochial concept like *mana* or *hau* as premises for 'general' theory (Lévi-Strauss 1987: 47–9, though see below). But while Lévi-Strauss' own remedy was to pursue universal theory in spite of the particular meaning of *mana*-terms (because, as we shall see, he deemed them not to have any particular meaning at all), in this paper I propose the opposite: to draw theory from the particular meaning of *mana*-terms – and not least from their peculiar claims to universality – while side-stepping aspirations to *theoretical* universality, if not as meaningless, then at least as irrelevant.

The question obviously comes down to what one takes theory to be. Like Mauss of the *Théorie Générale*, Lévi-Strauss assumed that the measure of theoretical strength is generality, with universality at the limit. This assumption rests on a further one, namely that the model of anthropological analysis is scientific explanation: the job of anthropologists' theories is to shed light on ethnographic data – the more data illuminated, the stronger the light. However, as argued in the Introduction to this volume, such an image ignores the reciprocal effects *upon* theory that ethnography has to offer – so evident in the strategy of Mauss' other great work, *The Gift*. At issue here is not a theory's extension over ethnographic data, but the data's capacity to extend our theoretical imagination. On such an image, anthropological analysis is best compared not to science but to philosophy: a reflexive project of inventively transforming analytical concepts, as opposed to applying them to data. The ideal of universality then emerges as a category mistake. To measure *The Gift*'s theoretical purchase in terms of the quantity of 'gift-economies' it explains is as silly as judging the merits of Platonism by the amount of Forms one can count (cf. Gregory 1997: 47).

As I have discussed elsewhere, such an approach to anthropology implies a strict methodological corollary: that the scope for theory (which is to say, the scope for inventing new concepts through the analysis of ethnography) is proportionate to the 'alterity' of the ethnographic data that motivate it (Holbraad 2003; forthcoming). Alterity is just a relational indicator of the contradiction between the ethnography and the initial assumptions the analyst brings to it. The more the alterity, the more work the analyst has to do in order to transform his assumptions to overcome the contradiction, i.e. the more he has to theorise. On this deliberate version of exoticism, few data on the ethnographic canon could be more theoretically enticing than *mana*.

190

If 'alterity' is a tag for phenomena that do not 'make sense' to us, then *mana*-terms are 'alter' in the most literal way. For, as we shall see, it is their very meaning that has always been at issue for anthropologists. In other words, if anthropological debate is supposed to be motivated by misunderstanding, as I am arguing, then the one about *mana* is exemplary. Unlike other canonical debates, in which misunderstanding has had to be proven as an underlying difficulty – as Mauss did for gifts, Dumont for hierarchy, Strathern for gender, and so on – the debate about *mana* has been about the difficulty of understanding all along.

Here my aim is to bring the theoretical mileage of *mana* to bear on the theme of this volume, namely the possibility of revising assumptions pertaining to 'material objects', as anthropologists sometimes call them, or as we prefer, in order to keep our ontological options as open as possible, 'things' (see Introduction). As we shall see, one of the sources of anthropologists' constructive misunderstanding of *mana*-terms is that they systematically cut across the concepts with which an analyst might demarcate notions like 'material', 'object' or, indeed, 'thing'. So attending anthropologically to what people call *mana* promises a field day when it comes to revising these concepts. In particular, I shall be arguing that *mana*-terms provide us with an analytical hold on the commonplace assumption that 'things' must necessarily be thought of as ontologically distinct from 'concepts'. Such a move is possible just because the 'universality' of *mana* cuts systematically across this distinction: it is both a thing and a concept.

In this sense my argument on *mana* is directly inspired by Mauss' on Maori *hau*. If the notion of *hau* provided the leverage to deny that the distinction between things and people is axiomatic (as we argue in the Introduction), then *mana*-terms do the same for the distinction between things and concepts. The main difference, however, between the strategy of *The Gift* and the one pursued here has to do with ultimate aims. Having subverted the distinction between people and things with reference to the ethnography of gift giving, Mauss stopped short of providing an alternative analytic frame that might account for such phenomena, other than to imply, in negative terms, that gifts presuppose a collapse of our guiding distinctions (Mauss 1990: 73). His positive project, after all, was political: to use the subversion of the distinction between people and things offered by the ethnography of gifts to advance a subversive polemic against the ethos of modern markets (see Introduction). By contrast, the positive aim of this paper remains analytical. After showing that *mana* cannot be articulated in terms of the commonplace distinction between concepts and things, I want to consider the possibility that the ethnography of *mana* might itself dictate an alternative analytic frame – one that goes beyond the distinction between concepts and things. So the question is this. If, as was so widely commented in the literature, *mana* is both, say, a stone and ritual efficacy – both thing and concept, as we would say – then might thinking through it provide us with an analytical standpoint from which we would no longer need to make this distinction? Might there be a frame for analysis in which *mana* does not register as an ontological anomaly, as it does when we say – surprised – that it is both thing and concept?

Taking a cue from earlier writers who considered *mana* as just an Oceanic version of a much wider phenomenon, this argument will be made from an otherwise parochial ethnographic standpoint, namely that of Cuban Ifá, a male diviner cult of West African origin that I have been studying in inner-city Havana since 1998. As will be shown, Ifá diviners' seemingly nebulous appeal to the notion of '*aché*' displays apparent 'anomalies' that are analogous to those anthropologists have associated with *mana*. But before getting to the ethnography, I wish first to identify in some detail what I take to be the import, as well the shortcomings, of the debate about *mana*, as it was conducted all those years ago.

Mana in debate

The anthropological debate about *mana* developed in two trajectories, which roughly correspond to the proverbial divide between French rationalism and British empiricism. In France, from as early as Comte, primitive concepts of 'force', of which *mana* was deemed exemplary, were set up as think-pieces for debates over the origins of thought itself. While such ideas did exert some influence on the evolutionary speculations of such figures as Tylor, Frazer and Marett, particularly in their now curious debates about the relationship of 'religion' and 'magic', British anthropologists' concern with *mana* has been mainly ethnographic, ever since the Anglican missionary Robert Henry Codrington put the concept on the map in 1891. The strategy of the present chapter, drawing analytical mileage from ethnographic particulars encountered in Cuba, is suspended across the two camps – pursuing rationalist ends with empirical means, as it were, jeopardising the foundations of both. But since my empirical concerns are limited to Cuba, well beyond the reach of the classical ethnographic controversies (which were fielded primarily in Oceania and North America), my focus here will be on the French-led debate about the general conceptual import of *mana*-terms.

Having said this, a good place to pick up the conceptual debate is precisely its relationship to the ethnographic controversy. Consider, for example, Malinowski's impeccably Anglo-Saxon complaint on this score:

> [. . . T]he theory of mana as the essence of primitive magic and religion has been so brilliantly advocated and so recklessly handled that it must be realized first that our knowledge of the mana, notably in Melanesia, is somewhat contradictory, and especially that we have hardly any data at all showing just how this conception enters into religious or magical cult and belief.
>
> (Malinowski 1954: 78)

In addition to Marett's (1914; 1915), the theory Malinowski had in mind was, of course, the one proposed in the *Année Sociologique* by Hubert and Mauss (Mauss 2001), and elaborated by Durkheim in the *Elementary Forms* (1995). But, while his point about the merits of fieldwork has been well taken ever since, Malinowski's complaint about *mana*-theorists' high-handed attitude to ethnography was wrongheaded. For the French, the contradiction of *mana* was not an ethnographic malaise but an ethnological datum. It was *mana* that was confused, not our understanding of it. In fact, the suggestion that 'our' contradictions were owed to ethnographic weakness (and that *mana* really was there to be known) was simply not borne out by subsequent research. As Bradd Shore writes in a more recent review of the ethnographic debate on the Polynesian term, '[a]n even cursory glance at the literature on *mana* suggests how difficult [. . .] understanding has been to come by' (Shore 1989: 137). So while the 'British' challenge – taken up by Hocart (1914), Hogbin (1936), Firth (1940), Keesing (1984), and Shore himself among many others – was to put order in what to them appeared an ethnographic morass, the 'French' one was effectively to explain why such attempts were bound to fail. What made *mana* so compelling theoretically was precisely the fact that being 'singularly ambiguous,' as Hubert and Mauss wrote, it is 'quite outside our adult European understanding' (Mauss 2001: 132).

Of course, the talk of 'adult' understanding expresses the automatic anthropological strategy in the face of alterity at the time, namely to relegate it to an earlier phylo/ontogenetic phase. The fact that *mana* was invariably relegated *all the way* back, to the beginning of whatever was at issue for each theorist (as we'll see, religion and magic for Mauss, society too for Durkheim, knowledge for Lévi-Strauss and Sperber), just proves my earlier point about its maximum alterity. But putting chronological considerations aside, here I want to consider the *form* that the alterity of *mana* took in these debates, and its intriguing relationship to the form of its anthropological 'explanations'.

Like all good debates, the French one about *mana* turned on a common premise, namely that the elusiveness of *mana* – its 'singular ambiguity' – was a matter of what one might call its *excess*. Summarising the state of play on *mana*, Lévi-Strauss explains that the problem *mana*-terms present to anthropologists has always been a matter of 'the apparently insoluble antinomies attaching to the notion of *mana*, which struck ethnographers so forcibly, and on which Mauss shed light: force and action; quality and state; substantive, adjective and verb all at once; abstract and concrete; omnipresent and localised' (Lévi-Strauss 1987: 63–4). The excess of *mana*, in other words, was from the start deemed as a systematic transgression of distinctions one could be expected to consider axiomatic.

Indeed, had Lévi-Strauss added concept and thing to the list, which Hubert and Mauss and Lévy-Bruhl had put on the agenda earlier, his summary of the debate's motivations would include my own here.[3] The difference, already outlined in general terms above, has to do with the way one chooses to view the confrontation between *mana* and the putative axioms it transgresses. The philo-philosophical route I propose is that of exploring how *mana* may in its transgression trump the axioms. This is in contrast to the tenor of earlier approaches, which was that axioms are after all axioms, and therefore their authority ought to be confirmed by showing how they can be used to explain *mana* – in other words, how they can trump its putative transgression. Rather than recognising that the 'problem' of *mana* was a function of the relationship between their own analytic tools and their object, analysts imputed the problem onto the object itself. Rather than asking why they might find *mana* excessive, they asked why *mana* might be excessive. And so anthropologists' own mystification by *mana* was projected as 'native mysticism', there to be explained as a perplexing 'phenomenon'.

In illustrating this predicament it pays to recount the debate backwards. While I would hardly wish to subscribe to a *faux* Heideggerian argument about the 'being' that is *mana* having been progressively covered up by anthropologists' 'idle' theory on the subject, it is nevertheless remarkable that the further back one goes in this debate, the closer one gets, if not to the truth, then at least to the kind of approach I wish to advance. So, while Hubert and Mauss may not be quite equivalent to Heidegger's Greeks in this context, I would propose that after *The General Theory of Magic* the *mana*-debate could have taken a more fecund route than it did. In terms of the guiding distinction of the present volume, while Hubert and Mauss' perspective on the relationship between *mana* and magic contains the rudiments for 'thinking through' *mana*, their capitulation to the positivist urge to *explain* this relationship set on its track a trajectory in subsequent debate of merely 'thinking about' it (see Introduction). But note the risk involved in the latter strategy. If the challenge of thinking 'about' things is that of explaining their alterity away, by showing how given axioms can account for it, then the risk of reckoning with alterity at its most extreme – as I have argued for *mana* – is that the axioms may be *shown up* as insufficient for the task. Indeed, I want to argue that in their effort to explain away the apparent contradictions of *mana*, anthropologists themselves have been led to similar contradictions. *Mana* has, as it were, been thinking itself through anthropologists, even as they were busy thinking about it, embedding the 'antinomies' of its own transgression into their theories. I start at the end, with Lévi-Strauss.

Lévi-Strauss' solution to the problem of *mana*'s 'antinomies' amounts to a dissolution. His strategy is analogous to that other famous disappearing act of his, performed a dozen years later, on the notion of 'totemism' (Lévi-Strauss 1964). The debate about totemism, the argument goes, was spurious because it turned on the assumption that the meaning of totemic symbols could be identified by examining their relationship to the social groups they symbolised. Thus framed, anthropologists' answers were as arbitrary as those relationships themselves, for the connection between totem and clan was no more revealing than that between, say, the signifier 'dog' and the animal category it signifies. Signifiers do not acquire their meaning by means of their bilateral relationships to signifieds. They acquire it by means of their multilateral relations with other signifiers. Meaning is a function, in the algebraic sense (Lévi-Strauss 1987: 42–3), of a signifier's position within a structured series. Provided as such, series of signifiers can *only then* be used to code a series of signifieds by establishing one-to-one relations between their respective elements (signifier-to-signified). Totemic classification is an example of this general principle, and therefore poses no more of a problem than any other instance of signification.

Lévi-Strauss' dissolution of the *mana*-debate is similar (although he does not draw the analogy). Anthropologists' intrigue with the antinomies *mana*-terms pose – abstract and concrete, concept and thing, and so on – was motivated by the expectation that, however ambiguous and hard to discern, the meaning of such terms could be identified by reference to the phenomena (or at least the field of phenomena) they signify. The case is made with Mauss in mind – both instigator and target of Lévi-Strauss' analysis in the eponymous article of 1950 – but applies as well to other ethnographers and theorists worried about how best to interpret the meaning of *mana*. Mauss' suggestion that the ambiguity of *mana* is what makes it 'magical' since magic is itself an inherently ambiguous phenomenon (see below) paradoxically places limits on the ambiguity of *mana* by tying it to magic as signifier to signified (Lévi-Strauss 1987: 52–3). On a structuralist premise, however, the matter of *mana*'s ambiguity cannot be settled by appeal to the ambiguous phenomena it signifies (i.e. the totemic illusion), but rather has to be seen in terms of the relations between *mana* and other signifiers. So if, as ethnographers report in desperation, *mana*-terms have no fixed position within indigenous semiotic structures, consisting 'of a series of fluid notions which merge into each other' (Mauss 2001: 134), then it follows that these terms have *less* meaning rather than more. They are signifiers that can 'float' from one semiotic position to the other precisely because, of themselves, they have no meaning. Having remarked on the varied (anti-nomous) meanings ethnographers have attached to these terms, Lévi-Strauss writes:

> And, indeed, *mana* is all those things together; but is that not precisely because it is none of those things, but a simple form, or to be more accurate, a symbol in its pure state, therefore liable to take on any symbolic content whatever?
>
> (1987: 64)

Now, ingenious as it is as a dissolution of the problem of mana, the suggestion that mana-terms are meaningless, much as words like 'thing' or 'stuff' are (1987: 54–5; and see Introduction), can be seen as perverse in two senses.

First, one of the reasons for which ethnographers have considered notions like mana so important in the first place is that their informants do. Whatever mana may be, it certainly isn't a thingamajig or a whatyoumay-callit to those who are concerned with it. Lévi-Strauss' provocation, in this respect, is no more convincing for being intentional. The second perversity of his analysis, less obvious, has to do with the more general point made above, regarding the confrontation between the transgressive character of mana and the analytical tools used to account for it. If the strategy I wish to advocate here is one in which analytical concepts are modified by ethnographic material, then Lévi-Strauss' occupies the directly opposite pole. The motivating distinction of his analysis – the opposition of signifier versus signified – does not only fail to be modified by mana: it flatly contradicts it. For even if the transgressive ambiguity of mana can be thought pacifically as a 'float', the point is that such a float traverses the axiomatic division between signifiers and signifieds, which is of course just a variant of mana's other famous 'antinomies', such as concrete versus abstract and thing versus concept.[4]

Of course, it would be circular of me to submit this contradiction as a capital crime – part of the point of this paper being to show that it is. Maybe we should just admit that ethnographic alterity just is there to be pacified, like the savages who first presented us with it were. But not if the armoury we use contradicts *itself* (this should, by our own reckoning, render *us* savage – cf. Lévi-Strauss 1966). Indeed, while a thorough critique of structuralist analysis is beyond the present remit, I would argue that Lévi-Strauss' appeal to floating signifiers indexes a deep fracture in his theoretical edifice.[5] On the one hand, meaning is posited as a function of semiotic relationships between signifiers, as opposed to one-to-one semantic relationships between signifiers and signifieds, which are arbitrary. On the other, the relationship between signifying and signified series taken as whole cannot be taken as arbitrary, for that would be just saying that signifieds have no purchase whatsoever on signifiers, thus not only rendering the very notion of a signified redundant, but also barring the possibility that signifiers may be used to express 'knowledge' or 'truth' about the world they signify (Lévi-Strauss 1987: 59–60). Now arguably this friction, between the contrasting demands of semiotics and semantics, has played itself out in the starkest terms historically, as Lévi-Strauss' dual legacy of 'post-structuralism' on the one hand (prone to revel in rootless signifiers) and cognitive theory on the other (positively obsessed with rooting them for the sake of reason) – e.g. see Barthes 1984; Sperber 1985; Boyer 1986.[6] But back in 1950 Lévi-Strauss thought that the idea of 'floating signifiers' ameliorated this tension, which he projected as a characteristic of the evolution of human thought:

> [A] fundamental situation perseveres which arises out of the human
> condition: namely, that man has from the start had at his disposition

a signifier-totality which he is at a loss to know how to allocate to a signified, given as such, but no less unknown for being given. There is always a non-equivalence or 'inadequation' between the two, a non-fit and overspill which divine understanding alone can soak up; this generates a signifier-surfeit relative to the signifieds to which it can be fitted.

(1987: 62)

The role of *mana*-terms, then, is to 'enable symbolic thinking to operate despite the contradiction inherent in it' (*ibid.*: 63). *Mana* plays sweeper, absorbing the signifier-surfeit in its contentless form – until, that is, 'knowledge' comes along to disaggregate it into signifiers that may be fixed with reference to *real* signifieds. But there is a contradiction here, and it is in Lévi-Strauss, not the 'human condition'. For on this view, what differentiates *mana* from other signifiers (ones that *have* 'symbolic content') is that it refers to no signified. In other words, while its 'meaninglessness' is defined in semiotic terms (contra Mauss, and in accordance with structuralist first principles), the actual work *mana* does for Lévi-Strauss' argument on 'knowledge' turns on a semantic definition of meaning. In this sense the concept of the floating signifier is indeed *mana*-like (cf. *ibid.*: 57), transgressing Lévi-Strauss' axiomatic distinction between semiotic and semantic analyses of meaning. We might as well speak of the 'floated signified', as Deleuze suggested (1990: 49) – although my argument would be that we should speak of neither, because *mana* is signifier *and* signified (and more).

Now, as I said, if one goes further back in the debate, before Lévi-Strauss, this tendency of *mana* to embed its transgressions into the very tools mobilised analytically against it becomes all the more evident, and ends up appearing less like a peccadillo and more like a viable theoretical strategy. Consider Durkheim's analysis of 'force' in the *Elementary Forms of Religious Life* (1995). Durkheim is concerned to show that, contrary to Comte's contention that scientific notions of force are illusory because of their 'theological' origins, these ideas are 'real' precisely because they originate in religion (Durkheim 1995: 206, cf. Comte 1975: 138–51). This places the argument on force at the very heart of Durkheim's analysis of religion, which, famously, aimed to provide religious representations with an objective foundation by grounding them in the reality of the social groups that collectively represent them. With a view to the debate, hot at that time (e.g. see Marett 1900), about the evolutionary sequence of different religious forms, he traces the origins of religious representations to the notion of a 'sort of diffuse power that permeates things' (Durkheim 1995: 201). Giving Austronesian notions like *mana* and North American ones such as *wakan* (Sioux) and *orenda* (Iroquois) as examples of this 'impersonal force' (*ibid.*: 191), he argues that such a notion is also at the heart of the most elementary form of religious life of all, aboriginal totemism. There, however, force is not conceived abstractly nor given a generic name, but takes the form of 'a material thing', the totem (*op. cit.*). But 'in reality', Durkheim writes, 'the totem amounts to [. . .] the tangible form in which that intangible substance is represented in the imagination; diffused through all sorts of disparate beings, that energy alone is the real object of the cult' (*op. cit.*). So, he argues totemism 'carried the idea [of force] in its womb' (*ibid.*: 194).

Durkheim's argument that, despite their illusory mystical connotations, these notions of force refer to the very real powers that social groups exert over their members is well known (1995: 207–31). Here we may draw attention to the implications of this argument for the question of the 'antinomies' of *mana*. Durkheim's central concern is with what he calls the 'objectification' of religious forces (*ibid.*: 230), most clearly instantiated in totemism, but also characteristic of concepts like *mana* insofar as they are taken to 'permeate things'. The usual analytical axioms are of course built into such an approach. Since sacred things are not identical to the forces they emanate (totemism, see *ibid.*: 190–1) or that permeate them (*mana*-concepts, see *ibid.*: 194–8), and the sacred character of these forces is in any case illusory (*ibid.*: 211), natives' beliefs to the contrary must be explained as some form of projection (*ibid.*: 207). But what is unusual about Durkheim's explanation is that by grounding these projections in a process of objectification he takes to be real (i.e. that of 'collective representation') he is effectively denying that they present an antinomy at all. For the contrast between a realm in which things are not imbued with abstract forces[7] and one in which they are, is not, for Durkheim, one between reality and illusion, but rather one between physical and social reality. The only illusion on the part of the religious is that of mistaking social origins for sacred ones. Thus, effectively, the transgression of *mana* is absorbed into sociological theory in the form of its central concept, that of society. Only a Polynesian speaking of *mana* could have transgressed the distinction between concept and thing any more boldly than Durkheim did himself in articulating the peculiar remit of sociology:[8]

> There is a realm of nature in which the formula of idealism is almost literally applicable; that is the social realm. There, far more than anywhere else, the idea creates the reality.
>
> (1995: 229)

The last step back in the debate, from Durkheim to Hubert and Mauss, is small, though not only for the obvious reasons. The canonical way to connect the *Elementary Forms* to the *General Theory of Magic* – the foundational text of French *mana*-theory – would be in terms of *Année* sociologism. For Durkheim's demystification of *mana* as a social force does lean heavily on his nephew's point in the *General Theory* that, though illusory, the idea of *mana* arises as a result of 'emotions, impressions, impulses [that] are ceaselessly produced [. . .] in communal life' (Mauss 2001: 171). But this early version of what today we would call social constructivism is the least interesting part of the essay (cf. Lévi-Strauss 1987: 56–7). Much more compelling, for the sake of the present argument, is the role Hubert and Mauss give to *mana* not as a phenomenon to be explained (a temptation to which they succumb only at the very end of the essay) but as an analytical tool in its own right.

Hubert and Mauss are explicit as to why *mana* must occupy a central position in their theory of magic – why, in Lévi-Strauss' words, 'the logical structure of the work [. . .] is entirely grounded in *mana*' (1987: 52). Familiar explanations of magic, they argue – in terms of 'sympathetic' syllogisms, 'magical properties', or 'animist hypotheses' – fail because they invariably leave a 'residue' with respect to magical phenomena taken as a totality (Mauss 2001: 120–31). Magic, in our terms, is transgressive – 'total', one might say (cf. Mauss 1990: 3–6; Goldman 2003: 134) – in that it fuses notions of abstract thought, concrete property and spiritual agency. In Hubert and Mauss' marvellous phrase, it is a 'practical idea' (Mauss 2001: 112). Therefore its explanation cannot be couched in terms of 'rigid and abstract categories which our language and reasoning impose' (*ibid.*: 133), but rather requires a conceptual repertoire that traverses these boundaries. Enter *mana*:

> This is the idea, or rather the category, which explains the logical possibility of magical judgements and avoids condemning them as absurdities. It is a remarkable fact that this obscure idea, which we have had such difficulty in separating from the vague nature of affective states, an idea which is almost untranslatable into abstract terms and which is inconceivable to us, should be precisely that idea which provides believers in magic with clear, rational and, occasionally, scientific support. The idea of *mana*, in so far as it is implied in all kinds of magical propositions, becomes, as a result, an analytical concept. Consider the following proposition: the smoke given off by aquatic plants brings clouds. If we were to insert, after the subject of the sentence, the word *mana*, we would immediately have the equation – smoke with *mana* = clouds. This idea [. . .] transforms magical judgements into analytical judgements.
>
> (Mauss 2001: 155–6)

Of course, Hubert and Mauss were hardly oblivious to the circularity of explaining one form of logical transgression in terms of another, and hence felt it necessary to make the buck stop with an argument about how *mana* gets constructed by collective 'powers of suggestion' (Mauss 2001: 171) – society as French magic once more. But I would suggest that my backward story about the increasing explicitness with which *mana*-like transgressions played a role in the analytics of the *mana*-debate, from Lévi-Strauss to

Mauss, could have had a different ending. For another way to make the buck of transgression stop would be to place it in an analytic frame within which it no longer appears transgressive. Hubert and Mauss' willingness to use *mana* for analytical ends, albeit temporarily, is a gesture in this direction – though perhaps a gesture too far, inasmuch as it amounts to adopting *mana* – 'going native' with it (cf. Lévi-Strauss 1987: 47–8). Indeed, my argument is that this move – of adopting *mana* – is just a more explicit and volitional expression of the pitfalls anthropologists have fallen foul of in trying to 'explain' *mana*. Be they transmuted as embarrassing contradictions (Lévi-Strauss), or translated as theoretical premises (Durkheim), *mana*'s transgressions are too 'hot' to handle, as the natives might have put it (Mauss 2001: 134; cf. Sahlins 1985: 18–19).

So, in summary, if the lesson of the story of *mana*-theory is that *mana* will always trump the analytic axioms one throws at it, then its challenge is to make a virtue of necessity, by giving the transgressive potential of *mana* full rein so as to reach new analytical departures – thinking neither about it, nor just with it, but through it. The closest French *mana*-theory came to this tack was with Lévy-Bruhl's argument about the primitive 'law of participation' (1926). Indeed, if Mauss was Lévi-Strauss' mirror, then Lévy-Bruhl was its other side (Goldman 2004; cf. Goldman 1994: 139–43 and *passim*). What *mana*-terms indicate, Lévy-Bruhl argued, is that primitive 'representations [must] obey some other system of logic than the one which governs our own understanding' (1926: 69, cf. 127–36). So the task of analysis is to chart out this system by exploring how primitive representations are constituted within it. His law of participation is the result. In 'primitive mentality,' he writes, 'objects, beings, phenomena can be [. . .] both themselves and something other than themselves' (*ibid.*: 76). The reason why we find this 'incomprehensible' is that the law of contradiction governs our logic, whereas primitive mentality is 'indifferent' to it (*ibid.*: 78). *Mana*-terms exemplify this principle perfectly. When faced with them, Lévy-Bruhl writes, logical thought – as opposed to primitive, 'prelogical' thought – 'is always dubious':

> Are they realities which exist *per se*, or merely very general predicates? [. . .] It is the nature of logical thought to demand a reply to questions such as these. It cannot admit at one and the same time of alternatives which seem to be mutually exclusive. The nature of prelogical mentality, on the contrary, is to ignore the necessity.
>
> (*ibid.*: 135)

Clearly, Lévy-Bruhl's distinction between 'our' logic and 'their' prelogic, criticised with effect by Evans-Pritchard (1965: 87–92; cf. Lévy-Bruhl 1973; Tambiah 1990: 87–8), is an attempt to protect the integrity of our logical axioms in the face of the transgressive logic of *mana*. Nevertheless, in substance Lévy-Bruhl's approach is much more interesting than it is in this aspect of its form. For what does Lévy-Bruhl's law of participation amount to other than an attempt on *his* part to elaborate an analytical frame in which notions like *mana* no longer appear transgressive? His insistence on imputing this logic onto the primitives, prevaricating on its analytic credentials, is detachable from his substantive exposition of the logic itself, and therefore, from the present perspective, can be excused as a sign of its times.

The real problem with Lévy-Bruhl's argument is that it is cast in essentially negative terms (as was, I argued above, Mauss' argument in *The Gift* about the fusion of persons and things). Stripped to its bare bones, Lévy-Bruhl's analysis amounts to the claim that primitive logic disobeys the law of contradiction.[9] At great length and detail he seeks to show that this principle (or is it an anti-principle?) is not only exemplified in all sorts of aspects of primitive life, but also lends them coherence. In terms of the aims of the present chapter, this is a half-measured strategy. Starting with a familiar axiom (the law of contradiction) it shows how its negation – which entails the fusion of our axiomatic distinctions, including the one between concepts and things – plays itself out coherently in primitive life. What it does not do is explore how 'primitive life' (or at least ethnography) might serve to elaborate an *alternative* set of axioms that may go beyond merely restating the insufficiency of our own in positive terms, as Lévy-Bruhl's 'law of participation' does (see quote above). In other words, my question is, if *mana* does not obey the logic of contradiction, then *what logic does it obey*? To get beyond tautology one must move on from the negation of axioms to the creation of new ones (see Introduction). I pursue this task in what follows, with reference to *aché*, the Afro-Cuban cousin of *mana*.

Aché in Cuban Ifá

Aché is relevant in one way or other to all aspects of Ifá worship – as well as Santería, the other main Yoruba-based cult in Cuba, with which Ifá largely shares its cosmology (cf. Brown 2003). Its 'universality', in this sense, renders it as much a 'mana-concept' as mana itself.[10] By way of illustration consider El Monte, the classic monograph on Afro-Cuban religion by Lydia Cabrera (2000), in which aché is mentioned eleven times, and characterised differently in each one of them. Sometimes Cabrera writes of aché in the abstract as 'grace'[11] (ibid.: 16), 'magical power' (ibid.: 99), 'all the powers, force, life, the secret of the earth' (ibid.: 103), or 'luck' (ibid.: 301). But elsewhere aché appears concretely as 'Orula's [i.e. the patron deity of Ifá] grace [kept by the Ifá priest] in his saliva' (ibid.: 106), a 'powder that belongs exclusively to a deity' (ibid.: 481), or, yet more specifically, as 'iyefá, the white powder full of virtues which is spread on to Orula's divining-board' (ibid.: 494). Furthermore, aché appears as something that deities are born with (ibid.: 314), or it may inhere in plants (ibid.: 113), or be invested in idols through consecration rites (ibid.: 103). But rituals themselves may 'accumulate' aché through the presence of plenty of initiates (ibid.: 108); indeed aché is also the kind of thing that initiates themselves can 'have' or 'give' (ibid.: 108).

Here I'll focus on the role of *aché* in the cosmology and practice of Ifá divination. This is hardly arbitrary, since it is mainly as diviners that Ifá initiates (called '*babalawos*') are distinguished from other Afro-Cuban cult practitioners, including practitioners of Santería, and divination furnishes the basic organising principle for other aspects of worship (Holbraad 2005; forthcoming). Furthermore, in terms of the present argument, it is in divination that abstract and concrete senses of '*aché*' come together most clearly.

Asked how *aché* relates to divination, *babalawos*' initial response is most often that *aché* is the power or capacity (in Spanish usually '*poder*' or '*facultad*') that enables them to divine in the first place: 'to divine you must have *aché*', they say. In fact conducting the séance, as well as other rituals, such as consecration, is also said to 'give' the *babalawo aché*, which he may also 'lose' if he uses his office to trick people or do gratuitous evil through sorcery. The importance of *aché* as an enabling condition or force is enshrined in the liturgy of the divinatory séance, with *babalawos* invoking it by name as part of the various Yoruba incantations that need to be chanted for a successful divination. But while these invocations were usually explained to me in rather vague terms – sometimes as appeals for the *aché* of ritual ancestors, other times as solicitations of the *aché* of nature, or of the deities, or specifically of Orula – there were evidently also senses in which *aché* was understood much more precisely, to refer specifically to the secret powders that are an indispensable ingredient in just about all Ifá ceremonials, including divination. I'll describe only the uses to which *aché*-powders are put, and not their ingredients, which *babalawos* guard closely, since – and this is really the point – powders are a principal source of their divinatory powers.

Unlike spirit-mediums and other seers, *babalawos* divine only with the help of certain consecrated paraphernalia. The method is basically similar to other geomantic systems found throughout sub-Saharan Africa and elsewhere (Peel 2003: 115). Most importantly, at initiation, *babalawos* receive a divining-board and a number of palm nuts (*ikines*) of which they use sixteen in order to divine for ceremonial occasions from then on. This is done by clutching all sixteen nuts with both hands, and then separating most of them off with the right hand so as to leave either one or two nuts in the left. If only one remains, the *babalawo* marks two lines with his middle and ring finger on a layer of *aché*-powder, also called *iyefá*, which is spread on the surface of his divining board. If two nuts are left, he marks a single line with his middle finger. The process is repeated until eight (single or double) marks are made on the board, arranged in two columns of four (referred to as 'legs'). In what we might call a random way, this yields one of 256 possible divinatory configurations, referred to either in Yoruba as *oddu* or in Spanish as *signos* (signs) or *letras* (verses). Each *oddu* is connected to a series of myths that are interpreted in various ways during the latter parts of the divinatory séance so as to give pertinent advice to consultants (see Holbraad 2003).

Practitioners emphasise that all the paraphernalia involved only work, as it were, provided they are properly consecrated during the ceremony of initiation, and this most crucially involves 'charging' or 'loading' (*cargar*) each item with *aché*-powder in secret ways (see also below). When I asked what would happen if one were to conduct a divination with 'Jewish' equipment (as yet-to-be-consecrated objects are called), *babalawos* dismissed the idea: Orula 'does not speak' with such objects, they said. The notion that Orula literally speaks in divination is important in this context. For the consecration of the palm nuts in particular is in fact conceptualised as the birth of Orula himself, or, better, the birth of *an* Orula, since each *babalawo* has his own, so there are many. As a general principle in the polytheistic cosmology of Ifá and Santería, while deities may be thought of as transcendent beings who reside in the temporal beyond of mythical time and the spatial one of nature or the sky, they are also given a radically immanent role in the form of idols (Bascom 1950; Peel 2003: 94). Unlike Christian icons and the like, these idols, which usually are stones (*otá*) placed inside decorated pots (*soperas*), are not taken to 'represent' the deity, but rather to *be* it, and are hence fed with blood, spoken to and generally taken care of in ritual contexts. So in this sense Orula simply *is* the palm nuts (which, by the way, when not being used to make Orula 'speak' in divination, are kept in a clay pot on a shelf in the *babalawo*'s home).

Connected to this is the idea that the divinatory configurations that the *babalawo* marks on the powder – the oddu – are also considered as divine beings. The exploits of each individual *oddu* feature in countless myths, wherein *oddu* may appear as kings, warriors, tradesmen, animals, etc., or even as guises of Orula himself. In fact on this score there is a certain amount of ambiguity inasmuch as *babalawos* do often speak of these divine personages as 'paths' of Orula (*caminos*), rather than minor deities in their own right, by analogy with the 'paths' that other popular deities (*orishas*) have – each *orisha* being basically a multiplicity of different 'aspects' or 'avatars' in Yoruba cosmology (Argüelles and Hodge 1991: 226; Bolívar Aróstegui 1994: 27–64; Brown 2003: 118). Be that as it may,[12] the point is that there is nothing 'arbitrary' about these 'signs', as they are often referred to in Spanish (*signos*). When the *babalawo* marks the eight single or double marks on the powder of his divining board, the *oddu* in question is said literally to 'come out' (*salir*), or, more actively, to be 'drawn' (in the gambling sense – *sacar*). And there is no mistaking its potency; crouching around the divining board, the *babalawos* and their consultants are in the presence of a divine being, a symbol that stands for itself if ever there was one (*sensu* Wagner 1986).

The power of powder

So *aché* is excessive like *mana*: power and powder, abstract and concrete, concept and thing. But I would argue that this does not index an antinomy, as Lévi-Strauss would have it. Nor, for that matter, are we faced with an ordinary ambiguity, to be compared, for example, with the English concept of love, which can hardly be said to have a single meaning that incorporates filial and erotic senses. For while *babalawos* certainly distinguish between the different senses in which they use the word '*aché*' – no one is confused about the difference between power and powder – they also assume (and, if invited, explicitly draw) a clear logical connection between the two senses. To have the power of *aché* as a diviner one must be properly consecrated as a *babalawo* and this, most crucially, involves receiving and knowing how to use the consecrated equipment, charged with the powder of *aché*. No powder no power, so to speak. Conversely, the secret knowledge required to prepare *aché* powders and use them for Ifá is possessed only by *babalawos* – a term they translate from Yoruba as 'father of secrets' (Menéndes Vázquez 1995: 51; cf. Bascom 1991: 81). In other words, preparing and using these powders is within the power of *babalawos* exclusively – so 'no power no powder' also.

It is worth being clear about the logical status of this mutual implication, since it goes to the heart of the 'anomaly' *aché* poses – the heart of the problem about concepts and things. For there are two ways of glossing this implication that make it appear quite unanomalous, so to speak, though clearly unusual – or even 'irrational', as the old phrase has it (Sperber 1985). The first would be to gloss the implication in causal terms: no powder no power and vice-versa, because each is a necessary causal condition for the other. The problem then would be simply one of showing why certain people 'believe' – to use a hackneyed word – in such seemingly strange causal sequences. We can all understand how, say, gunpowder was a necessary condition for the power of the Conquistadors, and how, conversely, the gunpowder's power was predicated on its Spanish makers' privileged knowledge of how to produce it. Why might Cuban diviners posit an analogous relationship between their power and their powder, given that no causal efficacy seems 'actually' to be involved?

The problem with this causal gloss is that it does violence to the ethnography. For, like all causal sequences, the circular one proposed here is cast in terms of logically contingent relations between discrete elements. On such a view, *aché*-powders and *aché*-power are first posited as logically independent from one another and then related 'externally' by what philosophers call 'physical' necessity. This hardly tallies with what practitioners say. As shown by their reaction to my suggestion that I might start divining with Jewish equipment, for them the notion of powerless powder, and of powderless power, is not just untenable as a matter of fact, but rather inconceivable as a matter of principle. A *babalawo* who hasn't been properly consecrated with *aché* powder just isn't a *babalawo*. And powder that hasn't been prepared properly by a *babalawo* – father of these secrets – just isn't *aché*. In other words, the relationship between power and powder is, philosophically speaking, 'internal': each is defined in terms of the other.

This suggests an alternative gloss on the mutual implication, in terms of logical rather than physical necessity. On this view, the slogan 'no powder no power' (and its converse) is to be taken as what philosophers call 'analytic', of the same order as statements like 'the queen is head of state', or '2 + 2 = 4'. Just like 2 isn't 2 unless added to itself it gives 4, so a *babalawo* isn't what he is (i.e. doesn't have the power of *aché*) unless he has been consecrated with the powder; and vice-versa. The question then would be: what is it about the meaning of power and powder in this context that makes them mutually definable in this way? Why do Cuban diviners consider these two concepts mutually constitutive while we, presumably, do not?

Persuasive though it may seem, inasmuch as it reflects the internal relationship of power and powder in Ifá, this analysis in terms of logical necessity is just as inadequate to the ethnography as the causal account, though for opposite reasons. The problem here is that by treating the relationship between powder and power as an analytic implication, one effectively ignores its irreducibly practical character. True, for a babalawo it is enough to contemplate what his power means to know that it required his consecration with aché powder (and vice-versa). But the point is that this logical operation presupposes a practical one, since it is only because aché powder is actually efficacious that it can be used to produce babalawos 'with aché' (i.e. with power). Babalawos only count as such provided they have been consecrated with powder, not because the meaning of powder logically implies their power (like the meaning of 'queen' implies being head of state), but because the powder itself gives them power. (And vice-versa for powder.) In other words, the difference between the relationship of powder and power and that described by an ordinary analytic statement is that while the latter states a conceptual identity, the former implies a real transference (of powder that gives power and of power that gives powder).[13]

Now, at this point my account of this dilemma will appear contradictory. It seems as if what I've done is to complain of the causal analysis that it distorts the logical implication that binds power and powder, only to reject the logical analysis on the grounds that it distorts the causal character of the implication. Which is it: logical or causal? But I would argue that this appearance of contradiction is a consequence of the Procrustean character of the analytical choices we seem to have at our disposal. The mutual implication of powder and power in Ifá is, indeed, not causal insofar as causal implications connect discrete matters of fact, whereas powder and power are inconceivable as independent variables because *aché* just is the kind of powder that gives power and *aché* just is the kind of power that makes powder. But this logically necessary mutual implication is not analytic, since power and powder are not conceptually identical but rather in a relationship of mutual generation: *babalawos* cannot conceive of one without the other because each cannot literally be conceived without a transference of the other.

Indeed we may note here that the distinction between causal connection and logical identity, which renders *aché* contradictory, is corollary to the distinction between things and concepts. And it is precisely because *aché* does not fall tidily into either of the latter categories that it does not lend itself to analysis in terms of either of the former relations. If *aché* powder and *aché* power were 'things' (in the sense of 'objects'), then they could be conceived of as discrete variables, which, as we've seen, they cannot. If they were concepts, then their internal connection would be a purely deductive matter, whereas, as we've seen, it is not. So properly speaking *aché* is neither thing nor concept but rather a bit of both: an indiscrete thing and a concept that literally transfers itself. Clearly for as long as we insist on thinking in these terms we can only articulate *aché* as a paradox, which, as we've seen, was the predicament of the debate about *mana*-terms in general.

The strategy of this paper is based on the idea that this negative analytical predicament prescribes a positive methodology that may lead to an analytical resolution. If *aché* is to be taken as both what we call a concept and what we call a thing, then it follows that the connection between the two sides of its 'double aspect', so to speak, is not arbitrary. That is to say, while the logical status of *aché* is still obscure due to its apparent 'excess', we do know one thing: that its abstract meaning as 'power' is internally related to its concrete nature as powder. So the meaning of *aché* (the 'concept') is literally constituted by the things to which it would otherwise be assumed simply to 'apply'. Its intension is modified by its extension, if you like, by what one might call a relation of 'hyper-metonymy' (imagine a crown that didn't just signify royalty, but actually made it – a 'magical' crown, then).

On this hypothesis, which – as we have seen – is motivated by the ethnography, the task is to understand *aché* in its very excess. And the opportunity for doing so is there, in the ethnography of the thing itself, in powder. For, with the axiom 'thing v. meaning' discarded, the ethnography of things like powder can no longer be assumed to be about 'interpreting' them in terms of the meanings the people we study 'attach' to them. Things carry their own context within themselves, as Marilyn Strathern has put it, writing of other things (Strathern 1990; and see Introduction). So the method *aché* dictates for itself could be captured by the old phenomenological injunction: 'back to the things themselves'. But only with the proviso that this is not because somehow the level of things and of people's 'practical' engagement with them is more 'primordial' than the level of theoretical manipulation of concepts, as some anthropological versions of phenomenology would sometimes have it (e.g. Ingold 1996; Willerslev 2004). Rather, because the internal relationship between concepts and things implies that in some important sense things just *are* concepts. So our job is to think through them, as the title of the volume would have it, rather than about them. In particular, this method allows us to determine the logical status of the 'hyper-metonymy' relating powder to power in Ifá, by attending to the role of the 'thing itself' – powder – in Ifá divination.

So what makes powder power in Ifá? The beginning of a reply may be given by making explicit what divinatory power consists in for *babalawos*. As we saw, the difference between unbaptised and consecrated equipment is that Orula only speaks through the latter, and this is because he is deemed to *be* the latter: when he speaks, he *is* sixteen palm nuts being cast into *oddu*-configurations, marked on the powder of the divining board; and those marks themselves *are* Orula's *oddu*, not just their representations. So the divinatory power of the *babalawos* can fairly be glossed as their ability to render Orula and his *oddu* immanent during the consultation: an otherwise transcendent deity, who is imagined to reside in natural features, the sky, or mythic time, is made temporarily present during the séance. Divinatory power, then, most crucially involves the capacity to engender what we might call 'ontological leaps' on the part of the deity, from transcendence to immanence or, more simply, from radical absence (the 'beyond') to presence. (These leaps are the polytheistic counterpart to the epistemological 'leaps of faith' associated with monotheism, though even God – in Christianity – needed his son as a one-off ontological transgression, or at least he thought we did.)

Before going on to explain how *aché*-powders may be said to condition such leaps, as the logic of 'no powder no power' would imply, it is necessary to comment on the problem they present – the 'problem of transcendence' let's call it. The problem, which *babalawos* have the power to solve, amounts to the danger that Orula and the rest of the *orishas* might remain in a state of transcendence, permanently separated from humans in the 'beyond'. Such a state of affairs, depicted in calamitous terms in Ifá myth (e.g. see Clark 2005: 56), would render all aspects of Ifá worship impossible, including not only divination, but also initiation, consecration, sacrifice, and magic, all of which are premised on the idea that deities and humans can enter into *relations* with each other (Orula's speech to the consultant through the oracle, mortals asking the deities for divine favour, feeding them blood, bringing divine power to bear on personal affairs in sorcery, etc.).

My argument depends on the idea that despite its theological twist, as it were, this problem is familiar at a more abstract philosophical level as the problem of 'individualism', to put a word on it. The question, which in modern times goes back at least to the social contract theorists of the seventeenth and eighteenth centuries, is how from a position of an aggregate of individuals, separate and self-contained units that are, in other words, transcendent with respect to one another, we might arrive at a position where these units are formed in relation to each other – how, in human terms, 'society' is created out of 'individuals'. A peculiarly anthropological dissolution of this question goes back at least to Mauss, and has in recent years become particularly associated with Melanesia due to the work of Marilyn Strathern (1988; 1995; see also Dumont 1970; Marriott 1979). That is to say, that the question of how relations might be engendered out of individuals is itself arbitrary, for one could perfectly well ask how individuals are engendered out of relations. Indeed, anthropologically speaking, phenomena like magic, or gifting, or certain kinds of tribal leadership, or caste, or hunting and shamanism, or affinity, or even anthropological analysis itself, will be endlessly misunderstood unless we perform exactly this kind of analytical reversal, viewing relations as logically primitive, and the terms they relate ('individuals') as derivative effects.

While I cannot comment on gifting, caste, affinity and so forth, I would suggest that with regard to Ifá divination the choice between giving priority to relations over individuals or vice-versa is at least problematic, and ultimately false. Crudely put, if one were to say that the problem of transcendence in Ifá is not really a problem because deities and humans mutually constitute each other in the relationships that divination implies, one would be denying the very condition that leads clients to the diviners in the first place, namely that the deities *are* transcendent most of the time, so that the diviners' powers are necessary in order to elicit them into relation. In this sense, relation and transcendence are symmetrical in Ifá cosmology, so a choice of giving priority to one over the other must be false (cf. Højer 2005). Therefore, the analytical question is how *relation and transcendence might themselves be related*, other than by antinomy.

Powder gives us the answer, and to see this we may pay attention to its role in divination. As we saw, spread on the surface of the divining board, powder provides the backdrop upon which the oddu, thought of as deity-signs, 'come out'. In this most crucial of senses, then, powder is the catalyst of divinatory power, i.e. the capacity to make Orula 'come out' and 'speak' through his oddu. Considered prosaically, powder is able to do this due to its pervious character, as a collection of unstructured particles – its pure multiplicity, so to speak. In marking the oddu on the board, the babalawo's fingers are able to draw the configuration just to the extent that the 'intensive' capacity of powder to be moved (to be displaced like Archimedean bathwater) allows them to do so. The extensive movement of the oddu as it appears on the board, then, presupposes the intensive mobility of powder as the medium upon which it is registered. Of course, physically speaking, this is always the case – movement presupposes movement. Even if the babalawo marked the oddu with a pencil on a piece of paper, the lead would only leave a mark provided the paper particles reacted accordingly. But the point is that powder renders the motile premise of the oddu's revelation explicit, there for all to see by means of a simple figure-ground reversal: oddu figures are revealed as a temporary displacement of their ground, the powder.[14]

This suggests a logical reversal that goes to the heart of the problem of transcendence. If we take seriously *babalawos'* contention that the *oddu* just *are* the marks they make on *aché*-powder – as we must if we are intent on thinking *through* these things – then the constitution of deities as displacements of powder tells us something pretty important about the premises of Ifá cosmology: that these deities are to be thought of neither as individual entities nor as relations, but rather as *motions*. Indeed, beyond the role of powder, this accords with the mechanics by which the *oddu* get determined in the first place, since, as we saw, Orula himself is a plural object: sixteen palm nuts that only 'speak' through motion – the diviner's cast. And it also accords with the otherwise perplexing idea that all *orishas* manifest themselves as one of a number of 'paths', as I mentioned.

If the *oddu* of Orula, as well as the *orishas* more generally, just are motions (or 'paths'), then the apparent antinomy of giving logical priority to transcendence over relation or vice-versa is resolved. In a logical universe where motion is primitive, what looks like transcendence becomes distance and what looks like relation becomes proximity. Motions through and through, the deities are never divorced from humans, stuck in the 'beyond' of transcendence – to say so would be to place limits on the logical priority of motion. Conversely, humans' relations with motile deities cannot be taken for granted, as the Melanesianist image would have it, for there is no guarantee that the deities' movement will be elicited in the right direction, as it were.[15] The relation, then, is potential, and it is just this potential – the potential of directed movement – that *aché*-powder guarantees, as a solution to the genuine problem of the distance deities must traverse in order to be rendered present in divination.

The notion of potentiality here, and particularly that of potential relation, is closely akin to arguments presented by Eduardo Viveiros de Castro and Marcio Goldman, on the 'virtuality' of Amerindian and Afro-Brazilian cosmologies respectively (Viveiros de Castro 1998a; 1998b; 2002; 2004; 2005; Goldman 2003; 2004). Drawing on Deleuzian conceptions of 'virtuality', 'difference', and 'becoming' (e.g. Deleuze 1994), their analyses of these cosmologies turns on a figure-ground reversal that is closely analogous to the one powder just performed for us here. Their point (and I paraphrase wildly across texts for the sake of brevity) can be summarised like this.

Anthropologists tend to describe the cosmologies they study as systems of classification. The assumption is that cosmologies are populated by different entities (gods, ancestors, spirits, and so on) that relate to one another in different ways (hierarchically, genealogically, temperamentally, or whatever). Cosmologies can be 'charted' by placing these entities in relation to each other in conceptual space – or, indeed, on paper – according to their differences, characterising their relations in the spaces that are provided – notionally or graphically – between them. Now, try imagining a figure-ground reversal on such a chart, as in an Escher sketch. Cosmological elements now feature not as self-identical marks relating to each other externally in space (the 'scheme', the 'paper'), but are rather extended across the spaces that previously divided them. What was assumed to be a scheme of entities now appears as a field of relations, so that the differences that previously distinguished one cosmological element from another 'extensively' now become 'intensive' characteristics of those elements themselves, now conceived of as 'self-differentiating' relations. Showing that such a 'plane of immanence' (2004: 6) underlies pan-Amerindian notions of myth, spirits, and shamanism, Viveiros de Castro writes:

> [T]he agents and patients found in origin myths are defined by their *intrinsic capacity to be something else*; in this sense, each mythic being differs infinitely *from itself*, given that it is 'posited' by mythic discourse only to be 'substituted,' that is, transformed. It is this self-difference which defines a 'spirit,' and which makes all mythic beings into 'spirits' too. [. . .] In sum, myth posits an ontological regime commanded by a fluent intensive difference which incides on each point of a heterogenic continuum, where transformation is anterior to form, relation is superior to terms, and interval is interior to being.
>
> (2004: 7–8)

While Viveiros de Castro does not add the priority of motion over rest to his list, it is clear that such a logical reversal, which I have argued is necessary to make sense of the 'intrinsic capacity' of Ifá deities to move from transcendence to immanence, is confluent with his argument. Furthermore, the role he has given elsewhere to Amerindian *mana*-concepts as a premise for what he calls the 'transductivity' (2004: 11) of spirits and other virtual becomings is largely analogous to the role of *aché* as a premise for the motility of Ifá 'paths' in divination (see Viveiros de Castro 1998a: 79–83; cf. Gray 1996).

Now, a full discussion of these analogies and their possible breakdowns would involve far-reaching comparisons between Amerindian 'animism' and Afro-American 'polytheism' – 'spirits' versus 'deities', so to speak. Here I shall only make use of the analogy with Viveiros de Castro's argument on virtuality to make two points – one positive and one negative – that may help to sharpen my own argument on motility. Both points pertain to the question as to how Viveiros de Castro's use of the concept of 'intensive difference' fares in relation to the problem of deities' transcendence, which, as we have seen, *aché* has the power to solve.

Firstly, it will be noted that the point of analogy between the virtual and the motile lies precisely in the idea of potentiality, which is a common corollary of both.[16] As we have seen, if *aché* forces us to conceive of the *oddu* of Ifá as motions, it also allows us to think of the *oddu* as having the potential to become immanent in divination, so as to enter into relations with the *babalawos* that invoke them. In this sense, being motions, *oddu* are also 'potential relations'. Analogously, if for Viveiros de Castro spirits are virtual in the sense that they are 'self-differential', then they too should be construed as potential relations inasmuch as their self-difference just amounts to their inherent potential to 'be something other than themselves' – to recall Lévy-Bruhl's formulation (1926: 76; see above). Indeed, more than just analogous, these two senses of 'potential relation' stand in a relationship of logical implication. For the *oddu*'s potential to enter into relations with humans is premised on what Viveiros de Castro calls 'self-difference'. *Oddu* do not simply 'travel' from the beyond of mythical transcendence to the here of the divining board, for their 'motion' is not one of a self-identical entity. As we have seen, the capacity of *oddu* to reveal themselves in divination implies a transformation, which resembles the one Viveiros de Castro envisages for Amerindian spirits (although there are contrasts too, as I'll argue). Be they conceived as 'paths' of Orula or as deities in their own right, the *oddu* are 'posited' as characters that live somewhere in the beyond as variable mythical guises, only to be 'substituted' during the divinatory séance, first as configurations of the palm-nuts and then as 'signs' on the aché powder. In other words, *oddu* can relate to 'others' just because they can 'other' themselves, inasmuch as their 'motion' from transcendence to immanence is premised on their capacity virtually to 'self-differentiate'.

The upshot of this is that the motion of the *oddu* as they 'come out' on the divining board should not be conceived in spatial terms at all, but rather in ontological ones. *Aché*, then, is the space in which ontological transformations happen, and its role on the divining board as a 'register' (*registro*)[17] is also 'ontological' through and through. In the motile universe of Ifá, the very act of registration on the surface of the divining board – as the *babalawo*'s fingers move through the powder to reveal the *oddu* – is not an *ex post facto* representation of an already pertaining state of affairs, but rather an act of ontological transformation in its own right, for it is in this act that the *oddu* is 'substituted' as an immanent presence in the séance.

Indeed such an analysis of *aché* as the premise/catalyst of transformation can arguably be generalised in Ifá, beyond the immediate context of divination. The point can be put with reference to an argument presented by Goldman in a recent conference paper (Goldman 2004; cf. 2003), regarding what he sees as three distinguishable 'logics' or 'dimensions' of Candomblé, the Afro-Brazilian cousin of Santería and Ifá.[18] First, Goldman argues, Candomblé involves a 'cosmology',[19] based on a complex system of metaphoric classifications. Second, it involves an 'anthropology', which places humans amidst these classificatory schemes by means of a series of ritual substitutions associated with the metonymic identifications of sacrifice and possession. And third, it involves a 'ritualistic' logic of 'manipulation' (Goldman 2004: 3), whereby metaphoric classifications and metonymic identifications are mobilised 'pragmatically' at the service of secret magical actions.

While Goldman does not provide specific examples from Candomblé in his short think piece, his notion of 'ritual manipulations' corresponds directly to what *babalawos* and *santeros* in Cuba call '*trabajos*' (lit. 'works'). Witchcrafts in the strict sense of the word, these are covert operations in which varied magical ingredients are mixed and matched according to secret recipes, with a view to bringing about specific desired effects, ranging from the relatively benign (e.g. protection from sorcery, healing of illness, and so forth) to the more interventionist (e.g. love magic, spells against enemies, precipitations of misfortune or even death). Elaborating on Roger Bastide's claim that Candomblé practice is characterised by a 'desire to blend', Goldman argues that this magical 'savoir faire' (*ibid.*: 3), displays a logic of what Deleuze called 'becoming', in the sense that it involves manipulations that deny 'all possible substantial identity', so that 'differences' are posited 'not in order to be reduced to similarity [. . .], but in order to "differ", simply and intransitively' (*ibid.*: 4).

This logical inversion, identical in import to Viveiros de Castro's notion of self-difference, does not only contrast with both the 'structural' (i.e. metaphoric) logic of Candomblé cosmological classifications and the 'serial' (i.e. metonymic) logic of Candomblé 'anthropology', but also ultimately encompasses both of them. For, as Goldman argues, as soon as one takes into account the focal significance of witchcraft in the practice of Candomblé, one is forced to conclude that the intellectual stipulations of Candomblé cosmology and anthropology are only posited in order to be transformed – to use Viveiros de Castro's language – or indeed *transgressed* – to use mine – in the pragmatics of witchcraft. Thus, Goldman suggests, 'classifications may be of service mainly to the extent that they are overcome, functioning more or less as trampolines for action and creation' (*ibid.*: 8).

While it would be too big a job to establish here the validity of this analysis in terms of the ethnography of Ifá, Goldman's main thesis about the 'deterritorialisation', as he calls it, of categories in witchcraft is, I believe, fully transposable. Indeed, it seems to me that the implication of Goldman's argument is not so much that the 'becoming' of witchcraft needs to be added as the third and most characteristic dimension of Candomblé logic, alongside the categorial dimensions of 'structure' and 'series' which it trumps, but rather that the fact that witchcraft appears transgressive when placed alongside categorial logic just shows the latter up as an inappropriate analytical frame for understanding Candomblé, and Ifá by the same token (see also Henare, Chapter 3 in this volume). So the point is not that witchcraft 'becomings' contradict cosmological structures and anthropological series, but rather that, since witchcraft properly encompasses cosmology and anthropology, the assumption that the latter pair (let alone witchcraft itself) can be understood in terms of structures or series of self-identical categories was wrong in the first place.[20] Goldman suggests such an interpretation of his argument when he recalls Bastide's observation that Candomblé classifications 'are not like our own', inasmuch as they do not operate over entities but rather over 'forces and participations'. He also points to the transgressive role of Exu (the West African trickster deity – called Echu in Cuba) within Candomblé cosmology and anthropology, who in ritual acts is posited as an indispensable intermediary between humans and deities (Goldman 2004: 6–7; cf. Pelton 1980: 133–63; and see below).[21]

Such pointers (and more evidence of Ifá's cosmological motility appears below), indicate that my argument that, in Ifá, deities are best understood as motions – denying 'all possible substantial identity', so to speak – can be extended beyond the context of divination, as a general cosmological premise. For present purposes the most pertinent ethnographic evidence for this has to do with the role of *aché*, as conceived by practitioners on this broader cosmological scale. Goldman touches on the issue at the very outset of his characterisation of Candomblé cosmology:

> [Candomblé cosmology involves] a kind of monism that supposes a single essence that diversifies into various modalities that constitute all that exists or that can exist in the universe. This essence, which is clearly similar to the Melanesian notion of *mana* [. . .], is referred to in Candomblé as *axé*. The diversification of *axé* is initially manifested in the divinities themselves, the Orixás, since each of them incarnates a specific modality of the general essence. In turn, each thing or being that exists in the world – stones, plants, animals, human beings, etc. [. . .] – 'belongs' to one of these Orixás to the extent that they share with him this essence, which is at the same time both general and individual.
>
> (Goldman 2004: 1–2)

Although *babalawos* in Cuba have not given me such a concerted cosmogony regarding *aché* (their varied accounts tend to focus on the generative role of 'major' *orishas* at the beginnings of time), Goldman's synthesis does reflect *babalawos'* common observation that the *orishas* and their worldly 'belongings' 'have *aché*'. Indeed, from the point of view of such statements, Goldman's paradoxical appeal to the notion of 'essence' (e.g. 'both general and individual') is perhaps unnecessary. Building on my earlier argument about *aché* in divination, an alternative analysis would posit *aché* not as diversified essence but as *the premise of diversification itself*.[22] Orishas 'have *aché*' precisely inasmuch as they are able, qua motions, rather than entities or relations, to 'become' the various elements of the world: stones, plants, animals, humans. . . . These in turn, 'belong' to the *orishas* just in the sense that they *are them*: they are varied outcomes of the *orisha*'s motile becoming, and hence 'have *aché*' also.

This, arguably, is the significance of the ritual requirement in Ifá (and Santería) that all consecrated items be physically 'loaded' with *aché*-powders.

This includes not only *babalawos'* Orula deity and the divinatory objects that go with it (see above), but also all the other deities practitioners receive as 'loaded' idols at different stages of their initiatory career (Holbraad forthcoming), as well as the initiates themselves, who are 'marked' with *aché*-powders at various parts of their body during initiation. Just as the powder *babalawos* use on their divining boards is powerful as a surface on which Orula's *oddu* can 'come out', so consecrated idols and initiates are powerful ('have *aché*') as conduits that render the presence of the relevant *orishas* immanent, particularly as and when this is required in ritual. In light of our earlier analysis of the role of powder as the pervious 'ground' on which deities manifest as immanent 'figures', it makes sense that powder should also be the 'active ingredient', so to speak, of consecration. Admittedly, its role as motile ground here is, literally, not as graphic. Powder is not itself marked, but rather is either 'loaded' in small portions into secret cavities of the idol-deities, or indeed used to 'mark' the bodies of neophytes. One is tempted to say that the power of these pinches of *aché*-powder is metonymic, though only on the proviso that this is a 'hyper-metonymy' in a strict and pertinent sense (see also above). Unlike ordinary metonymy in which a part comes to stand, symbolically, for the whole (e.g. crown for king), the pinches of powder that are used in consecration do not merely 'stand for' the whole from which they are partitioned (which in the case of Ifá consecration is the same *iyefá*-powder that is used, in larger quantities, to cover the divining board), but rather, literally, they reconstitute it *as wholes in their own right*. This follows from a second 'prosaic' property of powder. As a pure multiplicity of particles, powder is not only pervious, as we saw, but also 'partible': even pinches of powder constitute wholes, inasmuch as no qualitative difference (other than quantity!) distinguishes them from the wholes from which they were detached (cf. Reed, Chapter 2 in this volume).[23] So, even though in consecration powder does not actually *display* motility as it does in divination, it does retain literally the property (namely, perviousness) that would allow motile deities to be rendered immanent, and thus is powerful in the same sense – albeit, of course, *in principle*.

Be that as it may, it is clear that in consecration powder is power in the same sense as it is in divination, namely as a catalyst for the ontological transformation of the *orishas*, from a state of transcendence in the 'beyond', to a state of immanence in the consecrated items. This brings us back to a second point of comparison with Viveiros de Castro's notion of 'self-difference' – and arguably Goldman's notion of 'becoming', by the same token. For it should be noted that the kind of ontological transformation that is at stake in Ifá is in significant ways different from the ones Viveiros de Castro has in mind in the Amerindian context. With reference to Stephen Hugh-Jones' distinction between 'horizontal' and 'vertical' types of Amazonian shamanism – the former associated, among other features, with hunting, affinity, warfare, reciprocity and anarchic or egalitarian social relations, and the latter with gathering, descent, internal cohesion, heredity and hierarchical social reproduction (Hugh-Jones 1996; cf. Pedersen 2001) – Viveiros de Castro implies that the tendencies of his argument about the virtuality of spirits are 'horizontal' (2004: 5). By contrast, Ifá in many ways resembles Hugh-Jones' analysis of vertical shamanism. For example, as I have discussed elsewhere, Ifá cults are structured hierarchically, based on the regal prestige of initiation and training in mythical knowledge, and reproduce themselves along lineage branches, involving principles of ritual kinship, heredity and so on (see Holbraad 2005; forthcoming; cf. Hugh-Jones 1996: 32–47).[24] Indeed, projected beyond Hugh-Jones' immediate concern with shamanic (or, in our case, divinatory) practice, the contrast between horizontal and vertical cosmological arrangements captures an important difference between Amerindian spirits and Ifá deities.

Viveiros de Castro's account of spirits is 'horizontal' inasmuch as it is essentially anarchic. Spirits are conceived as endlessly multiplying, like 'forests of mirrors', and their multiplicity is irreducibly qualitative inasmuch as it implies 'modulations' of 'form' (2004: 11) – of 'ontic' form, we might say, mutating from species to species, from animal to human, minuteness to monstrosity.[25] Ifá, on the other hand, in accordance with its imperial associations in West Africa (e.g. see Bascom 1991; Peel 2003), presents the question of deities' potential for transformation in irreducibly vertical or, as practitioners also put it, 'hierarchical' terms. What I have in mind here is not primarily the much debated ranking of deities in the form of a systematic 'pantheon', whose historical evolution, as David Brown has argued convincingly, is heavily bound up with Christian and other 'theologising' influences both in Africa and in Cuba (Brown 2003: 114–28; Peel 2003).[26] Rather, what makes Ifá 'vertical' is the cosmological premise upon which such rankings are conceived, namely the idea that deities can be characterised by their degree of 'distance' from the human world. Brown writes:

> [R]ankings along the spirit–matter continuum can be flexible and ambiguous. For example, Echu is, in fact, 'everywhere and sees everything': he is a 'warrior' of the highly 'material' street and forest; he is also right up there as 'God's secretary'; at the same time, he is not merely a 'mischievous' orisha but is, in one road [viz. 'path'], Alosí, the Devil, who manifests himself in this world. [. . .] Obatalá [sky deity, patron of peace], too, defies ontological confinement. Numerous relatively more 'material' and more 'spiritual' Obatalás, who are 'younger' warrior types or 'older' sage types, respectively, populate this continuum.
>
> (2003: 127, references omitted)

So if the orishas are as multiple as Amazonian spirits, each of their 'paths' taking a different ontic form, their multiplicity is nevertheless 'vertically' distributed. They differ from the Amazonian paradigm in that their ontic transformations also imply shifts in what one might call *ontological status*, since their multiple becoming is inflected hierarchically as a 'continuum' of relatively proximate and relatively distant 'manifestations'. Indeed, the distinction between shifts of ontic form and of ontological status allows us to conceptualise the difference between (horizontal) shamanism and divination, as the respective modes of divine disclosure in Amazonia and in Ifá. The shamanic ability to 'call spirits', explains Viveiros de Castro, is a matter of 'vision': where non-shamans just see animals in the forest, for example, shamans see spirits (Viveiros de Castro 2004: 4; see also Pedersen, Chapter 7 in this volume). This makes sense, since the 'problem' that spirits present to humans is that there is more to them than meets the non-shamanic eye – *qua* intensive differences, they are always more than the sum of their ontic snapshot appearances (e.g. the forest animals, which are just a form of their becoming). The problem with the *orishas*, on the other hand, is not so much that they are invisible but rather that they are not fully 'here' in the first place. After all, insofar as the *orishas* are visible at all, it takes no special powers to see them. The idol-deities in which they manifest ceremonially, the natural features of which they are patrons, the devotees whose bodies they possess during Santería rituals, as well as the *aché* powder that Orula marks during divination – all these concretions are there for all to see. The problem is how to elicit the deities' presence in these concrete forms – how to elicit immanence, having posited transcendence. One might say that if the shaman's task is to see what is present, the diviner's is to render present what is already seen.

It follows that while Viveiros de Castro's notion of intensive difference is, as already shown, pre-supposed by the idea of motility, such a notion is nevertheless insufficient on its own to account for the peculiar verticality of Ifá deities' ontological transformations – the problem of transcendence. True, such a notion is in this respect an improvement on the Melanesianist concept of the 'relation', which precludes the possibility of ontological distance altogether (see above). Nevertheless, the distance admitted by the 'potential' relations of the virtual is not of a kind that allows us fully to make sense of deities' transcendence. A matter of ontic form rather than ontological status, the potentiality of virtual spirits is that of transforming themselves horizontally into what they are not ('becoming-other'), whereas the vertical axis of transcendence to immanence implies transformations that are also constituted as shifts between *orders* of otherness ('becoming-other-kinds-of-other', if you like).

The idea of motility, I argue, is able to capture these differences between difference. For by distributing virtual becomings across a continuum of *motion*, with its peculiar capacity to 'self-scale', if you like, in terms of the formal relations of 'distance' and 'proximity' (which, as we have seen, the notion of direction implies), we effectively add a second dimension to the concept of 'becoming' itself. Perhaps the clearest way to express this is in terms of the structuralist distinction between 'syntagmatic' and 'paradigmatic' relations. Virtual continua relate differences paradigmatically. Motile ones relate them syntagmatically, which is to say that they relate them ordinally, in sequences that provide them direction in terms of asymmetrical (positional) relations of 'before' and 'after'. So, no less 'intensive' than their virtual counterparts, motile differences are nevertheless more sophisticated from a logical point of view, in that they are able to render two dimensions of difference – paradigmatic 'form' and syntagmatic 'status' (or 'position') – at once. Both dimensions are needed in order to articulate the problem of transcendence, which, as we have seen, is so central to Ifá cosmology. Motile deities' transformations allow them to enter into relations with humans. And the fact that these transformations scale themselves as changes of ontological status shows that deity–human relations are not given as cosmological *fait accompli* (as virtual relations that are there for those who can see them, as in horizontal shamanism), but rather have to be *accomplished* by eliciting the deities from the relative ontological distance of transcendence to the relative proximity of immanence.

Conclusion: motile things are motile concepts

So the answer to the question as to why *aché* powder is power is that, in Ifá, powder provides the condition under which deities can manifest themselves immanently. If deities' moves to immanence are a function of their motility, then *aché* powder is an essential ingredient for eliciting such moves, since it allows them to be articulated as such – articulated quite literally, as we have seen, on the surface of the divining board as a series of intensive motions (inward displacements) of powder that reveal the 'figures' of Orula's *oddu*.

Now, there is an obvious objection to this line of argument, which I wish to address by way of conclusion, because it brings this discussion of *aché* straight back to the theme that motivated it, namely the relationship between concepts and things. A knee-jerk complaint against the notion of *aché*'s motile power is that it seems highly 'metaphorical'. Perhaps deities are indeed best thought of as motions, goes the objection, and powder may indeed serve to register these motions for the purposes of divination. But this is hardly proof of the power of powder. For the fact that the peculiar physical characteristics of powder (i.e the intensive motions of its particles) gave *us* an analytical clue as to the role of motility in Ifá cosmology does not imply that *aché* powders actually *contribute* to the motility of the deities or, for that matter, to the *babalawos*' power to elicit these motile deities into immanence. Indeed, isn't the whole strategy of our claim to having shown this quite circular? Isn't it only because we have already assumed – by 'magical' analytical fiat – that the distinction between things and concepts may be elided, that we now claim that in Ifá powder is power, on the grounds that *babalawos'* power *just is* their capacity to elicit deities on the divining board, and this capacity *just is* – in part[27] – the capacity of their *aché*-powder to move itself on the surface board so as to render the motile deities immanent? Had we not negated by stipulation the axiom of things versus concepts, such identifications would be shown up as quite illogical. For things like powder may perhaps be thought to be powerful by *babalawos* (and such a strange notion could surely be explained anthropologically in different ways, in the manner of 'twins are birds'), but the notion that powder *just is* power is either a rhetorical metaphor or logically absurd.

Indeed, one can imagine our putative critic going further with this line of reasoning, using the apparent circularity of the argument on power and powder to disparage the broader meta-anthropological strategy that was used to justify it. As a response to earlier failures to account for *mana's* systematic transgressions of the concept-versus-thing axiom, my suggestion was that an ethnographic analysis of the transgressions of *aché* might provide a conceptual frame within which such transgressions no longer register as logical absurdities. This line of inquiry led us to the analytics of 'motility' which, as we saw, are able to make sense of the claim that powder is indeed power. But is this not circularity writ large? For if such an ethnographic analysis has to *begin* from the stipulation that the distinction between concepts and things is not axiomatic, then how can it also purport to *show* it?

Such objections turn on a confusion between the charge of logical circularity and the virtue of what was called 'recursivity' in this volume's introductory chapter. True, in order to get to the concept of motility, and thus to show that a thing like powder can be identical with a concept like power, we had to proceed from the premise that such an identification might in principle make sense. And certainly this would have been circular if all that such an inquiry had produced was a confirmation of its own premise. However, the inquiry has offered more than that. Proceeding from a stipulative identification of concepts with things, it has yielded the analytics of motility. And the reason why this undertaking is not circular is precisely that motility does not merely presuppose a collapse of the concept/thing divide, but rather provides its logical justification. So if the initial stipulation allowed us, like Wittgenstein's ladder, to get to the concept of motility, then that concept in turn allows us to discard the ladder of mere stipulation, and accept a novel logical framework that denies the axiom of concepts versus things.

For the conclusion can only be this. If the motility of powder dissolves the problem of transcendence versus immanence for *babalawos*, then motility also dissolves the problem of concept versus thing for us. And this because the latter problem is just an instance of the former. After all, the notion of transcendence is just a way of expressing the very idea of ontological separation. And ontological separation is what a non-motile logic posits at the hiatus that is supposed to divide concepts from things. Motility, on the other hand, turns on the idea that ontological differences do not amount to separations at all, but rather to intensive and 'self-scaling' transformations. Thus, just like in a motile logical universe powder can *be* power, deities can *be* marks on the divining board, and so forth, so concepts and things can also *be* each other. All it takes is to stop thinking of concepts and things as self-identical entities, and start imagining them as self-differential motions.

Acknowledgements

A version of this chapter was presented to the Anthropology Seminar at Manchester University, whose members I thank for highly insightful comments. I am also particularly grateful to Rebecca Empson, Marcio Goldman, Keith Hart, Ami Henare, Stephen Hugh-Jones, Danny Miller, Chloe Nahum-Claudel, Buck Schieffelin, Marilyn Strathern and Eduardo Viveiros de Castro, who all commented on drafts. My profoundest gratitude goes to Javielito Alfonso, Victor Betancourt and Rafael Robaina for explaining so much of Ifá to me, though the misconceptions, as they know well, are all mine.

Notes

1 Recent works by Eduardo Viveiros de Castro and Marcio Goldman are inspiring exceptions. As my citations below would indicate, my argument here is intended as a contribution to this 'Brazilian' line of thought, which I take as 'post-structuralist' in the best sense: taking Lévi-Strauss' problems – like that of *mana* – seriously enough to criticise his structuralist attempts to dissolve them.

2 Pascal Boyer writes: 'Almost every ethnographer has, in the course of fieldwork, come across these notions, which seem virtually meaningless, yet are placed at the very heart of traditional discourse' (1986: 50).

3 For example, Hubert and Mauss note of *mana* (specifically in its Melanesian sense):

> First *mana* is a quality. It is something which possesses the thing called *mana*, not the thing itself. [. . .] Secondly *mana* is a thing, a substance, an essence that can be handled yet also independent. [. . .] By its nature it is transmissible, contagious: *mana* may be communicated from harvest stone to other stones through contact. It is represented as a material body. It may be heard and seen, leaving objects where it has dwelt. [. . .] Thirdly *mana* is a force, more especially the force of spirit beings, that is to say, the souls of ancestors and nature spirits. It is *mana* which creates magical objects.
>
> (Mauss 2001: 134–5)

Lévi-Bruhl uses the example of the Arunta in Australia who have

> certain words [that] are at times used as substantives, and then again as adjectives. For instance, arungquiltha to the Aruntas is 'a supernatural evil power.' A thin ostrich or emu is either arungquiltha or is endowed with

219

arungquiltha. The name is applied indiscriminately either to the evil influence or to the object in which it is, for the time being, or permanently, 'resident.'
(Lévy-Bruhl 1926: 133–4, citing Spencer and Gillen 1898: 548 (note); cf. Durkheim 1995: 199)

4 Sahlins' discussion of the changing meanings of *mana* and *tabu* in Polynesia, following the events of Captain Cook's arrival, can be seen as an attempt to correct the first 'perversity' of Lévi-Strauss' analysis by upholding the second (Sahlins 1985: *passim*). Having provided rich discussions of the meanings of '*mana*' and '*tapu*', he goes on to explain shifts in these meanings in terms of altering relationships between 'senses' and 'referents', 'meanings' and 'things', etc. (*ibid.*: 136–56).

5 For two inspired critiques see Godelier 1999: 23–9; and Deleuze 1990: 48–51.

6 The ancestral relation between Lévi-Strauss and Sperber appears to be particularly close. Sperber's coveted analysis of symbolism as 'not a means for encoding information, but a means of organizing it' (1975: 70) is identical in its implications to Lévi-Strauss' theory of the floating signified as structural prerequisite to knowledge (more of which below).

7 The widespread tendency to translate *mana*-terms as 'force', 'energy', 'power' is effective inasmuch as such concepts are the closest modern Euro-Americans (and, as we shall see, Cubans too) come to obscuring the distinction between concepts and things. Durkheim and others' implication that such translations are also theoretically illuminating is misleading since such terms do 'no more than provide difficult native concepts with an equally mysterious gloss' (Viveiros de Castro 1998a: 79; see also Keesing 1984).

8 Indeed, the first injunction of the *Rules of Sociological Method* could almost be the motto of the present volume: '*consider social facts as things*' (Durkheim 1982: 60; original emphasis).

9 These critical comments are based on my reading of Lévy-Bruhl's early and most controversial works (particularly *How Natives Think*). Marcio Goldman (pers. comm., and see Goldman 2004) points out that in his later writings Lévy-Bruhl moved from a 'logical' interpretation of 'participation' to a 'pragmatic' one. It may be worth remarking, however, that my aim in this paper is to advance a 'logic' that denies the very distinction between 'logic' and 'praxis', a distinction that draws much of its force from the axiom of 'concept v. thing'.

10 Parrinder also suggests such a comparison, though he does not mention *aché* by name (1951: 11).

11 Translations from the Spanish text are mine.

12 Rafael Robaina – a leading anthropologist of Ifá in Cuba and a *babalawo* himself – claims that, strictly speaking, this is a misunderstanding (pers. comm.). As he explains, in certain Ifá myths it is made clear that the 256 *oddu* are in fact Orula's children, conceived when Orula was in the sky with his first wife, who was also called Oddu.

13 Hubert and Mauss express exactly this point when they write that the idea of *mana* 'not only transforms magical judgements into analytical judgements but converts them from a priori to a posteriori arguments, since the idea dominates and conditions all experience' (Mauss 2001: 156). Saul Kripke put the possibility of a posteriori analyticity on the philosophers' table almost a century later, though not much to our use here since *mana*-terms like *aché* are anything but 'rigid designators' – as the terms of a posteriori analytic truths, for him, must be (e.g. 'water is H2O' – 1980: 48–9).

14 I have made a parallel argument regarding the role of money in Ifá cosmology (Holbraad 2005).

15 For an illuminating account of the logical implications of the notion of direction, framed in terms of the philosophy of evolution, see Ingold 1986: 12–13.

16 For a detailed account of the notion of potentiality, cast in relation to Ifá initiation, see Holbraad forthcoming.

17 The act of consulting the oracle is commonly referred to as 'looking at one's self with Orula' or 'registering one's self with Orula' (*mirarse con Orula, registrarse con Orula*).

18 While Goldman notes that his informants as a rule emphasise the Bantu origins of their Candomblé practices (pers. comm.), the cosmological commonalities with the (putatively) Yoruba-based practice of Ifá in Cuba are widely accepted and well documented (e.g. see Brown 2003: 115; cf. Palmié 2002: 159–62)

19 Translations from the original Portuguese are mine.

20 Such an interpretation, of course, serves to bring Goldman's strategy very close to my own, regarding the analytics of *mana*-concepts: their transgressions should be heeded rather than accommodated or explained away (see above).

21 For example, in Ifá divination Echu has to be offered coconut in order to ensure a successful séance with Orula. As Victor Betancourt, a notorious *babalawo* in Havana, put it to me, 'you can think of Echu as a police authority; if you want permission to conduct an orderly gathering, you go to the police to get the stamp'. A more common explanation as to why Echu (or Elegguá, the warrior-deity with whom Echu is often identified in Cuba) needs to be honoured at the outset of séances is that it is he who 'opens the paths' (*abre los caminos*). While the expression is ambiguous, and practitioners tended to improvise when I invited them to elaborate, such a conception would support my claim that Orula's *oddu* move into immanence during the séance. Goldman implies the opposite when he writes that in Candomblé divinities are posited as 'immovable essences, needing an intermediary – Exu – in order to communicate with people' (Goldman 2003: 135). Goldman's remark resonates with the notion, common among practitioners in Cuba, that Echu/Elegguá carries humans' sacrificial offerings (*ebbó*) to intended *orishas*. This, however, would not contradict the notion – so central to my argument – that in divination (as opposed to sacrifice) Orula's *oddu* themselves 'come out' on the divining board.

22 See Keesing 1984; 1985, for a critique of the tendency in Melanesian ethnography to view *mana* as a 'diffuse substance', as opposed to 'a process or a state' (1985: 203). The tendency, he argues, is characteristic 'of European, not native, theologians' (*ibid.*), by which he means anthropologists.

23 For a distinction, cast with reference to money, between this notion of partibility and Melanesianists' use of the concept of 'fractality' (e.g. Wagner 1991; Strathern 2004), see Holbraad 2005: footnote 21.

24 One of Hugh-Jones' themes is the co-dependence of vertical and horizontal shamanism in particular socio-historical junctures in different parts of Amazonia. Analogies could be drawn with Stephan Palmié's penetrating account of the co-dependence in Cuba (historically, socially and symbolically) between Ifá and Santería on the one hand, and, on the other, the cults collectively referred to as 'Regla de Congo' (after their mainly central Western African provenance) or 'Palo Monte'.

> If [Ifá and Santería] tend to be represented as imposing a civilizing process on an unruly world whose powers are made to enter domestic ritual space [. . .] as divine kings, palo prescribes an obverse directionality. It notionally leads ritual

actors out of the human oikos [. . . on], quite literally, an errand into the wilderness.

(Palmié 2002: 171).

25 For example, Viveiros de Castro writes that the 'gigantic' and 'anomalous' character of Yawalapíti 'kumã-beings' renders them 'at once an archetype and a monster, model and excess, pure form and hybrid reverberation (human and animal, for example), beauty and ferocity in a single figure' (2004: 22, emphases omitted).

26 Brown points out that the 'hierarchical protocols' that practitioners associate with the *orishas* 'can shift, depending upon socioritual context' (2003: 128). He explains:

> Formally, the ranking orisha elder, Obatalá [sky-deity, patron of peace], is the 'highest,' and Ochún [river deity, patroness of sexual love] is the 'smallest' or most junior. Yet, these relationships are fluid, since alternate patakín (legends) relativize and turn upside down, at least momentarily, any given hierarchy. In one important story, little Ochún, manifesting as the unprepossessing buzzard, saves the world from a scourge when all others have failed, demonstrating that 'a junior can be [. . .] the elder among elders'.
>
> (Brown 2003, citing Ecún 1986: 141)

Clearly this is not to argue that Ifá cosmology is less 'vertical' – in Hugh-Jones' terms – than practitioners represent it, but rather to show that its vertical coordinates, so to speak, are not fixed. Such a position is confluent with my argument about the motility of the *orishas*.

27 I say 'in part', of course, because invocations and offerings are also required in order to attract the deities, as I have described elsewhere – see Holbraad 2005.

References

Argüelles, A. and Hodge, I. (1991) *Los Llamados Cultos Sincreticos y el Espiritismo*, Havana: Editorial Academia.

Barthes, Roland (1984) *Mythologies*, trans. A. Lavers, New York: Hill and Wang.

Bascom, William R. (1991) *Ifa Divination: Communication Between Gods and Men in West Africa*, Bloomington: Indiana University Press.

——(1950) 'The focus of Cuban Santería', *Southwestern Journal of Anthropology*, 6: 64–8.

Bolívar Aróstegui, Natalia (1994) *Los Orishas en Cuba*, Havana: PM Ediciones.

Boyer, Pascal (1986) 'The "empty" concepts of traditional thinking: a semantic and pragmatic description', *Man* (n.s.) 21: 50–64.

Brown, David (2003) *Santería Enthroned: Art, Ritual, and Innovation in an Afro-Cuban Religion*, Chicago: University of Chicago Press.

Cabrera, Lydia (2000) [1954] *El Monte*, Miami FLA: Ediciones Universal.

Clark, Mary Ann (2005) *Where Men are Wives and Mothers Rule: Santería Ritual Practices and their Gender Implications*, Gainesville: University Press of Florida.

Comte, Auguste (1975) *The Essential Writings*, ed. Gertrud Lenzer, New York: Harper Torchbooks.

Deleuze, Gilles (1994) *Difference and Repetition*, trans. P. Patton, London: Athlone Press.

——(1990) *The Logic of Sense*, trans. M. Lester, London: Athlone Press.

Dumont, Louis (1970) *Homo Hierarchicus: the Caste System and its Implications*, London: Weidenfeld and Nicolson.

Durkheim, Emile (1995) [1912] *The Elementary Forms of Religious Life*, trans. K. E. Fields, New York: The Free Press.

——(1982) *The Rules of Sociological Method and Selected Texts on Sociology and its Method*, ed. S. Lukes, trans. W. D. Halls, London: Macmillan.

Ecún, Obá (Cecilio Pérez) (1986) *Itá: mitología de la Religión 'Yoruba'*, Madrid: Gráficas Maravillas.

Evans-Pritchard, E. E. (1965) *Theories of Primitive Religion*, Oxford: Clarendon Press.

Firth, Raymond (1940) 'The analysis of mana: an empirical approach', *Journal of the Polynesian Society*, 49: 483–510.

Godelier, Maurice (1999) *The Enigma of the Gift*, trans. Nora Scott, Cambridge: Polity Press.

Goldman, Marcio (2004) 'Serie, estrutura, devir: Lévy-Bruhl, Deleuze e o Candomblé', paper presented in round table dicussion on 'A Antropologia a Favor da Diferença, ou, Para que Servem os Autores "Menores", at XXVIII Encontro Anual da Associação Nacional de Pós-Graduação e Pesquisa em Ciências Sociais, 2004.

——(2003) 'Observações sobre o sincretismo Afro-Brasileiro', *Kàwé Pesquisa. Revista Anual do Núcleo de Estudos Afro-Baianos Regionais da Universidade Estadual de Santa Cruz I* (1) 132–7.

——(1994) *Razão e Diferença: afectividade, racionalidade e relativismo no pensamento de Lévy-Bruhl*, Rio de Janeiro: Editora UFRJ.

——(1985) 'A construção ritual da pessoa: a possessão no candomblé', *Religião e Sociedade*, 12(1): 22–54.

Gow, Peter (2001) *An Amazonian Myth and Its History*, Oxford: Oxford University Press.

Gray, Andrew (1996) *The Arakmbut of Amazonian Peru. I: Mythology, Spirituality and History*, Oxford: Berghahn.

Gregory, Chris A. (1997) *Savage Money: the Anthropology and Politics of Commodity Exchange*, Amsterdam: Harwood Academic Publishers.

Hocart, A. M. (1922) 'Mana again', *Man*, 22(79): 139–41.

——(1914) 'Mana', *Man*, 14(46): 97–101.

Hogbin, H. Ian, (1936) 'Mana', *Oceania*, 6(3): 240–74.

Højer, Lars (2005) 'The anti-social contract: enmity and suspicion in Northern Mongolia', *Cambridge Anthropology*, 25(1).

Holbraad, Martin (forthcoming) 'Relationships in motion: oracular recruitment in Cuban Ifá cults', *Systèmes de Pensée en Afrique Noire*.

——(2005) 'Expending multiplicity: money in Cuban Ifá cults', *Journal of the Royal Anthropological Institute*, 11(2): 231–54.

——(2004) 'Religious "speculation": the rise of Ifá cults and consumption in post-Soviet Havana', *Journal of Latin American Studies*, 36(4): 1–21.

——(2003) 'Estimando a necessidade: os oráculos de ifá e a verdade em Havana', *Mana*, 9(2): 39–77.

Hugh-Jones, Stephen (1996) 'Shamans, prophets, priests and pastors', in Nicholas Thomas and Caroline Humphrey (eds) *Shamanism, History and the State*, Ann Arbor MI: University of Michigan Press, 32–75.

Ingold, Tim (1986) *Evolution and Social Life*, Cambridge: Cambridge University Press.

——(1996) 'Hunting and gathering as ways of perceiving the environment', in R. F. Ellen and K. Fukui (eds) *Redefining Nature: Ecology, Culture and Domestication*, Oxford: Berg, 117–55.

Keesing, Robert M. (1985) 'Conventional metaphors and anthropological metaphysics: the problematic of cultural translation', *Journal of Anthropological Research*, 41: 201–17.

——(1984) 'Rethinking mana', *Journal of Anthropological Research*, 40: 137–56.

Kripke, Saul (1980) *Naming and Necessity*, Oxford: Blackwell.

Lévi-Strauss, Claude (1987) [1950] *Introduction to the Work of Marcel Mauss*, trans. F. Barker, London: Routledge and Kegan Paul.

——(1966) *The Savage Mind*, Oxford: Oxford University Press.

——(1964) *Totemism*, trans. R. Needham, London: Merlin Press.

Lévy-Bruhl, Lucien (1973) [1949] *Notebooks on Primitive Mentality*, trans. P. Revière, Oxford: Blackwell.

——(1926) *How Natives Think*, trans. L. A. Clare, London: George Allen and Unwin.

Malinowski, Bronislaw (1954) *Magic, Science and Religion and Other Essays*, New York: Doubleday Anchor Books.

Marett, Robert R. (1915) 'Mana', in J. Hastings (ed.) *Encyclopaedia of Religion and Ethics*, vol. VIII, Edinburgh: T. and T. Clark.

——(1914) *The Threshold of Religion*, London: Methuen.

——(1900) 'Preanimistic religion', *Folk-lore*, 11: 162–82.

Marriott, M. (1979) 'Hindu transactions: diversity without dualism', in B. Kapferer (ed.) *Transaction and Meaning: Directions in the Anthropology of Human Issues*, Philadelphia: Institute for the Study of Human Issues,109–42.

Mauss, Marcel (2001) [Hubert and Mauss 1902] *A General Theory of Magic*, trans. Robert Brain, London: Routledge Classics.

——(1990) [1950] *The Gift: Forms and Functions of Exchange in Archaic Societies*, trans. W. D. Halls, London: Routledge.

Menéndez Vázquez, Lázara (1995) 'Un cake para Obatalá?!', *Temas*, 4: 38–51.

Palmié, Stephan (2002) *Wizards and Scientists: Explorations in Afro-Cuban Modernity and Tradition*, Durham NC: Duke University Press.

Parrinder, Geoffrey (1951) *West African Psychology*, London: Lutterworth Press.

Pedersen, Morten (2001) 'Totemism, animism and North Asian indigenous ontologies', *Journal of the Royal Anthropological Institute*, 7(3): 411–27.

Peel, J. D. Y (2003) *Religious Encounter and the Making of the Yoruba*, Bloomington: Indiana University Press.

Pelton, R. D. (1980) *The Trickster in West Africa: a Study of Mythic Irony and Sacred Delight*, Berkeley: California University Press.

Sahlins, Marshall (1985) *Islands of History*, Chicago: University of Chicago Press.

Severi, Carlo (2004) 'Capturing imagination: a cognitive approach to cultural complexity', *Journal of the Royal Anthropological Institute* (n.s.) 10: 815–38.

Shore, Bradd (1989) 'Mana and tapu', in Alan Howard and Robert Borofsky (eds) *Developments in Polynesian Ethnology*, Honolulu: University of Hawaii Press.

Spencer, B. and F. J. Gillen (1898) *The Native Tribes of Central Australia*, London: Macmillan.

Sperber, Dan (1975) *Rethinking Symbolism*, Cambridge: Cambridge University Press

——(1985) *On Anthropological Knowledge*, Cambridge: Cambridge University Press.

Strathern, Marilyn (2004) *Partial Connections* (updated edn) Walnut Creek: Altamira Press.

——(1995) *The Relation*, Cambridge: Prickly Pear Press.

——(1990) 'Artefacts of history: events and the interpretation of images', in J. Siikala (ed.) *Culture and History in the Pacific*, Helsinki: Finnish Anthropological Society, 25–44.

——(1988) *The Gender of the Gift: Problems with Women and Problems with Society in Melanesia*, Berkeley: University of California Press.

Tambiah, S. J. (1990) *Magic, Science, and the Scope of Rationality*, Cambridge: Cambridge University Press.

Viveiros de Castro, Eduardo (2005) 'The gift and the given: three nano-essays on kinship and magic', in Sandra Bamford and James Leach (eds) *Genealogy beyond Kinship: sequence, Transmission, and Essence in Ethnography and Social Theory*, Oxford: Berghahn Books.

——(2004) 'The forest of mirrors: notes on the ontology of Amazonian spirits', Lichstern Lecture, Department of Anthropology, University of Chicago, May 2004. (e-version: http://amazone.wikicities.com/wiki/The_Forest_of_Mirrors).

——(2002) 'O nativo relativo', *Mana*, 8(1): 113–48.

—— (1998a) 'Cosmological Perspectivism in Amazonia and Elsewhere', four lectures delivered 17 February–10 March at the Department of Social Anthropology, University of Cambridge.

——(1998b) 'Cosmological deixis and Amerindian perspectivism', *Journal of the Royal Anthropological Institute*, 4(3): 469–88.

Wagner, Roy (1991) 'The fractal person', in M. Godelier and M. Strathern (eds) *Big Men and Great Men: Personifications of Power in Melanesia*, Cambridge: Cambridge University Press.

——(1986) *Symbols That Stand for Themselves*, Chicago: University of Chicago Press.

Willerslev, Rane (2004) 'Spirits as ready to hand: a phenomenological study of Yukaghir spiritual knowledge and dreaming', *Anthropological Theory*, 4(4): 395–418.

INDEX

226

Related titles from Routledge
Anthropology and Anthropologists:
The Modern British School (3rd edition)
Adam Kuper

'Its great merit is that it not only describes all major developments in method, theory and controversy; it also gives much biographical information about the persons responsible for those developments ... Kuper writes lucidly, economically, and occasionally with refreshing irreverence.'
British Book News

On its first publication in 1973 Adam Kuper's entertaining history of half a century of British social anthropology provoked strong reactions. But his often irreverent account soon established itself as one of *the* introductions to anthropology.

Since the second revised edition was published in 1983, important developments have occurred within British and European anthropology. This third enlarged and updated edition responds to these fresh currents. Adam Kuper takes the story up to the present day, and a new final chapter traces the emergence of a modern European social anthropology in contrast with the developments in American cultural Anthropology over the last two decades.

Anthropology and Anthropologists provides a critical historical account of modern British social anthropology: it describes the careers of the major theorists, their ideas and their contributions in the context of the intellectual and institutional environments in which they worked. It is essential reading for all students of social anthropology; it will also appeal to lay readers with an interest in the field.

Adam Kuper is Professor of Anthropology at Brunel University. He has taught at universities in Uganda, Britain, Sweden, Holland the the United States and was the founding chairman of the European Association of Social Anthropologists. He is the author of a number of books on the history of anthropology and on African ethnography, including *The Invention of Primitive Society* (1988) and *The Chosen Primate* (1994).

ISBN10: 0-415-11895-6 (pbk)
ISBN13: 978-0-415-11895-8 (pbk)

Available at all good bookshops
For ordering and further information please visit:
www.routledge.com

Related titles from Routledge

The Future of Visual Anthropology: Engaging the Senses

Sarah Pink

The explosion of visual media in recent years has generated a wide range of visual and digital technologies which have transformed visual research and analysis. The result is an exciting new interdisciplinary approach of great potential influence in and out of academia.

Sarah Pink argues that this potential can be harnessed by engaging visual anthropology with its wider contexts, including:

- The increasing use of visual research methods across the social sciences and humanities
- The growth in popularity of the visual as methodology and object of analysis within mainstream anthropology and applied anthropology
- The growing interest in 'anthropology of the senses' and media anthropology.
- The development of new visual technologies that allow anthropologists to work in new ways.

The Future of Visual Anthropology offers a groundbreaking examination of developments within the field to define how it might advance empirically, methodologically and theoretically, and cement a central place in academic study both within anthropology and across disciplines. This book will be essential reading for students, researchers and practitioners of visual anthropology, media anthropology, visual cultural studies, media studies, and sociology.

ISBN10: 0-415-35764-0 (hbk)
ISBN10: 0-415-35765-9 (pbk)

ISBN13: 978-0-415-35764-7 (hbk)
ISBN13: 978-0-415-35765-4 (pbk)

Available at all good bookshops
For ordering and further information please visit:
www.routledge.com

eBooks – at www.eBookstore.tandf.co.uk

A

e can
s e.

T cess
t n.

e
k earches
t would
f

N ccess
t

are

ke

w